CARL SCHMITT'S INSTITUTIONAL THEORY

In 1922, Carl Schmitt penned *Political Theology*, the celebrated essay in which he elaborated on the notorious theory that the heart of politics lies in the sovereign power to issue emergency measures that suspend the legal order. Ever since, Schmitt's thinking has largely been identified with this concept, despite him renouncing it over time. Offering a comprehensive analysis of Schmitt's writings, *Carl Schmitt's Institutional Theory* provides an ambitious, novel perspective on Carl Schmitt and his legal and political thinking. By delving into Schmitt's output over his decades-long career, Mariano Croce and Andrea Salvatore explore Schmitt's varied and developing thoughts on exceptionalism, societal pluralism, and the law as the progenitor and enforcer of normality. Challenging dominant interpretations, Croce and Salvatore dethrone the false centrality of certain key texts, and instead provide a more unified, coherent account of his institutional theory from across his long and controversial career.

Mariano Croce is Associate Professor of Political Philosophy at Sapienza University of Rome. He held the post of Marie Curie Fellow at the Faculty of Law of the University of Antwerp, where he is co-leader of the research line in kinship studies. His books include *The Legal Theory of Carl Schmitt* (2013, with Andrea Salvatore), *The Politics of Juridification* (2018), and *The Legacy of Pluralism: The Continental Jurisprudence of Santi Romano, Carl Schmitt, and Costantino Mortati* (2020, with Marco Goldoni).

Andrea Salvatore is Associate Professor of Political Philosophy at Sapienza University of Rome. His books include *The Legal Theory of Carl Schmitt* (2013, with Mariano Croce) and *Undoing Ties: Political Philosophy at the Waning of the State* (2015, with Mariano Croce).

Carl Schmitt's Institutional Theory

THE POLITICAL POWER OF NORMALITY

MARIANO CROCE
Sapienza Università di Roma

ANDREA SALVATORE
Sapienza Università di Roma

CAMBRIDGE
UNIVERSITY PRESS

CAMBRIDGE
UNIVERSITY PRESS

University Printing House, Cambridge CB2 8BS, United Kingdom

One Liberty Plaza, 20th Floor, New York, NY 10006, USA

477 Williamstown Road, Port Melbourne, VIC 3207, Australia

314–321, 3rd Floor, Plot 3, Splendor Forum, Jasola District Centre, New Delhi – 110025, India

103 Penang Road, #05–06/07, Visioncrest Commercial, Singapore 238467

Cambridge University Press is part of the University of Cambridge.

It furthers the University's mission by disseminating knowledge in the pursuit of education, learning, and research at the highest international levels of excellence.

www.cambridge.org
Information on this title: www.cambridge.org/9781316511381
DOI: 10.1017/9781009052474

First published 2022

A catalogue record for this publication is available from the British Library.

Library of Congress Cataloging-in-Publication Data
NAMES: Croce, Mariano, author. | Salvatore, Andrea, author.
TITLE: Carl Schmitt's institutional theory : the political power of normality / Mariano Croce, Sapienza Università di Roma; Andrea Salvatore, Sapienza Università di Roma.
DESCRIPTION: Cambridge, United Kingdom ; New York, NY : Cambridge University Press, 2022. | Includes bibliographical references and index.
IDENTIFIERS: LCCN 2022007047 (print) | LCCN 2022007048 (ebook) | ISBN 9781316511381 (hardback) | ISBN 9781009055598 (paperback) | ISBN 9781009052474 (epub)
SUBJECTS: LCSH: Schmitt, Carl, 1888-1985. | Law–Philosophy. | Political science–Philosophy. | Political theology. | Schmitt, Carl, 1888-1985. Politische Theologie.
Classification: LCC K230.S35 C76 2022 (print) | LCC K230.S35 (ebook) | DDC 340/.1–dc23/eng/20220430
LC record available at https://lccn.loc.gov/2022007047
LC ebook record available at https://lccn.loc.gov/2022007048

ISBN 978-1-316-51138-1 Hardback

Contents

Acknowledgements

Along the way, various portions of this book have been discussed at numerous workshops and conferences on Carl Schmitt's thinking and related themes. We are grateful for the feedback, comments and criticisms we have received from various colleagues, and especially Adalgiso Amendola, Daniele Archibugi, Sandrine Baume, Sandro Chignola, Emanuele Conte, Roger Cotterrell, Giuseppe Duso, David Dyzenhaus, Alessandro Ferrara, Filippo Fontanelli, Marco Goldoni, Martin Loughlin, Clara Maier, Francesco Mancuso, Giuseppe Martinico, Virginio Marzocchi, John McCormick, Reinhard Mehring, Jens Meierhenrich, Panu Minkkinen, Damiano Palano, Stefano Pietropaoli, Cesare Pinelli, Geminello Preterossi, Aldo Sandulli, William Scheuerman, Benjamin Schupmann, Luca Scuccimarra, Nadia Urbinati, Lars Vinx, Marc de Wilde, Lea Ypi and Samuel Zeitlin.

Thanks also go to the Rethinking Political Philosophy group (RePoP), which truly proves an experimental site of creative thinking.

We are particularly thankful to Martin Loughlin for believing in this project and for encouraging us to arrange a book proposal. A big 'thank you' to Finola O'Sullivan and Marianne Nield at Cambridge University Press for their valuable help and assistance. We are also very grateful to the anonymous readers, whose excellent suggestions significantly improved the book.

This is a revised and extended version of M. Croce and A. Salvatore, *L'indecisionista. Carl Schmitt oltre l'eccezione* (Macerata: Quodlibet, 2020). We are very grateful to Stefano Verdicchio and the Italian publisher Quodlibet for waiving their translation rights.

Introduction

It is somewhat ironic that this book publishes with the centenary of *Political Theology*, first published in 1922. In the end, one of the main claims we shall make here is that Carl Schmitt's celebrated essay has been unduly overemphasised and that it formulated a theory of law and a conception of normality that he himself dismantled a few years after its publication. A related claim will be that interpretations that identify a connection between *Political Theology* and successive works such as *The Concept of the Political* (1928) and *Constitutional Theory* (1928) are wrong in at least one important respect: through those works, Schmitt tried to pull himself out of the quagmire in which he was bogged down in 1922 – namely, the problematic conception that we shall dub 'exceptionalist decisionism'. But we shall have to go further. Works that are coeval with *Political Theology*, such as *Dictatorship* (1921) and *Roman Catholicism and Political Form* (1923), offer much leeway for criticising exceptionalist decisionism, either because the notions of exception and decision are thinner and more tenable (as is the case with *Dictatorship*), or because there is no room at all for any of them (as is the case with *Roman Catholicism and Political Form*). In sum, as a celebration of *Political Theology*, this book cuts a poor figure.

Nevertheless, this book is not a celebration of any specific Schmitt's text but an exploration of his work with a view to unearthing his theory of law and its bearings on his conception of politics. We shall soon see that it is pointless to look for *a* theory of law in Schmitt's overall oeuvre. As is the case with almost all great authors, most often his changes of mind are more enlightening than his firm points – and indeed we shall see that his firm points are the most hideous, such as his unshakeable conviction that the homogeneity of the social justifies political exclusion and the reduction of pluralism through administrative policies. We shall then be on the trail of Schmitt's smaller or greater amendments to his own theorising as he himself came to realise that he was on the wrong track. For there is little doubt that his chief theoretical objective was to understand how a state could secure the stability of the political community and make sure that a fixed set of loyalties and allegiances bind the populace to the state government. Yet, he explored different ways of thinking about the means whereby the state could achieve this. While most interpreters in the last hundred years have concentrated on the theoretical framework that he developed between 1922 and 1928, we shall contend that Schmitt could only get his project off the ground in between 1928 and 1934, when he elaborated on an institutional theory of law.

This book will not specifically focus on that span of years, since we have already offered our take on (what we called) Schmitt's 'institutional turn'.[1] Rather, we will discuss various interpretations of his writings and will put them to the test of his own rethinking of a few substantial points. In short, our central thesis can be summarised as follows. Schmitt is generally considered as the father of exceptionalist decisionism – that is, the theory that the heart of politics lies in the sovereign power to suspend the legal order and to create a new one *ex nihilo*. However, he held an exceptionalist view for a very limited period, and even in that period his thinking cannot be regarded as unwaveringly exceptionalist. By contextualising *Political Theology* and by looking at his output from the 1910s through to the 1950s, we shall make the case that Schmitt's is a *juristic theory of the legal order* that attaches special importance to the activity of the jurists and portrays jurisprudence as a vital complement of legislative power in the making of the law. Schmitt's most consistent view, after some overhauling, is an institutional theory of law and politics that exalts legal science as a jurisgenerative practice that shelters a community's institutional practices and its historical identity.

Needless to say, this will not amount to a defence of Schmitt's theory, let alone to an attempt to tease out a democratic residue in his thinking. Both routes are tortuous and hazardous. Schmitt was a highly conservative thinker who lent support to revolting ideas – such as the ethical and ethnic identity shared by the people and the Leader, which he defended in the hope of winning the sympathy of the Nazi regime. No liberal or democratic views can be advocated based on the conceptual resources Schmitt provided us with. However, this hardly makes his theory useless. Quite the contrary, he is an excellent case study to investigate the relation of the legal order to social practices, for his moving away from exceptionalist decisionism can be

[1] See, among other things, Croce and Salvatore, *The Legal Theory of Carl Schmitt*; Croce and Salvatore, 'After Exception: Carl Schmitt's Legal Institutionalism and the Repudiation of Exceptionalism'.

interpreted as the recognition of the foundational role of social life in the production and the maintenance of the legal order. To put it another way, between the 1920s and the 1930s Schmitt realised that the law is grounded on social practices and that therefore jurisprudence cannot disregard them as they endeavour to identify, reconstruct and describe the order; nor can law-making and law-applying officials. To make this point we shall examine a few crucial junctures in his extensive output. It is worth isolating the main steps of our overall argument.

The point of departure (Chapter 1) will be the deployment of a *jurisprudential reading* of *Political Theology*. It is jurisprudential in the sense that we consider such a key text first and foremost as an exercise in legal theory. More than this, many of the issues raised in *Political Theology* remain obscure unless one considers that Schmitt's main concern was with an answer to the question of what makes the legal order legible and intelligible as a unitary legal order. In other words, *Political Theology* tackled one of the perennial questions in the domain of jurisprudence, one that still haunts contemporary debates. To answer this question, Schmitt argued, jurisprudence cannot afford to set aside the issue of the genesis of law, because no legal norm or legal document can confer unity on the legal order – more generally, nothing that lies within its boundaries. Put another way, the legal order can be cognised and recognised as an order that derives from the decisional act whereby it was founded. If that is the case, it is part of the nature of the legal order to be suspended and abolished by that very decisional act if the circumstances dictate it – circumstances that are circularly established by the one who makes the decision.

It is not necessary to go into the details of our reading here. What matters is that it debunks the *exceptionalist reading* that centres on the sovereign decision as the unfounded foundation of modern politics. The exceptionalist reading deems *Political Theology* to be the nihilistic celebration of an impossibility: no rational justification for political authority is available once transcendence has ceased to lend legitimacy to secular power. While this is certainly a line of thought that crossed Schmitt's mind, we believe this argument was instrumental in the more vital thesis that sovereignty – or better, a personal sovereign in flesh and blood – is the normative acme of the legal domain. The exceptionalist reading, we shall hold, misses this point. It takes *Political Theology* to provide a portrayal of politics in late-modern settings once metaphysical resources have dried out and rational justifications seem to have run out of steam. But Schmitt was onto something different. He wanted to justify the notion of sovereignty as a jurisgenerative act, an essentially legal act; for the law exceeds the legal order, since the highest law is the activity whereby the sovereign forges and issues the legal order, and thereby ensures legal normality. This foundational act hovers over the formal constitution as well as all legal codes and all legal procedures.

Part of this book will be devoted to showing that this conception of law and its relation to politics were a sudden development of the early 1920s (Chapter 2). The jurisprudence of *Political Theology* effected a break with Schmitt's theorising in the 1910s. While he hardly ever inclined to normativism – that is, the theory that puts norms at the centre of the legal life – he certainly did not think that a personal sovereign brings about the law. For example, in *The Value of the State and the Significance of the Individual* (1914) political authorities are called upon to *realise* the law through decisions. Nonetheless, the law is not as much the positive legal order as it is a *Rechtsgedanke*, a meta-positive idea of law. Accordingly, the decision is a mediatory device whereby political power turns the meta-positive idea of law into positive statutory norms. By analysing other occurrences of the (thinly) decisionist lexicon in the 1910s, we shall spotlight the several differences between Schmitt's theorising in those years and his abrupt conversion to exceptionalist decisionism in 1922. This analysis of Schmitt's works in the 1910s along with our jurisprudential reading of *Political Theology* will provide the ground for rejecting the exceptionalist reading (Chapter 3).

A parallel and complementary line of inquiry will be the account of what we shall name the *pan-institutional reading* (Chapter 4). For in the last two decades some scholars have advanced alternatives to the exceptionalist reading to dig out Schmitt's enduring interest in the issue of institutions. While this interpretation sits easily with our own, we shall pinpoint what we see as a defect: it tends to obfuscate the difference between Schmitt's writings prior to 1928 and his later institutional writings. We regard this analysis as an important complement to our preceding account, because it shines some more light on the distinctive features of Schmitt's concept of institution after he encountered the works of the initiators of classic legal institutionalism, French jurist Maurice Hauriou and Italian jurist Santi Romano. The core of our argument will be the vindication of what we dubbed a *concretist reading*. We will maintain that after Schmitt's adhesion to institutionalism, his notion of institution changed in a few important respects. While before the early 1930s by institution Schmitt meant an organised agency carrying out public tasks, from the early 1930s it came to include the element of *concrete practice*. For he became concerned with the actual models of behaviour and the exemplary figures that are produced within established institutional settings. As we shall elucidate (Chapter 5), this effected a major change in his thinking. Let us linger on this aspect.

In the 1910s the law was a meta-positive idea to be realised within the empirical world through a decision, but the decision did not create the law. In the early 1920s, Schmitt revised this conception in that he came to believe that the decision brings about the legal order. In both theoretical scenarios, though, the law is removed from social practice. In the 1910s it is an ideal, in the early 1920s it is the creation of a sovereign. At the end of the 1920s and more clearly in the early 1930s, Schmitt changed his mind again. His novel conception had it that the law is grounded on the concrete models of behaviour and the exemplary figures that unfold within tradition-bound institutions. Unlike his preceding works, he affirmed that the law *is to be extracted from institutional practices*. This new conception involved a major amendment to how Schmitt conceived the normal. While in his earlier phases he regarded normality as that which is brought about by the realisation of the law or the making of a sovereign decision, at the end of the 1920s and especially at the onset of 1930s, normality became the seedbed of those models and figures that positive legal norms have to incorporate and make binding. The normal is the source of law, though it is not *ipso facto* legal.

The analysis of Schmitt's fresh institutional view will be the entry point to his novel account of how the law secures the homogeneity of the social. This is the crux of his ultraconservative political theory (Chapter 6). Contrary to the shared pluralist inclination of institutional paradigms, Schmitt employed institutionalism as a conceptual resource to make sense of the legal guardianship over normality. The law is the filter that allows extracting normative resources from social institutions – those institutions that are considered to be consonant with the history and tradition of the German people – and makes them binding for the whole population. What is normal within the social realm is turned into legal norms via an activity of selection and exclusion. It is no coincidence that in the 1930s Schmitt insisted that this filtering activity should be performed in compliance with the Leader's design of the German community and his idea of the public good. Even if we bracket off such a despicable assumption, the political theory that is coupled with Schmitt's institutionalism is essentially exclusionary – 'essentially' because the effacement of alternative institutions and their models and figures is (alleged to be) foundational to the subsistence of the community as an ethical and ethnic unity. Despite this, we shall argue two points. First, though abundantly objectionable, this theory did remedy the shortcomings of Schmitt's erstwhile exceptionalist decisionism. Second, it contributes to deciphering the tendency of state law – even within liberal states – to determine the substantive contents of the normal and to make the emergence of alternatives more difficult.

Our journey will conclude by illustrating Schmitt's most mature version of institutionalism, which we shall claim is a *juristic* one (Chapter 7). While he never abandoned the institutional conception of law that he espoused in the early 1930s, in the post-World War Two period he watered down the role of political authority and attached more weight to the role of legal science and its specialists. In *The Plight of European Jurisprudence* (1950), the political is pushed to the background while the salvaging activity of the jurists is brought to the forefront. For the first time in Schmitt's intellectual history, the juristic practice is completely detached from political tutelage and severed from domestic politics. The jurists are deemed to play a compositional activity as the guarantors of the unity of the whole European tradition in that jurisprudence is the only type of knowledge that can neutralise centrifugal forces. Quite the opposite, political authorities are described as the holders of a disruptive power and as a source of uncertainty insofar as they grow insensitive to the actual needs of traditional institutions and their members. To counter the weakness of politics, Schmitt held, jurisprudence should always remain conscious of its primary function as a repository of knowledge that provides the legal order with coherent and harmonious contents – those that are derived from the historical and cultural context – and should stand up against any attempts to reduce the legal order to a purely technical machinery.

In summary, Schmitt's subscription to an institutional theory of law in the 1920s and the 1930s had a durable impact on his subsequent work. It left a mark that visibly distinguishes his work prior to 1928 from that after this date. From the 1930s onwards, he certainly recovered some of the themes that he had mused on in the 1910s, but he relocated them in a different conceptual terrain, hallmarked by a notion of institution that was highly indebted to the institutionalist tradition – though tainted by illiberal features that are alien to that tradition. On this reading, the exceptionalist decisionism of *Political Theology* appears as a transitory response to a jurisprudential problem which he had to abandon shortly after 1922. To repeat, our reading does not make Schmitt's theory any more acceptable to those who think – as we do – that the exclusionary effects of legal frameworks and policy measures are an undesirable tendency to be counteracted. It does not make Schmitt's theory any more acceptable to those who think – as we do – that pluralism is the seedbed of alternatives for the construction of new bodies of law based on the normative resources of law-users themselves. However, it tells us something salient about the relationship between law and social practice. Effacing the political nature of law as it selects some models of life and backs them up with coercive force risks cloaking the exclusionary potential of the legal order. Paradoxically,

Schmitt's arguments for a bold politics of normality serve as a warning for those who are not alert to the normalising tendencies of the law.

Sure enough, to make the law more sensitive to its own normalising tendencies and to make sure that it remains open to the contributions of those law-abiders who are not comfortable with existing models of conduct, one can hardly pin one's hopes on Schmitt's legal and political theory. But this book is not meant to address this concern. Its more limited objective is to explain why and how he came to espouse his institutional theory and how he remained loyal to it until his last works. This comes with the modest invitation not to use the lexicon of exceptionalism to understand the present – as has happened in these latter times of truly exceptional crisis – because Schmitt himself realised that exceptionalist decisionism does not stand on its own feet. Yet, a modest objective is likely to be more promising than any Grand Theory, especially when it comes to the controversial figure of Carl Schmitt. For this book is an invitation to demythologise Schmitt's thinking and to lessen his enduring allure. He was a talented jurist and a shrewd thinker who was concerned with context-specific problems. He was intelligent (or strategic) enough to revise his previous positions as these contexts altered. And at the end of the day all that we can get from this is an interesting version of juristic institutionalism that grasps some (certainly not all) vital traits of the legal phenomenon. We suggest looking elsewhere if readers are searching for a fully fledged theory of the exception or a comprehensive conception of modern politics, and even more so if they hope to obtain any hints on how to revise today's constitutional orders. On the contrary, if readers are interested in how a leading jurist, sometimes wisely, other times myopically, conceptualised the exceedingly conservative role of law in the consolidation of a homogeneous institutional setting, Schmitt will do.[2]

Some of the material included in this book has appeared in earlier forms elsewhere. A version of Chapter 4 was published as Mariano Croce, 'The Enemy as the Unthinkable: A Concretist Reading of Carl Schmitt's Conception of the Political', 43 *History of European Ideas* 1016–28 (2017).

[2] Although this book is the outcome of a joint effort and ongoing collaboration, Mariano Croce is the author of this Introduction and Chs. 1, 4, 5, and 6, while Andrea Salvatore is the author of Chs. 2, 3, and 7 and the Conclusion.

1

What Is Exceptionalist Decisionism?

Reinterpreting *Political Theology*

This chapter begins with a caveat: its approach is deliberately reductionist. It dwells on one of the most debated issues of Schmitt's theory – the exception – in a way that falls short of an accurate study of the issue. For our goal is to set up an inquiry that will substantially downplay the role of the exception. In part, this reflects our own perspective on the matter – one that admittedly tends to minimise the role of the exception within Schmitt's overall thinking. Yet, the reductionism we pursue in this chapter does not ensue from this perspectival inclination. Rather, it has to do to with the main interest lying behind our investigation in the following pages. We shall pinpoint questions that, within Schmitt's intellectual biography, only became salient a few years after the publication of *Political Theology* in 1922. Accordingly, we shall treat this latter text – arguably the most debated along with *The Concept of the Political* (1928) – as the seedbed of ideas that he revised shortly after 1922.[1] This will undoubtedly affect the way this chapter unfolds.

Despite this, we believe such an 'oriented' reading is likely to uncover a few telling clues on *Political Theology*. In our account, this key essay puts forward a *jurisprudential* argument, more than a political, theological or metaphysical

[1] A most influential book on political theology and its impact on Schmitt's theorising is Meier, *The Lesson of Carl Schmitt*. There will be no opportunity to consider and discuss Meier's interpretation as much as it would deserve, and yet, as will soon become clear, we mostly disagree with him. For a more comprehensive account of Schmitt's political theology, see Nicoletti, *Trascendenza e potere*. On the relevance of political theology to Schmitt's conception of law, see Herrero, *The Political Discourse of Carl Schmitt*, especially Chs. 7 and 8. On the recent reappraisal of Schmitt's political theology, see various contributions in the third part of Arvidsson, Brännström and Minkkinen, *The Contemporary Relevance of Carl Schmitt*. A significant book that interrogates political theology with specific reference to US politics is Kahn, *Political Theology*.

one.[2] Accordingly, all of Schmitt's references to non-legal subject matters are ancillary. They are meant to corroborate the particular type of jurisprudential answer he thought he had found to the core question of his essay, that is: what allows one to describe a set of different norms and procedures as a uniform legal order? In other words, we take *Political Theology* to be an inquiry into the identity and the unity of the legal order in the first place. As we shall argue, Schmitt's mobilising theology and theological concepts was intended to bemoan the scant attention that coeval legal theorists afforded to the origin of law. This explains why a few pages of the present chapter will be devoted to Schmitt's disagreement with Hans Kelsen, as the latter was resolute in expunging the issue of the foundation of law from the domain of legal science. The scientific study of the legal order, Kelsen held, should not concentrate on anything that oversteps the law's formal structure – and this puts the law's original foundation out of the picture.

Our discussion of Kelsen's thinking in this chapter will come in handy for two further reasons. First, it will shine a light on how close Schmitt and Kelsen were to one another when they accounted for the unity of the legal order. Despite the obvious methodological clash, they both thought there is a privileged vantage point from which jurists can describe the law as a self-consistent whole. Doubtless, they disagreed on what this vantage point is. And yet, there is one – and this is a stunning point of contact between these two scholars. Second, our jurisprudential reading of *Political Theology* will help bring out the frictions between Schmitt's theorising in 1922 and some telling revisions that he made a few years later, as he drew his attention to other areas of legal knowledge and moved away from the issue of the origin of law. But at that point, the divergence with Kelsen's thinking became unbridgeable.

2 Contrary to the argument we are deploying here, some interpreters identify a fundamental connection between *Political Theology* and Schmitt's later institutional writings. See e.g. Brännström, 'Carl Schmitt's Definition of Sovereignty as Authorized Leadership'. Though this claim somehow resonates with our main thesis, we think Brännström's analysis is exegetically too liberal when it traces Schmitt's fascination with the concrete order back to the early 1920s: 'Quite consistent with the concrete-order approach, Schmitt establishes in *Political Theology* that order must be present for "a legal order to make sense"' (26). It is just as exegetically liberal when, based on the former claim, she writes that 'from the concrete-order perspective, the decision is not "new and alien" but guided by the normative parameters, behavioural patterns and expectations that are attached to the relevant normal situation. In other words, the decision is faithful to the legal substance of the concrete order in which the case unfolds' (25). Contrary to this interpretation, we believe that the kind of concreteness Schmitt had in mind in the early 1920s concerned the effectiveness of legal norms in normal times and hence is not comparable to the concreteness of Schmitt's later concrete-order thinking.

POLITICAL THEORY OR JURISPRUDENCE? THE EXCEPTIONALIST VS THE JURISPRUDENTIAL READING

There are many ways of interpreting such an emblematic work as *Political Theology*. Yet two readings look to us as the most compelling[3] – two readings that lead to scarcely reconcilable views of Schmitt's core claims in 1922.

The first reading can be dubbed *exceptionalist*. It takes the state of exception to be the main thread not only within *Political Theology*, but more generally within Schmitt's work as a whole. The exceptionalist reading alleges *Political Theology* to be both the epitome and the epilogue of the inner logic of modern politics. The form and function of politics in the modern era only come to the surface if they are observed through a theological-political lens. Therefore, on the exceptionalist view, Schmitt's political theology is not meant to revive the role of the divine within the secular. Quite the opposite, it intends to secularise the law and at the same time to emphasise the persistence of a political transcendence *within* the secular order. 'Transcendence' in this context entails the idea that politics is meant to impose a constraint on an always incipient, underlying chaos, one that is destined to remain unmanageable. Following in the footsteps of Thomas Hobbes, a constant reference point for him, Schmitt thought politics should mould, or even produce, the social world by domesticating the asocial, even antisocial, nature of human beings. However, the persisting risk of a re-emerging chaos implies that no political rationality can thoroughly purge itself of the fundamental irrationality of human nature. The pillar of state power, therefore, is the monopoly on the political whereby all individuals and groups give up the right to self-defence and entrust the state to ensure peaceable sociality.[4]

On this exceptionalist interpretation, the 'exceptional case' (*Ausnahmefall*) cannot be investigated, let alone justified, in the light of any existing legal norms or procedures. The exception conjures up a sovereign who is called on

3 As anticipated, owing to space limits, this chapter will not explore Meier's 'theological' interpretation of *Political Theology*, which emphasises the political relevance of religious faith. See Meier, *Carl Schmitt and Leo Strauss*; and Meier, *The Lessons of Carl Schmitt*. In support of Meier's argument, see Rae, 'The Theology of Carl Schmitt's Political Theology'. For a critique of the so-called 'theological turn' inaugurated by Meier's works, see Lievens, 'Theology without God', and Roberts, 'Carl Schmitt: Political Theologian?'. On Schmitt's conviction that theology is ill-equipped to deal with jurisprudential issues, also see Hoelzl, 'Ethics of Decisionism'.

4 Amongst the most illustrious advocates of this interpretative line, see Galli, *Genealogia della politica*.

to make an *unjustified* and *unjustifiable* decision (*Entscheidung*) by which, as per its etymon, the sovereign cuts something out and gives shape to the political community. This is why sovereignty – the supreme task of politics – is deemed to be foundational to social order. As a result, the exception that *Political Theology* extols is much more than a simple emergency (*Ernstfall* or *Notfall*).[5] It is a suspension of the order that serves a *creative* function. For a new order to be created, the existing one is to be suspended. That way, sovereignty unveils the paradoxical, unpredictable source of the legal order, which does not answer to any specific legal 'competence'. The exceptionalist reading takes this to be the (self-aware) culmination of the crisis of the modern conception of *an order that arises from disorder* – where the former is always emergent, while the latter remains fundamental:

> Schmitt's main scientific and political acquisition is indeed that through his decisionist theory of sovereignty he unveils the crisis of modern political language and thought and that this deconstructs the modern mediation and introduces an element of crisis, negation, and concrete contingency: that the order is the expression – not the resolution – of a crisis, and that this crisis traverses and exceeds every order; put otherwise, that sovereignty is internal and external to the order, while the latter is both destruction and creation.[6]

On this exceptionalist account, *Political Theology* celebrates the aporia of 'the political'. Modern politics cannot count on any ultimate solution and pivots on extreme measures that are as necessary as they are affected by unredeemable contingency. Political theology, along with its allusion to the extra-human dimension of the miracle, indicates the impossibility for modern sovereignty to be grounded on a stable foundation. The ideal of a rational justification for political and legal institutions founders on the catastrophe of modern meaning. Modernity's deep-seated tendency towards chaos is the starting point from which an order can be built from scratch while giving up hope for rational justification. The fundamental unit of politics is the state of exception, the suspension of the order, which gives politics a tragic tinge and makes sovereignty the prime mover that does not require justification.

There is, however, a reading of *Political Theology* that is alternative to the one we have just summarised: a *jurisprudential* reading, as we hinted above. It deems Schmitt's reference to theology to be more peripheral and downplays

5 The theoretical need for a sharper differentiation between exception and emergency – one that may better reflect Schmitt's thinking on them – is opportunely emphasised in Kennedy, 'Emergency and Exception'.

6 Galli, *Genealogia della politica*, 340–1.

the tragic elements that look so pivotal in the exceptionalist reading. On a jurisprudential view, Schmitt is not the advocate of the unfoundability of modern politics, but the 'theologian of jurisprudence'.[7] If so, his invoking theology takes a different shape. The exception, *pace* exceptionalist readers, does not mean to glorify the unfounded foundation of the political order; nor is it a eulogy for faith as the buttress of the political community.[8] In sum, the exception is not the cornerstone of Schmitt's theory. Rather, it is a pointer to the 'salvific' power of the jurists – and particularly the jurist Carl Schmitt, who interprets himself as the last mindful representative of the *jus publicum europaeum*.

In this light, *Political Theology* turns out to be an essay into the nature of jurisprudence, its boundaries, and its tasks. This is the interpretative key we shall adopt in the subsequent sections. This reading admittedly projects onto this seminal text the reasons for the theoretical amendments that Schmitt made a few years following its publication. But this is all the more needed, we think, if we are to understand *Political Theology* as a jurisprudential text, for this reading reveals the juristic problem that Schmitt realised he had failed to address in 1922. *Political Theology* – he concluded in the late 1920s – failed to unravel the issue of legal normativity. He also concluded that (what we shall dub) *exceptionalist decisionism* failed to capture the essence of law. While in 1922 Schmitt intended to 'normalise' the exception and to make it the main feature of law and the state, shortly afterwards he drew attention away from it. He recognised that exceptions are infrequent and extreme circumstances that provide no stable foundation for everyday life. He therefore revised the role and the scope of the exception as something to avoid, to prevent, to fend off, as it is a potentially disastrous event that brings disorder and chaos, rather than order and stability.

In brief, according to our jurisprudential reading, Schmitt's exceptionalist decisionism in *Political Theology* is a transitory, flawed jurisprudential option, rather than the funeral dirge of modern politics. We shall vindicate this interpretation by investigating the core theme of *Political Theology* – that is, the nature and function of legal normativity. As we noted above, his main problem, especially in his polemic with positivist scholars, can be summed up as follows: what is it that turns a set of norms into a unified legal order? Or better: from what vantage point and with what instruments can jurists describe

7 Schmitt, *Glossarium*, 23.

8 Here we are alluding to Meier's hypothesis. It is worth noting that the exceptionalist reading is at variance with Meier's theological reading, as faith is certainly not taken to be the cornerstone of politics. Quite the reverse, as we insisted, the exceptionalist reading argues for the secularisation of the theological element, so much so that politics can never be founded on anything that transcends it.

the legal order *as an order*? If this is so, then, the kind of transcendence Schmitt had in mind in 1922 did not concern the exception as the unfounded foundation. Instead, it concerned the exception as a creative moment that transcends and exceeds any set of norms that, *qua* norms, do not contain their own unifying principle.

To put it another way, we think exceptionalist decisionism was an attempt at restoring the exceptional case within the conceptual tapestry of legal science. It was a resolute stance against legal positivists who believed they could leave aside the inquiry into the origin of law and only concerned themselves with the formal structure of the legal order – to wit, the norms, the way they are related to each other and the constitution, which positivists believed is what primes the validity of the legal order. Nothing, positivist legal theorists assumed, comes before the constitution – nothing, of course, which falls within the scope of legal science. Schmitt's exceptionalist decisionism in 1922 was a rebuttal of this conclusion on the part of positivist scholars. However, as we emphasised, exceptionalist decisionism was a transitory solution that Schmitt dropped shortly after the publication of *Political Theology*. For it hollowed out legal theory and also made it difficult to account for how the law works on a daily basis. As we shall demonstrate throughout the present book, it was to free himself of this burdensome legacy that Schmitt at the end of the 1920s fed off bits and pieces of other jurisprudential traditions, particularly French and Italian institutionalism. But it was not until the beginning of the 1930s that Schmitt gave a convincing twist to his argument against positivism and disposed of the naïve anti-normativism of the early 1920s. On this account, *Political Theology* should be regarded as an anti-normativist writing that seeks to find an entry point to the proper cognition of law. It is anti-normativist in that legal norms, for Schmitt, offer no reliable access to the phenomenon of law, unlike the exception – namely, the circumstance in which the decision brings about the legal order – which reveals all secrets about it.

HOW TO DESCRIBE THE LEGAL ORDER AS AN ORDER

In the first chapter of *Political Theology*, entitled 'Definition of Sovereignty', Schmitt's claim is straightforward: sovereignty lies in its subject: 'It is precisely the exception that makes relevant the subject of sovereignty, that is, the whole question of sovereignty.'[9] From the point of view of the theory of state and law, why should one know who the subject of sovereignty is? Schmitt's answer is

[9] Schmitt, *The Concept of the Political*, 6.

just as straightforward. Knowing who the sovereign is lays the condition for knowing what the existing legal order is. From a jurisprudential point of view, therefore, one knows what the valid system of norms is if and only if one can identify the subject of sovereignty. This is no facetious question for a jurist, in that it concerns the set of norms and imperatives that a whole body of state officials is required to apply both in normal and exceptional times. While this question haunted twentieth-century jurisprudence, Schmitt attached almost no importance to it in normal times – that is, when legal norms are generally complied with and a valid constitution is in force. On the contrary, he thought the question becomes salient, even vital, in extreme circumstances, when the existence of the political community is in jeopardy and its members are in need of clear normative guidelines.

It is worth emphasising that, for Schmitt, the exception cannot be reduced to a socio-political state of things, however unpredictable or unregulated it may be. Nor should it be reduced to the abrupt suspension of normal life. The exception is much more than this. It is a 'borderline concept' that belongs to 'the theory of the state'.[10] This concept is key to identifying the subject of sovereignty and thus is key to identifying the valid legal order. It is true that the exception is an extreme case, but this does not mean that it falls outside the scope of law.[11] Quite the contrary, it is foundational to the legal order, because it responds to the question of who the subject of sovereignty is. This reeks of paradox. In order that one may know what the valid legal order is, one must identify the one who can suspend or abolish it. But this is exactly what Schmitt was getting at. The jurisprudential (neither political-theological nor

[10] Ibid., 5.

[11] The theme of the state of exception figures prominently in studies that bring Schmitt's thinking to bear on the present and refer to it, mostly critically, for examining the exponential growth of emergency measures after 9/11. Seminal works are Dyzenhaus, *The Constitution of Law*; Fatovic, *Outside the Law*; Honig, *Emergency Politics*; Lazar, *States of Emergency in Liberal Democracies*; Scheppele, 'Law in a Time of Emergency'; Scheppele, 'Legal and Extralegal Emergencies'. On the valuable points of Schmitt's challenge to liberal constitutionalism about the role of exception, see Tushnet, 'Emergencies and the Idea of Constitutionalism'. Some theorists go so far as to rehabilitate Schmitt's theory of exceptional powers for revising contemporary constitutionalism – see e.g. Posner and Vermeule, 'Demystifying Schmitt' and Vermeule, 'Our Schmittian Administrative Law'. One of the most thorough accounts of Schmitt's take on the state of exception and emergency powers is Gross, 'The Normless and Exceptionless Exception'. It ought to be noted, though, that one of Gross's main criticisms is that Schmitt in 1922 took no account of normality and only concentrated on the exception, which is correct as far as *Political Theology* is concerned, yet much less so as far as his later writings are concerned (as the present book goes to great lengths to prove). So, we disagree with Gross's conclusion that 'Schmitt obviously finds no reason to rethink his theory' (Gross, 'The Normless and Exceptionless Exception'). Finally, an influential work that explores the philosophical relevance of this concept is Agamben, *State of Exception*.

theological-political) battle that he was engaged in concerned the nature of the exception as a borderline concept of the doctrine of the state – one that provides an *epistemic* perspective from which jurists can describe the legal order as a unity.

In other words, the exception is a conceptual tool at the service of legal science. It allows overcoming the limits of normativism, as the latter's exclusive focus on legal norms leaves the question of sovereignty unanswered. Normativism takes the system of legal norms as an unquestioned matter of fact and thereby neglects the act that brings it about. By doing so, Schmitt continues, normativist theorists delude themselves that they can know what the valid legal order is by simply interrogating its form – that is to say, the norms and procedures that make it a mechanical system of regulation. Normativist theorists also delude themselves that there can be a norm dictating the procedures to be carried out in the event of an emergency. Against this view, Schmitt argued that knowing what the valid legal order is entails looking beyond legal norms and procedures to get to the core of the legal phenomenon: namely, the deciding act whereby a law is established.

As we shall specify in the subsequent section, from a normativist standpoint, Schmitt's juristic interest in the foundation act when the legal order is brought to life dragged him into sociological premises. He put himself outside the boundaries of legal science and relocated within a different, somewhat incompatible discipline, which is meant to investigate the conditions that make the law socially effective. The bottom line of this normativist critique is that sociological methods, pivoted on the effectiveness of the legal order, are unfit to account for the validity of legal norms. Sociology fuses and confuses the two issues, and thus reduces norms to some prior facts. But Schmitt was quick to turn this critique on its head. Normativists who claim that what comes *before* the state legal order falls outside the scope of legal theory fall short of their task as legal theorists – they fail to see, to explain, to account for what law is. While replying to Gerhard Anschütz, who maintained that legal theory cannot face the question of the suspension of law, Schmitt put emphasis on the need for a 'philosophy of concrete life', which does not retreat from 'the exception and the extreme case, but must be interested in it to the highest degree'.[12] It is worth clarifying, though, that the notion of concrete life implied in this and other junctures of *Political Theology* is much thinner than the 'institution-based' one that is at the core of his later texts. In 1922 he simply meant the concreteness of an order grounded on the exceptional case.

[12] Schmitt, *The Concept of the Political*, 15.

In summary, the jurisprudential argument put forward in *Political Theology* reads as follows: one can cognise and recognise the existing legal order only by looking at what happens if the order needs to be suspended – that is, if a state of exception (*Ausnahmezustand*) is declared. The state of exception, in its turn, produces the subject of sovereignty the very moment she makes the sovereign decision of suspending the law. As we shall point out in Chapter 2, this argument attaches much more importance to the sovereign decision than Schmitt did in his works from the 1910s. Yet, the overemphasis on the foundational decision provides the ground for laying a claim that is as clear as it is tautological – though this is plainly intentional on Schmitt's part: 'Sovereign is who decides on the state of exception.'[13]

This is a main consequence of Schmitt's reasoning as well as the linchpin of his exceptionalist decisionism: the subject who decides on the state of exception is not bound by the rules of the existing legal order. Were the decider to be bound, she could be identified through the legal norms that bind her. But this is not the case, according to the legal epistemology of *Political Theology*. First comes the exception, then the rule – consequently, under no circumstances can a legal norm regulate the exception.

Therefore, it is the decision that turns the decider into the sovereign. Only the *effective* decision, though – which is to say, the one that efficaciously suspends the constitution in its entirety and makes it unusable. Any such effective decision is generative of sovereignty. In a way that creates frictions with earlier texts,[14] in *Political Theology* Schmitt maintained that the suspension of the constitutional order can yield two results. First, the decider can restore the suspended order. Second, she can bring about a new one.[15] This makes sense of the famed incipit we quoted above. It is certainly a provoking statement, as are many Schmitt's incipits, but it is far from enigmatic.

[13] Ibid., 5. Translation partially revised.

[14] On the remarkable discrepancy between *Dictatorship* and *Political Theology* on the nature of the exception, see Gross, 'The Normless and Exceptionless Exception'. See also Chs. 2 and 5 of the present book. In contrast to our reading, on the connection between these two writings, and above all on *Dictatorship* as the laboratory of Schmitt's most radical claims in *Political Theology*, Giorgio Agamben writes: 'The relationship between *Dictatorship* and *Political Theology* must be seen in the light of this complex strategy of inscribing the state of exception within the law. Jurists and political philosophers have generally directed their attention chiefly to the theory of sovereignty contained in the book from 1922, without realizing that this theory acquires its sense solely on the basis of the theory of the state of exception already elaborated in *Dictatorship*' (Agamben, *State of Exception*, 35).

[15] It ought to be noted that, whether the order is the restored pre-emergency legal order or a brand new one, the novel source of the order is the sovereign – therefore, in this sense, *Political Theology*, unlike *Dictatorship*, seems to imply that the order is always a new one, even if the contents of the new order are identical to the pre-emergency one.

Sovereign can be anyone who makes sure that the condition of utmost emergency is neither disorder nor chaos, but a state of exception – a pivotal jurisprudential notion – where the constitutional order in force before the decision was made is no longer in force. The decision suspends everyday normality and introduces exceptional norms that are appropriate to the extreme case.

In short, the first chapter of *Political Theology* can be read as an anti-normativist manifesto concerning the proper cognition of the legal order. Neither a particular norm nor a whole system of norms provides the answer to the crucial question of what the valid legal order is. This is an issue that only finds an answer in the notion of the state of exception – which is quintessentially jurisprudential. This notion, in its turn, leads to the related notion of decision, in that the existence of the state of exception depends on a decision that proves effective – no matter how and why. The effective *decision* grants sovereignty to the one who made it insofar as it is an *effective* decision.

ON COERCION AND THE BASIC NORM

The idea of a decision evokes a cut, as the etymon suggests in English, German, and other languages. Something needs to be cut out, eliminated, however painful this may turn out to be; a troublesome surplus that is to be removed for the political community to take shape. Most interpreters believe that, while *Political Theology* is elusive on this aspect, Schmitt came to clarify the issue a few years later, in *The Concept of the Political* (1928). In this latter writing, a decision is (alleged to be) made on the 'enemy' – that is, a menace looming large for the existence of the community, a menace posed by someone who is to be *physically* eliminated. Along this interpretative line, which ideally glues together *Political Theology* and *The Concept of the Political*, the sovereign Schmitt spoke of in 1922 is the one who in 1928 decides on the enemy who is to be fought to bring friends together. On this view, the friend is *constructed* and *shaped* by means of this antagonistic movement: the community of friends emerges out of a reaction to a threatening enemy. We shall cast doubt on this interpretation in Chapter 4, where we shall argue that the enemy who takes centre stage in *The Concept of the Political* has little to do with the notion of decision exposed in *Political Theology*. As further evidence for our case later on, the jurisprudential reading advanced in the previous section will remain the mainstay of our argument in this section, since it also helps make sense of the second chapter of *Political Theology*. Here Schmitt engages in polemic with Kelsen to place stress on the concept of sovereignty as the key to the legal order. We think it is worth expanding on the disagreement between these two scholars, which was destined to take a different flavour after 1922.[16]

Kelsen's overall theoretical framework pivots on the distinction between 'is' and 'ought' – a typically neo-Kantian distinction that implies the separation of the truth of empirical claims from the validity of legal norms. 'Is' and 'ought' mark out areas that are to be distinguished on logical grounds in the first place, although the distinction has a series of methodological consequences on all fields of knowledge. For it lays the foundation for the further distinction between *descriptive* and *normative* theories. Descriptive theories have to do with reality; they concern 'is'. Normative theories have to do with *ideality*; they concern 'ought'. Sociology, Kelsen continues, is a natural science of human society intended to explain what happens in the domain of actual behaviour. The science of law is a normative theory that describes a particular 'mode of thought', a particular point of view that differs from those of other theories. It describes *what one ought to do*, rather than describing *what one does do*. From this point of view, one can account for the validity of a legal norm – not the way it is used to certain ends or become effective. Legal validity does not correspond to law's effectiveness – that is to say, the fact that norms are generally complied with. The way in which norms are understood and used by officials and/or by the citizens bears no jurisprudential significance; the inquiry of legal effectiveness is to be left to such scholarly fields as sociology and psychology. The science of law is only required to determine if a given legal norm can be considered as valid – that is, as belonging to the legal system.[17]

This succinct description of Kelsen's ideal of theoretical pureness shines some light on the normativist conception of legal norms. In the eyes of the purely theoretical jurist, norms fall within the scope of ought. Within this

[16] See Ch. 5 of the present book.

[17] This methodological stance is clearly articulated as early as 1911 by Kelsen in *Über Grenzen zwischen juristischer und soziologischer Methode*. It should be noted that this understanding of the Kelsenian notion of validity is not universally agreed upon. For a deft analysis, see e.g. Nino, 'Some Confusions around Kelsen's Concept of Validity'. The dispute is revived, with a few interesting polarities coming to surface, in Paulson and Litschewski Paulson, *Normativity and Norms*. A useful summary of the various faces of validity in Kelsen's theory is Guastini, 'Kelsen on Validity (Once More)'. A recent book that interestingly toys with this issue is Duarte d'Almeida, Gardner and Green, *Kelsen Revisited*, Part I – see in particular the debate on whether legal validity is endowed with binding force and thus on the degree of realism of Kelsen's theory. An outstanding guide to Kelsen's theory, which sensibly discusses the notion of validity with reference to the link between the Pure Theory and the theory of democracy, is Vinx, *Hans Kelsen's Pure Theory of Law*. It is vital to stress that in the present book our interest in Kelsen's thinking is limited to the impact it had, whether directly or indirectly, on Schmitt's thinking.

realm, norms can neither be validated nor nulled by the concreteness of conforming or nonconforming behaviour. A norm is a relation of meaning-attribution: coercion is a meaning which is attributed by the legislator to an act, while the act, by virtue of this attribution, is qualified as unlawful and is located within the field of law as a delict. This attribution is described in terms of a *normative imputation*. Normative attribution or 'imputation', according to Kelsen, is such that statements about ought cannot be reduced to statements about is.[18] Coercion is the distinctive trait of the unlawful act. This is the theoretical move that will meet with Schmitt's criticism in the early 1930s – which we shall have to consider in some depth later in this book. In doing so, Kelsen portrayed the illegal act in a truly positivist fashion: a norm is legal because the legislator wants it to be so, and not because the legal norm identifies a conduct which is intrinsically wrong.[19] A crime is nothing other than the outcome of the association of a sanction to an act on the legislator's part.

In sum, for Kelsen, the definition of unlawful acts through the attribution of legal meanings – sanctions – is primary not because it identifies *mala in se*, but because it designates *mala quia prohibita*. In qualifying coercion as the primary norm, Kelsen moved away from the traditional German doctrine, which conceived the state as the decider of what is prohibited. It is not the will of the state-person that determines the legal act, but the inner logic of the way the legal system works. In *Reine Rechtslehre*, published in 1934, Kelsen wrote:

> What makes certain human behaviour illegal – a delict (in the broadest sense of the word) – is neither some sort of immanent quality nor some sort of connection to a metalegal norm, to a moral value, a value transcending the positive law. Rather, what makes certain behaviour a delict is simply and solely that this behaviour is set in the reconstructed legal norm as the

18 Imputation can be usefully described as a 'bridging principle', which explains how one's knowledge of legal norms can be derived from one's knowledge of concrete conducts. This (less onerous) conception views imputation as a principle that 'constrains the possible mappings from any given set of such facts to multiple meanings and provides a bridge between the relevant set of lower level facts and the objective meaning of a legal norm' (Pavlakos, 'Kelsenian Imputation and the Explanation of Legal Norms', 50). For a thorough presentation of imputation, see Paulson, 'Hans Kelsen's Doctrine of Imputation'. On the philosophical backdrop of Kelsen's theory of imputation and how it changed over time, see Langford and Bryan, 'Hans Kelsen's Concept of Normative Imputation'.

19 In 'Hans Kelsen and Carl Schmitt', Paulson takes Schmitt's most effective critique of this view to be developed in *Political Theology*. We disagree on this point. As we shall clarify in later chapters, while Schmitt in 1922 was primarily concerned with Kelsen's inability to account for sovereignty as the genuine starting point for the cognition of the legal order, it was not until the early 1930s that he clarified (what he saw) as the defects of a normativist conception of norms.

condition of a specific consequence, it is simply and solely that the positive legal system responds to this behaviour with a coercive act.[20]

The unlawful act is that which the norm connects to a sanction while the legal norm associates specific conditioning material facts with specific conditioned legal consequences. The unlawful act, then, is an essentially intralegal predicate. It is a condition that determines a consequence. To put it another way, the legal norm is a statement establishing that, if a given conduct is performed (one that a legal norm qualifies as unlawful), then, a coercive act *ought* to be performed. The norm's extra-factual character makes sure that legal normativity be unprejudiced by the potential occurrence of unlawful acts. Legal normativity is never conditional on the effectiveness of the distinct norms. While the conceptual tenability of the notion of the unlawful act is debatable, it is evident that Kelsen's objective was to locate the source of legal validity outside the sphere of effective behaviour. To this end, he postulated a link between legal validity and an intralegal process of meaning-attribution. He denied that the law originates, and draws its resources, from a pre-existing social practice. He denied that the law holds a *necessary* relation to social life. Therefore, by separating the issue of effectiveness from that of the conceptual justification of law, Kelsen emphasised that, from a jurisprudential point of view, there is no relation whatsoever between the validity of legal norms and their effectiveness within social life.

Later in this book it will be important to analyse the difference between Schmitt's critique of positivism in *Political Theology* and his critique of it about twelve years later, in *On the Three Types of Juristic Thought*.[21] In 1922 Schmitt claimed that the major flaw of positivism relates to the dissolution of the concept of sovereignty, which in his view was the key to the law and its origin. This does not dovetail with his critique in 1934, when Schmitt claimed that the major flaw of normativism, and *a fortiori* positivism (as a fruitless blend of decisionism and normativism), was the wedge that it drove between concrete life and the law. The dismissal of sociological considerations, Schmitt argued in *Political Theology*, led Kelsen to devote exclusive attention to the form of the legal order, while the legal order turns out to be synonymous with the state. However, Schmitt reasoned, as long as one deems the state and the legal order to be one and the same thing, one remains blind to the jurisgenerative (quintessentially *legal*) force of sovereignty, which

20 Kelsen, *Introduction to the Problems of Legal Theory*, 26.

21 See Ch. 5.

comes before any legal order is set in motion.[22] And indeed, Schmitt is right on this point. In Kelsen's view, the issue of the creation of the law simply fades away. This could well be a problem of utmost historical or political relevance, and yet, as a historical or political problem, bears no relevance to the science of law. Kelsen thought that if one tries to investigate the original establishment of the constitution from a jurisprudential perspective, one comes to a point at which validity will have to be taken as a hypothetical presupposition:

> [O]ne may ask why a certain coercive act is a legal act and thus belongs to a certain legal system – the coercive act of incarceration, say, whereby one human being deprives another of liberty. The answer is that this act was prescribed by a certain individual norm, a judicial decision. Suppose one asks further why this individual norm is valid, indeed, why it is valid as a component of a certain legal system. The answer is that this individual norm was issued in accordance with the criminal code. And if one asks about the basis of the validity of the criminal code, one arrives at the state constitution, according to whose provisions the criminal code was enacted by the competent authorities in a constitutionally prescribed procedure. If one goes on to ask about the basis of the validity of the constitution, on which rest all statutes and the legal acts stemming from those statutes, one may come across an earlier constitution, and finally the first constitution, historically speaking, established by a single usurper or a council, however assembled. What is to be valid as norm is whatever the framers of the first constitution have

[22] One should bear in mind that, for Schmitt, the legal order does not exhaust the legal domain. Like the state, the law continues to exist even when the legal order is suspended. If this were not the case, the activity of the sovereign who decides on the state of exception would be tantamount to pure violence – a conclusion that Schmitt always rejected. Rather, the decision is already and always legal in the sense that it yields a new law the very moment it puts the legal order in abeyance. In a formula, the sovereign decision cannot be lawful (based on the legal norms it suspends), but is always legal, because it is the source of law and as such is the heart of the legal phenomenon. The same holds true for the state – that is, the multifarious apparatus comprising law-making and law-applying agencies and the state officials who operate them. As Schmitt disallowed the identity of the state and the legal order, when the latter is suspended the former does not founder. Rather, the state continues to operate in compliance with the exceptional law of the sovereign and the state chain of command obeys a line of authority that does not end with the pre-existing constitution but with the sovereign decision. This consideration only applies to *Political Theology*. When Schmitt extensively revised his own theory in a sense that we shall clarify later, he also revised the notion of decision, the idea of the source of law, and the relation between the decision and the legal order. In particular, from the early 1930s onward, because of the importance he attached to social practices, he came to believe that the continued existence of the state was not conditional upon the new law yielded by the sovereign, but on those very practices as the kernel of a historical tradition. This implies that the point we made in this footnote is inapplicable to writings posterior to *Political Theology*.

> expressed as their will – this is the basic presupposition of all cognition of the legal system resting on this constitution.[23]

In other words, while the constituent power cannot be considered as authorised by the constitution, for the constitution to be interpreted as valid, its validity is to be *presupposed*. This, and nothing else, is the content of the *Grundnorm*, the basic norm. This hypothetical norm serves two functions. First, it enables anyone, and especially the judges, to interpret an imperative, a permission, or an authorisation as an objectively valid legal norm. Second, it enables legal scientists to interpret legal norms as valid – that is, as belonging to the legal order.[24] But it is not up to the science of law to ascertain the validity of the basic norm as a hypothetical grounding principle. To put it otherwise, precisely when it purports to expunge all the data that have no legal-scientific character, Kelsen's methodological pureness cut out the concept that Schmitt believed to be the most important and decisive within the theory of the state – namely, the origin of law.

Despite these methodological divergences, however, there is a striking convergence between these two authors that should not go unnoticed. They came to quite similar conclusions on what it is that determines the identity of the legal order. They merely disagreed on the intra- or extra-legal nature of the foundation of law, and whether or not it falls within the scope of legal science. According to Kelsen, as we have seen, the original foundation of the order is not of the jurist's concern. The order acquires its own identity, unity and completeness in the light of the hypothetical basic norm. However, the role played by the decision in Schmitt's theoretical framework recalls the role played by the basic norm; for the decision is meant to determine who the sovereign is and, in the light of that, what the valid legal order is. For either of these scholars, therefore, the law has a positive nature, and so can have any content.[25] Both deny that law acquires its validity from extra-legal contents. Both concur that legal validity originates from the logic of the legal

[23] Kelsen, *Introduction to the Problems of Legal Theory*, 57.

[24] For a discussion of these two functions, see Raz, *The Authority of Law*, 122–45, and Vinx, *Hans Kelsen's Pure Theory of Law*, 11–15.

[25] In *Hans Kelsen's Pure Theory of Law*, Lars Vinx offers a fully fledged argument to explain why he does not agree on this point. He maintains that there is an unbreakable tie between Kelsen's pure theory and Kelsen's theory of democracy. Contrary to interpretations that isolate and distinguish the theory of law from the conception of politics, and even contrary to Kelsen's own lack of clarity about the tie that binds them, Vinx maintains that Kelsen's theory of the validity of law should be read against his theory of democratic institutions, the rule of law and the constitution.

machinery – which for Kelsen, contrary to Schmitt, does not include the moment of its establishment.[26]

The reason lying behind this fundamental convergence is to be found in their common objective. Both of them aim to identify the element that confers identity and coherence on the legal order and therefore permit one to gain knowledge of it. Most likely, the deepest root of this common objective, which makes their theoretical strategies comparable, is their staunch aversion to natural law theories. The basic norm and the decision are the mainstay of two theoretical strategies that are intended to identify the unified structure and the completeness of the legal order with no recourse to a natural law foundation and at the same time avoiding a *regressus ad infinitum*.

THE STRUCTURAL NATURE OF THE SOCIOLOGY OF LEGAL CONCEPTS

As we argued, Schmitt's and Kelsen's conclusions converge, as they revolve around the point of view from which jurists can vindicate the identity and the unity of the legal order. However, in *Political Theology*, Schmitt never got tired of bemoaning the limits of jurisprudential approaches that programmatically neglected the role of sovereignty. Scholars who identify sovereignty with the state, or the state with the legal order, turn a blind eye to the condition of existence of both the state and the law. But how did Schmitt think he should remedy this limitation?

In Chapter 3 of *Political Theology*, Schmitt coined the term 'sociology of legal concepts' to designate his endeavour to trace the historical forms of legal concept back to their origin. He thought this method of investigation is the most appropriate to study the fundamental concepts of politics, and sovereignty in particular. While this type of investigation could certainly be interpreted as a 'metaphysical' approach, it should better be regarded as a 'structural' approach to the basic categories of a form of life – though the

[26] Although this is not the main thread of our analysis, it should also be noted that, for either author, the application of legal norms always requires a decision – one that is nowhere to be found in the contents of the norms themselves. Indeed, in *Statute and Judgment* (1912), Schmitt's criticism of Kelsen was more moderate than in other works, since they had not entirely parted ways yet. Towards the end of the 1910s, both gave the decision a prominent role, with one main difference. Schmitt radicalised the autonomy of the decision as he considered it to be the foundation of legal normality. Kelsen narrowed down the area of the application of the decision by assigning it a normative role within the scope of a dynamic conception of the legal system as a pyramidal structure of normative acts of implementation. On the (poorly) decisionist nature of *Statute and Judgment*, see also Ch. 2 of the present book.

method is obviously not empirical but conceptual.[27] Schmitt's idea is that the foundations of the legal-philosophical theory of sovereignty should be recovered through an analysis of metaphysical or structural kind, rather than a purely normativist or purely sociological one.

The sociology of legal concepts can be viewed as *structural* in the sense that it reconstructs the entire conceptual grid of a given form of life. Any particular instance of this grid should be read against the background of the whole. Schmitt writes: 'This sociology of concepts transcends juridical conceptualization oriented to immediate practical interest. It aims to discover the basic, radically systematic structure and to compare this conceptual structure with the conceptually represented social structure of a certain epoch.'[28] In other words, this method looks for a kind of intelligibility in the light of which the 'situated' ideas of politics and law can be fully understood as belonging to a common metaphysical frame. For example, more than the sociology of the concept of sovereignty as an autonomous entity, for Schmitt it is vital to trace the correspondence between the historical-political status of the monarchy of a given period and the general political consciousness that characterised Western Europe in the same period.

Schmitt thought of a sort of metaphysical image of the world that shapes an entire epoch and presents to the consciousness of an entire civilisation certain forms of political organisation as the only possible ones. It should not slip one's attention, though, that, in stark contrast to the classical portrait of Schmitt's political thinking, this understanding sets a limit on the autonomy of the political. Indeed, based on the arguments offered in the first two chapters of *Political Theology*, the link between legal-political concepts and the metaphysical image of the world comes across as a fully fledged critique of theories that reduce legal knowledge to the study of the formal system in force. In the third chapter, Schmitt combined his interest in a more complete legal science with the dismissal of sociological reductionism: legal-political concepts are not the reflection of economic or other types of mechanisms, but enjoy a structural autonomy of their own. The multiple relations among the concepts inhabiting the various spheres of a community build the conceptual frame in which the ensemble of concepts gives rise to a community view in which everything holds together. Though underdeveloped as a research methodology, Schmitt's reference to the sociology of legal concepts is a

[27] On the nature of the sociology of legal concepts as an attempt to counter Max Weber's reductionism, see Colliot-Thélène, 'Carl Schmitt versus Max Weber'.

[28] Schmitt, *The Concept of the Political*, 45.

reference to a form of life in which concepts are caught in a relation of mutual dependence.

As far as the analysis of the concept of sovereignty is concerned, Schmitt's methodological framework pivots on three phases. First, he opens, as usual, with a seductive sentence: 'All significant concepts of the modern theory of the state are secularized theological concepts.'[29] Second, he evokes his sociological type of inquiry by presenting it as key to understanding the transformations in the political and the legal spheres. Finally, he introduces the analogy between pre-modern theology and modern sovereignty – the analogy consisting in the fact that both are exposed to the will of an absolute power that originates and organises the order. It is in this light that, for Schmitt, the analogue of the concept of the sovereign decision is the divine miracle: 'The exception in jurisprudence is analogous to the miracle in theology.'[30] As the latter suspends the laws of nature, so does the former suspend the laws of the state.

However, Schmitt's analogy does not imply the absence of an objective foundation of politics *tout court*. Rather, the miracle unveils the groundlessness of the sovereign decision, which can only be explained through the study of the broader and more integrated conceptual fabric of a form of life. The problem, therefore, is not so much the unjustifiability of the decision as a sovereign decision as it is its integration in the wider conceptual frame shoring up the community life. Based on this, one could argue that Schmitt was looking for the best way to ensure the integration of the unfoundedness of the decision with the complexity of the metaphysical image of the modern age. On this interpretation, the problem of the modern political form is grafted onto the relationship between the concreteness of political life and its transcendence in the form of an underlying conceptual constellation.

Schmitt's search for concreteness, however, got off on the wrong foot. For he was caught in a double bind. He wanted to celebrate the unjustifiability of the decision and at the same time claimed the decision to be anchored to an overarching conceptual frame. In doing so, he extolled an origin that is utterly heteronomous and hence not very 'original', as it springs from the metaphysical resources of a culture as a whole. At the same time, however, he insisted that only this origin, which is embodied in a decision on the case of exception, fends off the always incipient disorder.

It is pointless to dive deeper into this double bind, in that it betrays a fundamental oscillation concerning a solution that, from the end of the

[29] Ibid., 36.
[30] Ibid., 36.

1920s onwards, Schmitt was less and less happy with; for it created a short-circuit between the unjustifiability of the decision and its belonging to a conceptual background. As we shall illustrate later in this book,[31] he significantly scaled down the decisionist character of his theory and relocated the decision in a broader triangulation with norms and what in 1934 he called 'concrete order' (*konkrete Ordnung*). There is no need here to anticipate an argument that we shall have to detail as we go along. The objective of this chapter, with its jurisprudential reading of *Political Theology*, was to advance the hypothesis that in 1922 Schmitt placed the sovereign decision at the heart of the theory of law as a conceptual strategy to make the legal order legible and intelligible as an order. However, his insistence on the unjustifiability of the decision came at a price: the total devaluation of the ordinary life of the law.

In *Political Theology* Schmitt wrote: 'The exception is more interesting than the normal case. The normal proves nothing, the exception proves everything; it not only confirms the rule, the rule lives only from the exception.'[32] It is exactly this conclusion that Schmitt began to question year after year, up to the works of the early 1930s, where he made what we call an 'institutional turn'.[33] Not only was the exception an unreliable entry point to the foundation of law. It also brought instability into his general theory, in that it complicated, rather than explained, the normal case. This is the reason why Schmitt abandoned exceptionalist decisionism soon after 1922 and gradually began to look for a steadier basis for the normality of everyday life. Before moving on to the analysis of Schmitt's institutionalism, the next two chapters will discuss a few preliminary aspects that are key to understanding the institutional turn: first, Schmitt's durable interest in the concreteness of life – which, after all, is only silenced in *Political Theology* and timidly resurfaces in the guise of the sociology of legal concepts; second, the criticisms his exceptionalist theory received over the course of the heated debates on decisionism.

[31] See in particular Chs. 5 and 6.
[32] Schmitt, *The Concept of the Political*, 15.
[33] We first advanced the institutional turn thesis in Croce and Salvatore, *The Legal Theory of Carl Schmitt*.

2

Looking Backwards

Schmitt before Exceptionalist Decisionism

The unequivocal identification of Schmitt's thinking with exceptionalism (and, the other way around, of any form of exceptionalism with Schmitt's thinking) gets caught in a circle. It takes it for granted that Schmitt's genuine and most interesting advances are to be confined to less than a decade: from 1921 to 1928. In this span of years – quite a short one, for sure – the two pillars of exceptionalist decisionism are generally identified with *Political Theology* and *The Concept of the Political* – though one is left wondering why exceptionalism is associated with this latter book, since there is no exception to be seen in there. Based on such a periodisation, one cannot help but imagine Schmitt as obsessed with such an utterly extreme political scenario as the suspension of the constitution whereby a 'miraculous' sovereign, with a jurisgenerative act, makes so radical a decision as to establish a whole new order and a brand-new normality. However, as we noted at the very outset, such an approach to Schmitt's oeuvre is, to say the least, viciously circular, in that the conclusion that his most interesting works are, self-evidently, those he produced between 1921 and 1928 forms part of the premise.

However, if one cares to enlarge the scope to include Schmitt's whole publication record, the picture looks different. His first work, *Über Schuld und Schuldarten*, is dated 1910, while his last significant essay, 'The Legal World Revolution', celebrates Schmitt's turning 90. We do acknowledge, of course, that writings should not be counted but weighed (and meditated). Nor do we dare to question the salience of Schmitt's Weimar writings and more generally the great relevance of his thinking during those crucial years for Germany and Europe. Not at the price, however, of reducing sixty-eight years of intellectual effort and publishing activity (which stretches over two world wars and four constitutional regimes in his country alone) to less than ten years. While advocates of the exceptionalist reading can legitimately argue that the decisionism of the 1920s is his only phase worth considering and debating, those who are dubious of this latter conclusion can legitimately argue that Schmitt neither was born nor died as a decisionist. And this is a fact – as far as an unequivocal and compelling textual evidence can be.

Building on this fact, the present chapter sets out to mount three cases:

(1) Well before he became famous as the advocate of decisionism, Schmitt was an accomplished jurist. At that time, his view of law and the legal practice was scarcely reconcilable with his subsequent sovereign decisionism (even less so if decisionism takes the semblance of exceptionalism). By rejecting any 'continuist' interpretation, we make the claim that Schmitt's theorisation in the 1910s anticipated a few constitutive features of his legal institutionalism of the 1930s, particularly the close relation between normality and the judicial practice.
(2) The 1921–8 period can be portrayed as essentially and exclusively decisionist only if one turns a blind eye to some important lines of thought that he developed in those very same years.
(3) Even if one chooses to be blind to the various theoretical tensions between Schmitt's own lines of thought in that period, the books that open and close it, namely, *Dictatorship* (1921) and *Constitutional Theory* (1928), do not easily lend themselves to a resolutely decisionist interpretation.

THE ANTI-DECISIONIST STANCE OF SCHMITT'S EARLY WRITINGS

One is amazed, or at least should be, at the scant attention that the young Schmitt's writings have attracted. Particularly, we refer to *Über Schuld und Schuldarten. Eine Terminologische Untersuchung* (On Guilt and the Types of Guilt: A Terminological Investigation) (1910) and *Statute and Judgment: An Investigation into the Problem of Legal Practice* (1912).[1] However, both these

[1] The recent translation of this latter work by Vinx and Zeitlin, *Carl Schmitt's Early Legal-Theoretical Writings*, will certainly draw due attention to these overlooked texts. See, in particular, their introduction to the book, where they deftly contextualise *The Value of the State and the Significance of the Individual* and the other Schmitt's text included in the book, *Statute and Judgment*, and offer precious interpretative guidance. In a passing remark in their highly informative and comprehensive introduction ('Carl Schmitt and the Problem of the Realization of Law', 32), Vinx and Zeitlin claim that, in emphasising the relevance of *On the Three Types of Juristic Thought*, our interpretation of Schmitt's legal theory (see Croce and Salvatore, *The Legal Theory of Carl Schmitt*) does not take into due consideration that 'all three elements of legal order Schmitt distinguishes in this work – positive norms, sovereign decisions that contravene such norms and a concrete order that underpins the legitimate applicability of norms – are already present in the early legal-theoretical works'. Vinx and Zeitlin are certainly right that the three elements can be traced back to Schmitt's early texts. Nonetheless, this is not enough to debunk the claim that the early 1930s mark a turning point in Schmitt's thought.

texts show remarkable traits of intellectual originality and theoretical cogency – especially if compared to other occasional texts by Schmitt that have been subjected to the most searching scrutiny. This calls for a closer look into them. While they are valuable for their specific, original contents, they also mark interesting lines of rupture and continuity with Schmitt's later works – as is evidenced by their republication, respectively, in 1977 and 1969 (the latter with a new Preface by the author). Nor should their original versions go unnoticed, if only because of the number of reviews devoted to them and the prestige of the reviewers. This is all evidence that as early as 1912 Schmitt was considered as much more than a promising jurisprude of the Wilhelmine period.

Within the purview of a purely juristic inquiry, *Über Schuld und Schuldarten* investigates the notion of guilt in order to derive a fully juristic definition of it – one that does not rely on subjective motives to be reconstructed etiologically. In short, the argument reads as follows. To foreground the logical and semantic requirements and preconditions of a legal order, the concept of guilt cannot be based on subjectivist aspects and motives, such as dispositions, urges, drives, etc. Rather, guilt must be construed in *essentially juristic terms* – that is, in such a way for it to be 'recognised' and included within the legal order. In other words, culpability cannot be something that, *based on subjective reasons external to the order*, results in the simple infringement of a particular legal rule. Quite the reverse, it must be characterised as one's disposition to act in such a way that the legal order can interpret and qualify it as inadmissible *based on objective reasons internal to the order.*

To obtain a juristic, formal definition of guilt – and this is crucial to our overall argument in this book – Schmitt presupposes that the entire legal order (and not only the single norms) should be ascribed specific and concrete ends,

Indeed, it is Schmitt himself who specifies that '[e]*very* jurisprudential thought works with rules, as well as with decisions, and with orders and formations. But only one of these can be the ultimate jurisprudentially formed notion from which all the others are always juristically derived: either norm (in the sense of rule and statute), or decision, or concrete order' (Schmitt, *On the Three Types of Juristic Thought*, 43 (emphasis added)). Then, to be distinctive of a given legal approach, according to Schmitt, as well as an interpretation that builds on his categories, it is not the coexistence of rules, decisions, and orders as such, but the hierarchical – and jurisgenerative – order in which these elements are brought together. If viewed through this lens, it is easy to see that in Schmitt's early works there is no reference whatsoever to an institutional order, at least if conceived as a concrete web of basic institutions (whose primacy, in the hierarchy of the three elements he refers to, was yet to come). Rather, in the 1910s a combination of norms and (only judicial) decisions enjoyed priority over any concrete orders and formations. For a further discussion of these aspects, see Croce and Salvatore, *Little Room for Exception*.

a sort of *direct normative orientation* that turns the different legal prescriptions into a consistent body. At the same time, culpability is manifested in the offender's opposition to the aims of the order *as a whole*, not simply in the infringement of particular rules. Criminals are guilty not because of some criminal law provisions that make them so, but because of the *objective contradiction* between their conduct and that which the norm mandates as part of the more comprehensive set of purposes that saturates the legal order as a unity. Guilt is hallmarked by the *anti-juridical nature* of the criminal's purpose, or better, the straightforward, irreconcilable opposition between ends. While criminals perform conduct prohibited by legal rules, the thrust of the opposition is the conflict arising from the clash between the criminals' ends and the legal order's ones. In other words, guilt is more a matter of practical contradiction than one of rule-breaking: what is broken is not primarily the law, but the cohesion of a collective will.

Another significant feature is the fact that, despite its undeniable normativist nuance, in *Über Schuld und Schuldarten* Schmitt posited that the aim pursued by the legal order is not a simple ideal presupposition. Rather, it is a *concrete orientation*, which is realised both in the positive nature of the law and in the system of existing institutions. This makes sense of the definition of culpability as 'the concrete disposition of ends (*Zwecksetzung*) not corresponding to the ends of the law, put in place by a subject capable of understanding and willing, for whom it was possible to be aware of it being contrary to duty'.[2] Punishment is not intended to repress criminals, but to emphasise that they contravened the ends established and pursued by the legal order – as criminals themselves practically demonstrate by engaging in effectively and ostensibly criminal conducts.

As we noted, Schmitt's debut work is a text with a clear normativist tinge – though obviously not in a Kelsenian sense. For Schmitt's normativism is of a thin kind, to say the least. The claimed legal self-sufficiency (in a sense, non-evaluative) of the formal concept of guilt gets contaminated by considerations and features that are strongly evaluative; for one thing, the 'judgement of being unworthy' (*Unwerturteil*),[3] which Schmitt evoked to define what the illicit act is from the point of view of the legal order; for another, the peremptory qualification of the conscious attitude of the criminal as 'a legally malevolent will' (*böse*).[4] This is evidence that Schmitt believed the legal order pursues concrete ends based on which culpability can be characterised as non-conformity. And it is also evidence that he recognised the actuality of the ends

[2] Schmitt, *Über Schuld und Schuldarten*, 16.
[3] Ibid., 16.
[4] Ibid., 17.

that are incorporated into a positive legal order, which includes *de facto* institutional entities that exist in the legal realm and affect it.[5]

Regardless of how one assesses the type of normativism that permeates *Über Schuld und Schuldarten*, it is undeniable that *Statute and Judgment* (1912) broke with it as it introduced a notion of *decision*, which thus made its first appearance in Schmitt's intellectual history. However, there is a substantial difference that makes it difficult to compare this notion with the decisionism of the early 1920s: it is not a *sovereign* decision, the *Entscheidung* that brings about the state of exception, but a *judicial* decision, the *Urteil* that figures in the title. As such, it is not pitted against the law. In *Statute and Judgment* Schmitt advanced a theory of the decision essentially based on the normativity of the law, and not on the founder (or re-founder) of the legal order. As such, norms are certainly exposed to various degrees of indeterminacy, but it is an indeterminacy that exists within the legal order itself. Law's uncertainty can be overcome by means of the operational and epistemic resources available to the system – that is, the commonly adopted judicial practice that Schmitt eulogises in this book.[6] This theory of the decision eventuates not so much in a 'weak decisionism'[7] as in a theory of deliberation. *Statute and Judgment* aimed to identify an objective criterion to establish the conditions under which a judicial decision can be deemed to be correct from a point of view that is internal to the judicial practice.

5 The implicit conflictual potentialities, not only intra-legal, are nicely captured by Michele Nicoletti, who underlines that the aim of the criminal 'is the establishment of a concrete order; and it is this "position" of an aim, such an ordering intentionality governing the human will that undercuts the ordering will of society and that, by contradicting it, manifests itself as "guilt"' (Nicoletti, *Trascendenza e potere*, 22).

6 As has been convincingly argued, 'while in Schmitt's first writings one can certainly identify the incubation period of *Political Theology*, they nevertheless constitute an original and critical vantage point within the normativism of the early 19th century. In other words, if it is true that in *Über Schuld und Schuldarten*, *Gesetz und Urteil*, and above all in *Der Wert des Staates und die Bedeutung des Einzelnen* there are many elements that will be re-elaborated in the successive phase, it is just as true that the most fundamental of them – the role of the judicial decision – shows no character of foundation, let alone any autonomy with respect to the practical and juridical context from which it derives its legitimacy and force. *Right decision* means nothing other than a decision made in conformity with the existing legal order. On the contrary, in the decisionist phase, the deciding act is completely detached from the criterion of rightness. For the decision is not characterised by its conformity to something, but by the fact that it constitutes an origin that emerges out of normative and legal nothingness. Therefore, the topic of *Political Theology* is not the decision in general, but the sovereign decision that is at the root of the modern state, that is to say, the concrete act that is normatively indeterminable and indeducible, and despite this creates law and situates itself at the origin of the legal order itself' (Calabrese, *Colpa e decisione negli scritti giuspenalistici di Carl Schmitt*, 62–3).

7 See Portinaro, 'Che cos'è il decisionismo?', 258.

What matters for our purposes in the present book is the decisive role that the concept of *normality* plays in the proposed solution. It is already introduced in the Foreword, where Schmitt commented on the role of a uniform practice and a recurring regularity: 'The true endeavour of any judge, according to this treatise, is to decide the case at hand in the way that contemporary practice in general would have decided it. The demand for regular and uniform practice, hence, is the basis of all efforts to reach a correct decision.'[8] Here is the final formulation: 'A judicial decision is correct, today, if it is to be assumed that another judge would have decided in the same way. "Another judge", in this context, refers to the empirical type of the modern, legally trained jurist.'[9] A few pages later, Schmitt qualifies this 'other judge' as the 'the normal, legally trained judge. The word "normal" is used here in a quantitative sense that refers to the average, not as the designation of an ideal type and not in a qualitative-teleological sense.'[10] The judge is thus called upon to decide in such a way that the reasonableness of her decision in relation to the individual case (that has to comply with the dual requirement of predictability and calculability) may presumably be adopted by any other judge as an effective rule. This rule, which should ideally be general and generalisable, should then be applicable to any other concrete case related to the case at issue.

Basically, the anti-decisionism of *Statute and Judgment* pivots on the internal relationship between normality and the judicial practice of ordinary courts. Normality in this context plays out as the reiterated and consolidated adoption of judicial resolutions that proved effective and reliable in past circumstances – effectiveness and reliability that are largely due to the performative capacity inherent in judges' converging on a limited set of adjudications. The 'normal, legally trained judge', tasked with the Herculean job of safeguarding the order as a whole, is called into play to inhibit and neutralise any form of exception and creativity, whatever its origins and aims. And this is certainly worth stressing, as it conspicuously runs against the grain of Schmitt's exceptionalist decisionism in the early 1920s, where the sovereign decision is first and foremost framed in terms of exception and creativity. But there is more to this. As mentioned above, this pivotal activity of normalisation is entrusted to ordinary (not high) courts, within the frame of a systemic judicial strategy that Schmitt recovered in the early 1930s. Albeit in a completely different context and with completely different aims, *Statute and Judgment* and the early 1930s texts share the proclivity for a kind of determinacy that is more *judicial* than

8 Schmitt, *Statute and Judgment*, 43.
9 Ibid., 103.
10 Ibid., 109.

legal in that it is to be obtained primarily through and within the judicial practice. As we shall explain later,[11] with the early 1930s texts Schmitt finally embraced an institutional view of law – and, not by chance, in a legal horizon that was entirely centred on the idea of living law. It was at this stage that he came to consider widespread interactional practices, embodied into the institutional order, as the material foundation for the legal order.

Let us comment on one last, yet no less decisive, point of contact between Schmitt's approach in *Statute and Judgment* and his later institutional approach. Although norms and actual behaviour are close to one another, even contiguous, they do not coincide. Indeed, normality in Schmitt is never configured as the immediate and legally certified hypostatisation of the status quo, whether this is to be identified through judicial practice or in a sociologically describable institutional reality. On the contrary, normality emerges out of a constant mediation between two poles – an irreducible mediation, as Schmitt maintained many a time, that preserves and makes binding two key legal features: the normative force of the 'normal judge' (not of the whole body of actual judges) and the normative force of the *exemplum* of models of conduct carved into ideal-typical figures (the brave soldier, the loyal official, the good family man, etc. – we shall have to discuss them later).[12]

Lest we be misunderstood, we are not suggesting that there is continuity between this writing from the 1910s and those from the 1930s.[13] By simplifying a far more complex and nuanced thinking, a 'continuist' interpretation would make the same and opposite mistake as the one made by those who exclusively identify Schmitt with exceptionalist decisionism. Quite the opposite, we want to underscore that the exceptionalist output of the early 1920s marks an irreconcilable and irreversible break with the conceptual categories that Schmitt had hitherto adopted. In the 1910s he loudly reclaimed the autonomy of the legal field vis-à-vis the looming menace of colonisation, even the mere influence, on the part of the political (not yet theorised as *das Politische*).

In other words, what we want to emphasise here is that a few basic categories mobilised in the texts of the 1910s, above all *normality* and *regularity*, were destined to be retrieved and reinterpreted in a completely different context in the early 1930s – the main link between these two periods being Schmitt's anti-decisionist stance (if by decision we mean the absolute or sovereign decision).

[11] See Chs. 4 and 5.

[12] This is an issue that is as thorny as it is crucial to an adequate interpretation not only of the texts under scrutiny. With Schmitt *contra* Schmitt (and the reference here is above all to the unrepentant Schmitt who approved of Nazism), one should consider the decisive arguments that he himself offered against any attempt to reduce the law to the mere imposition of power: see Schmitt, *The Value of the State and the Significance of the Individual*, Ch. 1.

[13] We shall discuss a 'continuist' interpretation, the pan-institutional reading, later in Ch. 4.

In brief, the exceptionalist decisionism of the early 1920s constituted not only a change of direction with respect to the initial theoretical project – one that covered a span of years no shorter than the more famous Weimarian twelve-year period (1921–32). It also inaugurated a theoretical trajectory that was completely alien, even opposite, to the theory of the 1910s. As has been convincingly argued,[14] up to the end of the 1910s Schmitt played the part of the traditional jurist, the deft and diligent defender of a juristic conception of law that seeks to make up for the shortcomings of statutory law. In sum, until the end of World War One and the proclamation of the Weimar Republic, there is no sign of decisionism in Schmitt's works.

CORRECTIO OPPOSITORUM: AN INSTITUTIONAL DETAIL IN THE DECISIONIST PAINTING

In the twelve years that most interpreters consider as the most relevant period of Schmitt's output (1921–32), there is at least one work – whose correct interpretation and 'collocation' is still the object of heated debates – that is hardly amenable to an exceptionalist reading. This is the essay titled *Roman Catholicism and Political Form*. It is difficult not to notice that it was published in 1923, only one year after the publication of *Political Theology*. The divergence between these two works is intensified by their thematic proximity. Still, in *Roman Catholicism and Political Form* there is no mention of 'political theology',[15] just as in *Political Theology* there is no trace of the word 'institution' (either as a legal or as a merely political reality).[16]

[14] See Fioravanti, 'Kelsen, Schmitt e la tradizione giuridica dell'Ottocento'.

[15] It seems to us that *Political Theology II* proves beyond all doubt – of course with the limitations of any retrospective interpretation, especially when provided by the author (and mostly when the author is Carl Schmitt) – that his main interest is very far from any theological speculations on politics. A few quotes will suffice to illustrate this point: 'The book [*Political Theology*] does not deal with theological dogma, but with problems in epistemology and in the history of ideas: the structural identity of theological and juridical concepts, modes of argumentation and insights' (Schmitt, *Political Theology II*, 42). In a similar vein: 'This [the analysis developed in *Political Theology*] belongs to the research area of the history of law and sociology' (148). Even more clearly, Schmitt defines *Political Theology* – that is now interpreted in a perspective that takes for granted the institutional turns leading to a concrete-order approach to politics – as 'that juridic book' (49). Finally, and more generally, Ch. 3 as a whole makes the point that the mundane counterpart of theology is not – or at least, no longer – politics, but jurisprudence (misleadingly translated as 'theory of law' (108)).

[16] To refer to one of the interpretations that most insist on the radical opposition between the two writings we are considering, 'the contrast between *Politische Theologie* and *Römischer Katholizismus und politische Form* is so striking that it is hard to believe that the author had written one book right after the other. The Church's capacity to arbitrate, which was portrayed

Those who advocate an exceptionalist reading of Schmitt's theory inevitably relativise, if not dissolve, the thick institutionalist orientation of *Roman Catholicism and Political Form*, as it defies the comforting interpretive frame of decisionism. To water down the striking dualism between these two writings, the 1923 book is granted a minor role in Schmitt's output. *Political Theology* is claimed to tackle the issue of the unfounded foundation of political modernity – a reading that we have challenged in the previous chapter. *Roman Catholicism and Political Form* is claimed to be nothing but a digression – if not occasional, certainly cursory[17] – about the glorious, pre-modern (more than anti-modern) *plenitudo potestatis* (fullness of powers) as an endowment of the Church, the Church's bygone ordering power that had to give way to the constitutive groundlessness of the modern political horizon.

Certainly, the selection and excision of (written) texts is marked by a degree of arbitrariness that always calls for justification. That said, we are not claiming that this reconstruction of the duality between these books is misguided. Rather, we claim that, couched in these terms, it comes across as all too peremptory. We think it necessary to reframe the relation between *Political Theology* and *Roman Catholicism and Political Form* in a less rigid opposition, with a view to striking a balance that accounts for the mutual conceptual permeability of the two positions. Once again, with respect to both those readings that underestimate and those that overestimate the role of *Roman Catholicism and Political Form* in the frame of Schmitt's overall work, we do not mean to say that it represents a sort of snake in the grass of exceptionalist decisionism. Nor do we believe that exceptionalist decisionism was the counterpoint to an underlying, embryonic institutionalism. However, the idea that the 1923 text is substantially alien to the core of the Schmittian discourse is

here as the office of a great 'representative' institution, was based on a conception of politics almost diametrically opposed to the "political theology" of a Cortes, with its eschatological image of a counter-revolutionary civil war. Although *Römischer Katholizismus und politische Form* was published two years later, and probably after many revisions, its diametrical opposition to *Politische Theologie* on this point is symptomatic. An eschatological vision of catastrophe and renewal at one pole, and a more sober vision of a mediating classical political civilisation at the other, formed the antipodes between which Schmitt's thinking would continue to move' (Balakrishnan, *The Enemy: An Intellectual Portrait of Carl Schmitt*, 51–2).

17 Carlo Galli defines it as 'an almost second-hand booklet' in the afterword to the most recent Italian edition of this writing (Galli, 'La gloria e i nemici della Chiesa Cattolica', 83). A more convincing interpretation, in our opinion, reads: 'Too often overlooked within Carl Schmitt's oeuvre, *Roman Catholicism and Political Form* is crucial for a proper understanding of the moral content and political motivations of his writings from the early Weimar Republic' (McCormick, 'From Roman Catholicism to Mechanized Oppression', 391).

untenable. In our opinion, the decisionism of the 1920s was streaked and in part 'troubled' and almost 'corrected' by clots of an institutional thinking which would take over a few years later. Let us explain how and why.

It is not for this chapter to analyse *Roman Catholicism and Political Form* with the care it would deserve.[18] Still, its anti-decisionism potential does not require further evidence, if one thinks of the famous definition of the Church as a *complexio oppositorum*, an attitude to composition such that '[t]here appears to be no antithesis it does not embrace'.[19] The *proprium* as well as the *raison d'être* of the Church are to be found in such a unique capacity to hold opposites together; to include in a superior unity that which would otherwise be disjointed, separated, scattered; to adhere to the contradictory aspects of reality without succumbing to it; to give and give itself political form by recomposing the opposites (both internally and in relation to other political entities) within a unity that maintains and at the same time positively rearticulates its intrinsic divisions. As such, it is the opposite of the incurable break implied by deciding acts (in the way Schmitt theorised them in *Political Theology*). To put it otherwise, there exists no alienness in the Church as well as in the mundane world it is called upon to govern. Nothing (and nobody) can be perceived, defined, or treated as not belonging to an all-encompassing institution within which any existing element participates in the brilliance of a common identity. Of course, an other-than-self – evil and devil, privation of good and corruption of nature, what is literally or theologically outside the Church – does exist and this very existence is bound to affect both the self-understanding of the Church and the orientation of its political conduct and pastoral activity. Yet, this opposition to a total otherness, even if ontologically conceived, does not lead to a corresponding opposition within the Church. To rephrase it in the agonal terminology Schmitt used a few years later (and not before then), there is no internal enemy within (and in the eyes of) the Church. This is evidence that decisionism finds no room here.

[18] For a careful analysis of the text, see Galli, *Genealogia della politica*, 229–80. The most complete survey of the relations between Schmitt and German Catholicism, which is imperative for gauging the relevance of the text under scrutiny, is Dahlheimer, *Carl Schmitt und der deutsche Katholizismus*. On the topicality of the essay at stake and its relevance for a proper understanding of Schmitt's thought in the Weimar period, see McCormick, 'From Roman Catholicism to Mechanized Oppression'. While we remain unconvinced that *Roman Catholicism and Political Form* sheds further light on the kind of decision and on the meaning of state of exception that are present in *Political Theology*, we entirely agree with the claim, convincingly substantiated by McCormick, that there is neither philosophical nor political continuity between *Political Theology* and *The Concept of the Political*.

[19] Schmitt, *Roman Catholicism and Political Form*, 7.

It is just as clear that the peculiarity of the Church's order cannot in any way be considered as a replicable institutional model or one that can be reproduced outside the range of action of the Church itself, and even more so if one intends to use *Roman Catholicism and Political Form* as the foundation (or the inspiration) for Schmitt's later concrete-order thinking. The Church's extraordinary ability to give form is due to the uniqueness of a person, even before that of an experience – that is, the figure of Christ. In his dual nature, divine and human, Christ immediately mediates (that is to say, *ab origine* and by dint of his very essence) the plane of transcendence and the plane of immanence. What makes the Church truly unique as an institution is precisely this original surplus: it enjoys a public dimension and at the same time it is not exhausted by it, as it represents a transcendent uniqueness. As we shall explain later, the institutionalism of the 1930s is a totally worldly institutional form, without any metaphysics or any reference to an origin other than a normality administered through juristic means.

That said, however, one cannot easily dismiss *Roman Catholicism and Political Form* as a sort of *détour* with respect to the decisionist theoretical line. First, it may be true that the *complexio oppositorum* and its glorious jurisdictional uniqueness are to be confined to a pre-modern era (so much so that *Roman Catholicism and Political Form* turns out to be a kind of archaeology of the quasi-present). Yet, the fact remains that Schmitt raises questions that were topical at the time. He mentioned the names of William E. Gladstone and Otto von Bismarck, among others. He referred to nineteenth-century democratic and parliamentary regimes. He recalled the action of the League of Nations and explicitly states that 'Catholicism will continue to accommodate itself to every social and political order, even one dominated by capitalist entrepreneurs or trade unions and proletarian councils.'[20] Second, the accusation of occasionalism is shaky. Not only because, as such, it is by itself a flimsy argument, in that almost all of Schmitt's texts, even *Constitutional Theory*, despite its relatively systematic nature,[21] can reasonably be said to be occasional. However, one cannot help but connect *Roman Catholicism and Political Form* to that sort of preparatory essay, certainly less interesting but thematically very close, and somehow complementary, which is 'The Visibility of the Church' (1917).[22] Thirdly, *Roman Catholicism and Political Form* introduces a series of concepts, and more generally, a collection of terms, that Schmitt retrieved almost in their entirety in the institutionalist writings of the 1930s, although within the purview of a largely different theory.

20 Ibid., 24.
21 On this point, see Cumin, *Carl Schmitt. Biographie politique et intellectuelle*, 49–53.
22 Published as an appendix to Schmitt, *Roman Catholicism and Political Form*, 45–59.

These are expressions such as 'matter of human life',[23] 'the concrete foundation for a substantive form',[24] 'concrete existence'[25] and 'the visible institution'.[26] These terms formed a conceptual panoply that in the early 1930s replaced the exceptionalist toolkit.

There is even more than this. *Roman Catholicism and Political Form*, in a way that resonates with 'The Visibility of the Church', isolates four fundamental themes to which Schmitt returned in more detail in his institutionalist writings of the 1930s. Very briefly these are:

(1) the close link between institution and organisation
(2) the idea of concreteness as the capacity to give form to reality
(3) the attribute of 'visibility' – that is to say, an effective presence ('the concrete present – the visible institution'[27])
(4) the institution as a mediation that ties the concrete historical process to the present within an unbroken continuity which takes the form of a working legal structure.

To repeat: these four themes do not lessen the radicality of Schmitt's decisionism in *Political Theology*, nor do they form an alternative perspective of its own. Arguably, it makes more sense to interpret them as fundamental requirements that, according to Schmitt, all legal orders should meet beyond the specific political regimes within which they are in force. These are the characteristics that the exceptionalist jurisprudence of *Political Theology* failed to meet. And in this sense, *Roman Catholicism and Political Form* and 'The Visibility of the Church' can be regarded as a counterpoint, a sort of indirect, internal critique that identified the insufficiencies and aporias of the sovereign creationism of 1922. As far as the theoretical legacy of an occasional piece of writing (or two pieces of writing) is considered, this is no small achievement.

A DICTATORSHIP UNDER PRIOR AUTHORISATION

The fact that *Dictatorship* opened the door to decisionism is hard to dispute. The dictator, at least if she is a sovereign,[28] is very similar to the sovereign who

[23] Ibid., 8.
[24] Ibid., 30.
[25] Ibid., 8.
[26] Ibid., 32.
[27] Ibid., 53.
[28] As we shall discuss at some length in Ch. 4, it should be noted that the separation between sovereign and commissarial dictatorship proves very flimsy and, in any case, once power is conferred, it becomes completely indiscernible: 'Indeed, when a decision is made for the

stands at the forefront of *Political Theology*. There is one difference, however, which is by no means secondary. It is not the dictator who decides on the state of exception and then the necessity to suspend the constitution. The dictator rather figures as a delegate. The decider is the same body of jurists who are the protagonists of Schmitt's works in the 1910s, so much so that *Dictatorship* proves to be somehow in line with them. If the 1921 text inaugurates the exceptionalist decade, the new course seems to owe more than some debt to the jurisprudential and anti-decisionist approach of the 1910s.

In *Dictatorship* there is no sovereign who *ex post* legitimises herself based on the efficacy of her decision. It is the creators, and the interpreters, of the juristic practice who reveal the urgent need for such a solution. They declare the existing legal framework to be insufficient to tackle the mounting crisis and thereby authorise the exceptional and temporary suspension of the legal order. More than this. The exceptional circumstances that make the work of the dictator necessary can be conceived only from the point of view of the juristic practice and in purely juristic terms. For it concerns the possibility of a defensible distinction between the concrete application of the formal constitution and the normative constraint of constitutional provisions, together with the related possibility of an effective non-coincidence between the two moments.

The divergence between the recognition of the state of exception through a juristic lens, as outlined in *Dictatorship*, and the sovereign decisionism of *Political Theology* is all but negligible. Nor is it easy to reconcile the theoretical perspectives that they actualise. In *Political Theology* it is the sovereign who decides on the state of exception – that is, who decides whether there is concretely, in the here and the now, a condition that makes ordinary law ineffective (which is to say, to decide whether or not the state of exception exists). It is also up to the sovereign to decide what to do to put the legal order back into work. It is the sovereign who determines whether the order is the same as before or a new one – that is, to decide how to remedy the situation of lawlessness that characterises the state of exception. Instead, in *Dictatorship* it is the jurists who decide whether it is necessary to suspend the existing order. On the one hand, the jurists make the distinction – which certainly cannot itself be based on the law – between rules of law and rules for the

commissarial dictatorship, this does nothing but inaugurate a situation that can well lead to the complete restoration of the old constitution, but can also evolve into a sovereign dictatorship: it will be the practice of the dictatorship itself that will decide whether the "law" that is to be protected can have a new content within old forms or it is destined to morph into a new constituent power' (Fioravanti, 'Kelsen, Schmitt e la tradizione giuridica dell'Ottocento', 79–80).

implementation of the law. On the other hand, they declare that any available corrective remedies are inadequate and that the alternatives at (their) disposal to save the constitution in force without derogating from legal procedures have been exhausted. In this framework, the dictator, far from being a sovereign demiurge, is nothing more than a mere delegate: 'There is not a "subject" who has "decided" on the need for a dictator, but there is a practice, governed by the class of jurists, which has pushed the situation towards the dictatorial ending.'[29]

At least two factors urge caution when one associates *Dictatorship* with decisionism, as though this book were the laboratory of (or a historical introduction to) 1922 exceptionalist decisionism – if this is not already deployed in progressive evolution. It would be tempting to define these two factors as *katechontes*, as brakes on the inclined and wonky plane of a sovereignty with great ambitions but little effectiveness. First is the need for the dictatorial intervention to be previously authorised, and therefore the conceptual and legal subordination of the dictatorial intervention. Second is the coexistence of a jurisprudential practice and a body of jurists as counterparts. Not only does this set up a *de facto* diarchy that is at odds with the absolute sovereignty of *Political Theology*. Even more importantly, these factors put stress on the concrete functioning of concrete interactions within a given community context as a necessary presupposition. The dictator does have a power and competences of his own that allow him to operate over and above the real needs of the concrete situation. Yet the premises, the legitimation procedure, and the leeway of the dictator's activity are far narrower than those of the sovereign decider in *Political Theology*.

But there is a further and more fundamental aspect whereby one can fathom the chasm between the 'authorised' decisionism of *Dictatorship* and the sovereign decisionism of *Political Theology*. This aspect is closely connected to the *de facto* diarchy emphasised above and has to do with what could be defined as the 'degree of arbitrariness' in governmental action; which is to say, with determining whether or not – and in case, to what extent and how – those who are called upon to decide are bound to comply with a pre-existing state of affairs that actually channel and orient their political conduct by widening or narrowing the range of (legitimate) intervention.

In *Dictatorship* – not least because Schmitt was an eye-witness to the state of exception in Bavaria and the following military resistance by the revolutionary government – the extraordinary conditions for the legitimacy of the dictatorial action are precisely and unambiguously determined, as far as it is possible in

[29] Ibid., 81.

practice. The crucial questions are: under what conditions can a suspension of the law still be lawful; what is the difference, if any, between a legitimate and an illegitimate infringement of the legal order? To put it differently, is there the possibility of providing for lawful exceptions in extraordinary circumstances without so dissolving the legal order as such? What is generally regarded as Schmitt's final answer reads as follows: in order to be distinguished from arbitrary despotism, the dictatorship cannot trump norms as it pleases, but the norms whose authority is concretely undermined and can thus be restored by suspending the law (in order either to re-establish the previous order or to establish a new one). In other words, dictatorship is legitimate if and only if it aims to make itself redundant, a sort of temporary bridge to cross the troubled water of the contingent ineffectiveness of legal norms.

Yet, this is only half the story, and not even the most interesting one. Indeed, Schmitt added a crucial observation:

> The justification for dictatorship consists in the fact that, although it ignores the existing law, it is only doing so in order to save it. This is, of course, not a formally accurate deduction, and therefore it cannot be a justification in the legal sense, because neither the really nor the seemingly purposeful goal can justify a breach of law; and the creation of a situation that conforms to the principles of normative correctness does not constitute any legal authority. The formal characteristic is the empowerment of a supreme authority, legally capable of suspending the law and of authorising a dictatorship.[30]

This second half of the story (and of Schmitt's answer) makes it clear that the three criteria implicitly set out in the first half – dictatorship must be (1) an *extrema ratio*, (2) limited in time and (3) limited in its normative scope – are necessary but not sufficient conditions for legitimacy. There exists a further and decisive requirement: the empowerment by a supreme authority – an authority, therefore, that is not the authorised dictator. The emphasis Schmitt put on 'the absolute identity of task and authorisation, discretion and empowerment, commission and authority'[31] should not mislead us: in the work we are discussing, a self-legitimising dictator (as well as any other extra-legal source of power) is conceptually and legally inconceivable.

The substantial consequence of what could be erroneously perceived as merely formal empowerment is that effectiveness alone is by no means a compelling reason to declare an extra-legal decision as a lawful one. This is why Schmitt claimed that 'every dictator [including the sovereign one] is necessarily a

30 Schmitt, *Dictatorship*, xliii.
31 Ibid. (translation revised).

commissar'.[32] The supreme authority that empowers the dictator, Schmitt added, is the state, conceived either as an endangered legal order or as an emerging constituent power. More precisely, at least in our interpretation, those who are called upon to decide whether or not what is legally dictated (or legally foreseeable) is also actually enforced (or potentially achievable) can only be the jurists.[33] If this is true, then the really binding pre-existing state of affairs any dictatorship has to comply with is not merely the actual or the foreseeable existence of a constitutional order, but the jurisprudential orientation, in that the jurists are the ultimate interpreters of the legitimacy of any *prima facie* (and otherwise) unlawful initiative.

Political Theology tells a different story, or rather, it has quite a similar plot but with other characters and a more impressive setting. The two-act opera of *Dictatorship* turns into a one-character drama. Accordingly, the parts performed by the jurists are written out and an omnipotent sovereign takes the role formerly played by the dictator and – it is no use denying it – steals the spotlight. The proof is that the scene shifting in the background, although impressive, goes unnoticed. The crux of the matter is that in *Political Theology* there is no subject who mediates between the legal order and the sovereign decision. Once the jurists are dismissed, the only deciding player on the state of exception is inevitably the sovereign, since the general norm, conceived as an ordinary legal prescription, cannot speak for itself. The problem of competence arises, and could be abnormally and purposely emphasised by Schmitt, precisely because the competent deciders – namely, the jurists – were confined more to a deleted scene than to the backstage. Of course, Schmitt would reply that if they prove to be concretely able to decide on the state of exception, then they are the sovereign. But the problem is exactly this lack of distinction of different (and differently conditioned) ways of interpreting and performing the role of the sovereign.

Anyway, the new decision is unbound:

> What characterizes an exception is principally unlimited authority, which means the suspension of the entire existing order. In such a situation it is

[32] Ibid., xliii.

[33] This is even more evident in the case of sovereign dictatorship, since it is hardly conceivable that someone other than the jurist is able to grasp a power 'that, without being itself constitutionally established, nevertheless is associated with any existing constitution in such a way that it appears to be foundational to any existing constitution in such a way that it appears to be foundational to it – even if it is never itself subsumed by the constitution, so that it can never be negated either (insofar as the existing constitution negates it)' (ibid., 119). The opposition of the existing constitution to another that is still to come is thus to be viewed in continuity with the stabilising function that Schmitt assigned to the jurists in the works of the 1910s, where it is applied to hard cases, and not with the demiurgic power of a sovereign decision that was, again, still to come.

> clear that the state remains, whereas law recedes. Because the exception is different from anarchy and chaos, order in the juristic sense still prevails even if it is not of the ordinary kind. The existence of the state is undoubted proof of its superiority over the validity of the legal norm. The decision frees itself from all normative ties and becomes in the true sense absolute. The state suspends the law in the exception on the basis of its right of self-preservation, as one would say. The two elements of the concept legal order are then dissolved into independent notions and thereby testify to their conceptual independence.[34]

With the dismissal of the jurists, the pre-existing state of affairs, the defence of which still seems to remain the only way to distinguish a sovereign decision from bare and arbitrary violence, is reduced to the persistence of an 'order in the juristic sense'. The two sources of legitimacy foregrounded in *Dictatorship* – the partial suspension of the legal order (commissarial dictatorship) and the essential connection to a constituent power (sovereign dictatorship) – lose their legal character and are presented as the remnants of a somewhat obscure juristic order. Schmitt concluded: 'The decision parts here from the legal norm, and (to formulate it paradoxically) authority proves that to produce law it need not be based on law.'[35] We shall come back to this sort of (problematic) duplication of the law in Chapter 3. The point we would like to stress here is that the juristic order turns out to be a merely *de facto* ordering of a given social context. In the end, the dividing line between lawfulness and unlawfulness coincides with the distinction of ordered and unordered social interactions.

The major consequence is not that the state of exception becomes a matter of dispute – one that is resolved by the unpredictable effect of an unstable compromise between legal perspectivism and a proven ability to prevail over any other competing political course. What is most relevant – and even more so with reference to what Schmitt claimed in *Dictatorship* – is that in *Political Theology* legal effectiveness (that is, the establishment of an order whatsoever) turns to be the sole criterion for the legitimacy of an extra-legal decision. Certainly, the state continues to exist, but it is up to the decider to establish what a state legal order is and when it can be assumed as an existing state of affairs (that is, as an endangered situation, beforehand, and as a restored condition of normality, afterwards).[36] On this account, the reference to

34 Schmitt, *Political Theology*, 12.

35 Ibid., 13.

36 It is no coincidence that in *On the Three Types of Juristic Thought* Schmitt provided a very different and more consistent account of decisionism, in which the pivotal role is no longer played by the concept of exception for the simple reason that there is no pre-existing order to be suspended. The decision is now freed from any normative ties not only with reference to the

Maistre's claim that 'any government is good once it is established' – with two famous corollaries (i.e. 'making a decision is more important than how a decision is made' and 'no higher authority could review the decision')[37] – sounds quite like a full endorsement.

If we go back to the stage, it should be clear that the similarities between the two performances are only on the surface. *Dictatorship* looks less the historical prelude of *Political Theology*, as it is still generally interpreted, than a significantly different account of the ordering potential of the decision and its degree of independence from an overarching legal frame – a somewhat 'deflationary' account, which ties up to the jurisprudential approach developed in the 1910s more than to the radical decisionism of 1922. At a closer look, these two texts do not complement each other as though the historical perspective of 1921 could be completed by the theoretical enquiry of 1922. Rather, they disagree at least on a key aspect. In *Dictatorship* it is up to the legal order (or at least in reference to it) to lay down the conditions under which the decider can lawfully operate; quite the reverse, in *Political Theology* it is up to the decider to establish the conditions under which a legal order can emerge.

If we move to 1932 – in our reading, far beyond the end of the exceptionalist period – the essay *Legality and Legitimacy* is part and parcel of a conception of order that can hardly be reduced to the exclusivism of the sovereign decision. The very formulation of the problem, as the title itself suggests, presupposes the distinction between two levels of discourse about the order. For Schmitt, a 'decisive opposition' is manifest in the fact that 'the normative fiction of a closed system of legality emerges in a striking and undeniable opposition to the legitimacy of an instance of will that is actually present and in conformity

enforced legal order but also to any juristic order: 'As genuine and pure decision, this establishment of order can neither be derived from contents of a preceding norm nor from a previously existing order. Otherwise, it would be conceived either normativistically as pure self-application of the valid norm, or in concrete-order thinking, as the emanation of an already pre-existing order – reestablishment not establishment of the order. The sovereign decision is, therefore, juristically explained neither from a norm nor from a concrete order, because for a decisionist it is, on the contrary, the decision which first establishes the norm as well as the order. The sovereign decision is the absolute beginning, and the beginning (also in the sense of *Arche*) is nothing but sovereign decision. The sovereign decision springs from the normative nothing and a concrete disorder' (Schmitt, *On the Three Types of Juristic Thought*, 61–2). As the extensive reference to Hobbes further clarifies, in the beginning is disorder, anarchy, lawlessness, and not an 'order in the juristic sense'. Through the conceptual tools of his concrete-order thinking, Schmitt finally came to realise that the ontological and normative primacy of any order – be it legal, juristic or even political – is, in a purely decisionist perspective, utterly inconsistent and even unthinkable. Before the decision – which is absolute creation *ex nihilo* – there is nothing other than chaos.

[37] Schmitt, *Political Theology*, 55–6.

with law'.[38] Schmitt pits statutory law not against a sovereign decision, but against an existing legal practice, once again in the hands of the jurists (though in this case they are mainly represented by a large number of ministerial officials and high-ranking bureaucrats). He pits parliament not against a sovereign, but against the administration, which acts for the achievement of those law's purposes that statutory norms can no longer ensure – or at least it cannot ensure without a massive supplementary job that may make the normative guidelines effective and, if necessary, reorient them. Schmitt's aim in this last Weimarian text was not to pave the way for a sovereign able to compound the sacred and the mundane. Rather it was 'to provide a new autonomous legitimation for the bureaucracy' with a view to realising the law,[39] while the (fragmented and institutionalised) decisions that were needed for the realisation of the law were left to the activity of a body of civil servants who were regarded as enacting a political, even a constituent, role.

Based on the above, it seems plausible to raise doubts about the legitimacy, and above all the tenability, of an exceptionalist reading of such works as *Constitutional Theory* (1928) and *The Guardian of the Constitution* (1931) – if only because the decision does not come out of nothing (as for the former text), nor can it claim to create an order out of nothing (as for the latter text). Admittedly, both these writings imply two types of fundamental decision, and hence some form of decisionism. Yet, it is not an exceptionalist decisionism. The decisions Schmitt speaks of are very different from the demiurgic archetype outlined in *Political Theology*. With the exceptional decision they only share a deficit of implementation and a limited ability in securing and stabilising an order – two basic flaws that shall be discussed in the next chapter.

What is more interesting for our purposes, however, is not to question the decisionism (*sans phrase*) that in our view has long been overemphasised. Instead, it is important to understand when it really was that Schmitt began to move towards legal institutionalism. Certainly, the laconic endorsement expressed in the Preface to the second edition of *Political Theology* (November 1933) is a turning point, as we shall have to discuss in Chapter 4. At that stage, Schmitt's thinking hardly squared with his previous exceptionalism – and this change is way more significant than others that he made over the course of his long intellectual career. Yet, it is questionable that this turning point coincides with the inception of his institutionalism, which includes other, preceding texts that were crucial steps to his overall rethinking.

38 Schmitt, *Legality and Legitimacy*, 6.

39 Fioravanti, 'Kelsen, Schmitt e la tradizione giuridica dell'Ottocento', 91.

What is more relevant to our argument here is that these texts – generally overlooked (with the partial exception of the first one) even in the most comprehensive accounts of Schmitt's thinking – prove once and for all that his shift towards legal institutionalism predates the rise to power of the Nazi Party and therefore was not a sudden turn motivated by self-interest. We are referring to three essays that are key to outlining the incubation period of Schmitt's revisions – that is, 'State Ethics and the Pluralist State' (1930), 'Freiheitsrechte und institutionelle Garantien der Reichsverfassung' ('The Liberty Rights and the Institutional Guarantees of the Reich Constitution') (1931) and 'Grundrechte und Grundpflichten' ('Basic Rights and Basic Duties') (1932). This sort of (proto-) institutional trilogy is more the connecting than the missing link between the shaky decisionism of *Constitutional Theory* and the concrete-order thinking fully developed in *On the Three Types of Juristic Thought*, after the desperate and ultimately failed attempt to appeal to the extraordinary powers of the Reichspräsident in *The Guardian of the Constitution* (1931).

It is also based on these three works that Chapter 4 of the present book will consider in some detail the train of thought that led Schmitt to the concreteness of his institutional theory. A short excerpt from the note he added in 1958 on the occasion of the re-edition of 1931 essay (in a collection comprising, among other works, 'Grundrechte und Grundpflichten') will do for now:

> One can also see the essence of the Constitution itself in the institutional guarantees. This would correspond to the doctrine of concrete order thinking and would be convenient to overcome both normativistic functionalisations and decisionistic simplifications. Of the three types of legal thinking – normativism, decisionism and institutionalism – it is institutionalism, in the form of concrete order thinking, that is in all circumstances most appropriate than normativism and its hybrid concept of a hierarchy of norms and an abstract normative control.[40]

At the time of this statement, Schmitt was 70 years old, while the alleged occasionalism of his institutionalist digression turned 30. Evidence is conclusive enough, we believe, to argue that from the institutional turn of the early 1930s onwards, Schmitt's thinking, at least in his self-understanding, was marked by an unbroken continuity that went hand in hand with the blanket rejection of any exceptionalist decision. For once, Schmitt's self-understanding looks convincing.

[40] Schmitt, 'Freiheitsrechte und institutionelle Garantien der Reichsverfassung (1931)', 172.

3

How Exceptionalist Decisionism Came About

Schmitt and Coeval Critics

While the previous chapters brought into question exceptionalist decisionism as the distinguishing mark of Schmitt's entire output, the present chapter will argue that it did not even derive its origin from the two Schmittian writings that are supposed to be the cradle of decisionism. Even more than that, the idea of there being a basic connection between *Political Theology* and *The Concept of the Political* was not Schmitt's own idea; nor was it contemporary with the first editions of the two writings in question (separated as they were by five years, 1922 and 1927, a period of time that effected a major break in the brief and adventurous life of the Weimar Republic[1]). It is indeed significant that Schmitt made use of the term 'decisionism' for the first time – as referred to his own thinking – only in retrospect, when, in the Preface to the second edition of *Political Theology* (dated November 1933), he placed stress on the distance separating his new understanding of law, the concrete-order thinking, from his previous decisionism. After all, *habent sua fata libelli*.

Of course, the sovereign decision is there in 1922 and the friend–enemy antithesis is there in 1927. However, it was not until the end of the Weimar Republic that an unequivocal connection between the sovereign decision and the excision of the enemy – whereby the former concept is alleged to explain and integrate the latter and vice versa – was foisted upon Schmitt's works, mostly by his critics.[2] Schmitt self-interestedly recognised the existence of this connection in the hope of getting a more coherent and less ambiguous image

[1] In brief, between 1923 and 1926 Germany went through a period of political stability characterised by a decrease in violence, the successful containment of extremist fringes, the normalisation of its relations with France, the effective control of inflation and an unsteady economic recovery. This culminated in the Locarno Pact (1925) and the admission of Germany to the League of Nations (1926).

[2] The connection, more or less justified, between *Political Theology* and *The Concept of the Political* will be discussed in Chapter 4.

of himself across to the Nazi hierarchies, who were quite dubious of his loyalty.

As evidence for the disputable complementarity of *Political Theology* and *The Concept of the Political*,[3] only one year after the publication of the former, *Roman Catholicism and Political Form* still depicted the political as the expression of a planning ideality.[4] Here Schmitt for the first time referred to 'the political' by using the desubstantivising neutral form that shortly thereafter became the key feature of an entire theoretical *Weltanschauung*. Even more significantly, in *Political Theology* there is not the slightest reference to the notion of enmity, nor is there any reference to the figure of any enemy, let alone to the identity-building function that enmity was given in *The Concept of the Political*. Similarly, reference to the political is made only in passing in the Preface to the second edition (late 1933).[5] And this speaks volumes, if one thinks of Schmitt's well-known propensity to readapt his texts (as well as his ideas) to the various contexts with massive revisions when he got down to re-editing his works. Schmitt made cuts and additions to draw new conceptual links and undermine existing ones so as to adjust his positions on the issue at stake, to such an extent that his bibliography looks something of a sequence of deforming mirrors.

Not only was exceptionalist decisionism a later invention. It was also inversely proportional to the positive reaction that the two *Referenztexte* under scrutiny elicited after publication. It is necessary to distinguish – in general, but even more so in the present case – the reception met by the *issues* broached in these two texts from the critical assessment of the *arguments* advanced therein as well as the *lines of reasoning*. In this context, it is worth considering contemporary reviews published after the publication of these two works, above all those produced in the months following the publication of the book edition of *The Concept of Political* (1928). For they are not yet affected by a judgement on the biographical and intellectual trajectory of Schmitt as the (quasi-)*Kronjurist*, and therefore they were specifically centred on the conceptual aspects and methodological choices of the two books in their own right.

From this point of view, *Political Theology* and even more so *The Concept of the Political* (due to the less scholarly character of the topic and Schmitt's

3 We shall have to return to this issue in Chapter 4, though with a different objective.

4 'No political system can survive even a generation with only naked techniques of holding power. To the political belongs the idea, because there is no politics without authority and no authority without an ethos of belief' (Schmitt, *Roman Catholicism and Political Form*, 17).

5 Schmitt, *The Concept of the Political*, 2.

growing fame after the publication of the latter) met with a specular and somehow paradoxical destiny. *Political Theology* boastingly relaunched the concept of political theology to trigger a multidisciplinary reflection on it and to feed a debate that (increasingly though with ebbs and flows) has enjoyed durable success ever since.[6] In its turn, *The Concept of the Political* rearticulated and redirected the controversy on the conditions of politics (its nature, origins, aims and functioning), while the neutral *das Politische* intended to reclaim the intrinsic autonomy of the political domain. From this point of view, the two terms 'political theology' and 'the political' caught the wave. If, however, one draws one's attention to the critical reception of how Schmitt dealt with the issues at stake, this becomes a whole other matter. Almost all reviewers and commentators, regardless of significant ideological differences between them, expressed quite a few doubts – sometimes stronger, sometimes more cautious, but in any case explicit – on the tenability and the cogency of the arguments advanced by Schmitt. As we shall discuss in the following pages, in most cases the doubts voiced by Schmitt's critics hit the mark and laid bare the weaknesses of *Political Theology* and *The Concept of the Political* – to such an extent that these writings can be considered among the weakest works of his overall output as long as (and this is obviously a conditional statement that we should like to advance as such) they are measured against three criteria: their argumentative rigour, the plausibility of the (few) pragmatic indications they offer and the actual contribution they make to a realistic, viable and effective theory of politics and law.[7]

IRRATIONAL CONDUCTS

Before coming up on stage as the theorist *par excellence* of decisionism and exceptionalism, Schmitt was basically three things: a jurist, a Catholic and a

6 For the centrality of Schmittian reformulation of the theme, as such and for the subsequent debate, see Arvidsson, Brännström and Minkkinen, *The Contemporary Relevance of Carl Schmitt*, Part III; Baume, 'On Political Theology'; Diamanteis and Schütz, 'Political Theology beyond Schmitt'; Hell, 'Katechon'; Kahn, *Political Theology*; Koskenniemi, 'International Law as Political Theology'; McCormick, 'Political Theory and Political Theology'; Meier, *The Lesson of Carl Schmitt*; Meyer, Schetter and Prinz, 'Spatial Contestation?'; Motschenbacher, *Katechon oder Großinquisitor?*; Rae, 'The Theology of Carl Schmitt's Political Theology'; Roberts, 'Carl Schmitt: Political Theologian?'.

7 To avoid misunderstanding, we are not talking about Schmitt as a 'diagnostician' – that is, his genealogical interpretation of sovereignty and, more generally, of that peculiar break called 'Modernity'. Such aspects are certainly important but are not of our concern in the present work. Interpretations that insist on this aspect are Galli, *Genealogia della politica*; Ojakangas, *Philosophy of Concrete Life*; Storme, 'Maintenir l'histoire en mouvement'.

conservative. These three identities contributed, to various degrees, to his writings and that, beyond frictions about points that are certainly not secondary, in the 1920s still converged on a basic assumption: the idea that the state is the ultimate guarantor of political unity – with typically Prussian nuances, whereby the founding stones of the state are a strong executive, a powerful army and an efficient bureaucracy. Despite the common tendency to read Schmitt's works before *Political Theology* in the light of the sovereign decision, it was not until 1922 that it came into being. Accordingly, at least until 1922, Schmitt's held onto a distinction between law and politics that did not imply any separation, let alone a fracture. The state, founded on the administration and strengthened by the jurists' thoughtful and reflective contribution, stood out as the centre of politics and the only mediating power between centrifugal forces and different ways of assembling the social.

One needs to keep this in mind if one wants to make sense of two typical traits of the initial critical reaction to Schmitt's works: first, the connection that came to be established between such different texts as *Political Theology* and *The Concept of the Political*; second, the charge of irrationalism that was advanced by various critics against that which appeared to them as an existential philosophy within whose scope the political was no longer a field of mediation, but the bearer of a destabilising power against the state and its prerogatives. Schmitt was regarded by many detractors as a sort of sneaky enemy in the area of public law. He was held responsible for jeopardising the centrality and effectiveness of the state. As a member of the group of custodians of the state order, he irresponsibly opened the door to political existentialism and its unfathomable forces.

In the eyes of the early reviewers, the cause for concern was that which they interpreted as the desire of conservative jurist Carl Schmitt to relativise, if not to deny, the primacy of state law that had so far gone unquestioned. A serious menace lies beneath a notion of sovereignty, shrouded in nihilistic overtones (especially in *Political Theology*), whereby the sovereign decides and legitimises herself by exploiting exceptional circumstances. According to these critics, Schmitt gave away his dangerous intentions in the famous incipit of *The Concept of the Political*: 'The concept of the state presupposes the concept of the political.'[8] *Political Theology* and *The Concept of the Political* were thus put in relation not because critics thought that decisionism constituted a common interpretative thread. Rather, they took these writings to advocate an exceptionalist origin not only of the foundation of politics but also of its

[8] Schmitt, *The Concept of the Political*, 19.

ordinary activity. And in this regard, the re-publication of these two works, *The Concept of the Political* in 1932 (and then again in the fateful 1933) and *Political Theology* in 1934, played a major role in connecting these two texts and their fundamental themes.[9] In many of the vibrant and passionate pages of the first reviewers, the autonomy of the political was alleged to amount to an existential irrationalism that opened the Pandora's box of the centrifugal forces yielded by the political – those forces that the European civilisation and, more contextually, the flimsy Weimar democracy, had somehow managed to kerb.[10] It is no coincidence that one of the accusations that was most frequently levelled at Schmitt's theoretical approach was a gross insensitivity to the ordering power of law. His was interpreted as the quintessence of a somewhat obscure philosophy of the margin that oscillated between a sociological inquiry and a concealed invitation to sedition.[11]

As existentialism is a notoriously polysemic term (and intellectual stance), so is irrationalism a slippery concept. For our purposes (and those of some of the first reviewers of *Political Theology* and *The Concept of the Political*), either term can be rephrased as a constitutive impossibility (or unwillingness) to channel life practices and political energies into self-sufficient institutional structures. Existence does not only cover Hobbesian subsistence but includes a thicker conception of the political as the source of meaning and identity. According to these critics, existentialism stands for the impossibility to predict and regulate one's individual life, mostly in its politically relevant effects. Similarly, irrationality captures Schmitt's idea that the origin of politics goes well beyond any rationalisation of the dynamical forces that originate from it. In both cases, politics is no longer conceived as the government of social life, in that it is no longer in the hands of the members of a society. The order,

9 Pier Paolo Portinaro captures an element that is evidently common to these two works, both in their approach and in their theoretical scope. He points out how *The Concept of the Political* eventuates in a form of 'hyperrealism, since emphasis is placed not simply on physical force as a means – which is something all realist theories stress – but on the extreme consequences of the use of force. More precisely, it could be argued that this is merely the decisionist variant of a realist conception of politics: just as decisionism focuses particularly on the critical case, on the state of exception, so does the theory of the political draws for its definition from the extreme situation, in which the use of force becomes a concrete threat to human existence' (Portinaro, *La crisi dello ius publicum europaeum*, 235).

10 On the vexed question of whether Schmitt was a defender or one of the enemies of the Weimar Republic, see the thoughtful analysis offered by Cumin, *Carl Schmitt*, 93–134.

11 For a general review of the first reception of Schmitt's writings, see Surdi, 'Critica della categoria del politico'.

therefore, originates somewhere else, in unfathomable circumstances that cannot be contained (in the double sense of located and bridled) within institutional structures, whereas these structures are robbed of their traditional capacity to give themselves a form. For they lack the ordering resources that are necessary for the creation of a legal order and therefore cannot but procure them from outside sources.

It is in this sense that in 1932 Marxist theorist Siegfried Marck believed he had identified a conflict between existence and norm within Schmitt's theory: 'The actual functioning of a legal order refers to a decision that falls beyond the normative scope, that is, in the existential sphere.'[12] But there is an aspect that makes Marck's critique particularly useful for mapping the evolution of Schmitt's subsequent developments as he decided to put forward a novel conception of how the legal order works. Marck pointed out that the conflict between what falls within and what falls outside the legal order cannot itself be conceived through the conceptual categories of exceptionalist decisionism. Saying that a circumstance is not subject to legal regulation (this is the case, for example, of war) *ipso facto* determines the extra-juristic nature of that very circumstance. This implies an inescapable epistemic unspeakability in the first place, on top of legal ineffectiveness. Even beyond Marck's not always well-placed remarks, this begs two main questions. The first concerns the inability of the exceptionalist paradigm to account for the legal character of what is not (entirely) translatable into normative patterns. The second concerns the poor conceptualisation of the interlocked relation of facts and norms, and particularly of the normative force of social reality.[13]

This is a major problem, especially if one considers that it is precisely from what falls outside the normative realm that originates an existential 'priority of the political', as Helmut Kuhn put it.[14] This primacy consists in the fact that the legal domain can only receive the effects of what is decided at the political level: the ordering principles established by the political cannot be either

[12] Marck, '"Existenzphilosophische" und idealistische Grundlegung der Politik', 441.

[13] All the more so, since a certain fatality, as Leo Strauss notes, is certainly present in at least one central juncture of Schmitt's justification of the autonomy of the political, as he claimed that the latter depends on a pessimistic anthropology that frames political subjects as prone to risk and exposed to it: 'Schmitt describes the thesis of the dangerousness of man as the ultimate presupposition of the position of the political: the necessity of the political is as certain as man's dangerousness. But is man's dangerousness unshakably certain?" (Strauss, 'Notes on Carl Schmitt, *The Concept of the Political*', 111). On the 'hidden' dialogue between the two authors, see Meier, *Carl Schmitt and Leo Strauss*.

[14] Kuhn, 'Carl Schmitt, *Der Begriff des Politischen*', 191.

filtered or encompassed or mediated by judicial actors. But the self-sufficiency of the existential aspect, Kuhn continues, proves more difficult than expected. Pitting existence against the norm does not so much mean replacing the latter for the former as it means to elevate existence to a norm (where norm is to be understood in the minimal sense of a kind of normality that comes about without any mediation). In doing so, Kuhn centred one of the key issues of Schmitt's concept of the political and at the same time one of the major problems of his overall approach to the law developed in the 1920s – that is, the risk of reducing the existential foundation of exceptionalist decisionism to a sort of anti-normativism typical of the most brutal power politics.[15] The main problem here is not so much a sovereign who can do anything because the rightness of her decision is reduced to her effective clutch on society (which, by the way, is by no means a minimal condition). Rather, the main problem is that the decision is unable to extend over the boundaries of such a preordained and decisive existential plan and to account for the way in which it exists before, and independently of, any possible form of regulated social interaction.

In summary, Schmitt's position – whether or not it is a form of political existentialism – is beset by a twofold limit. This deficiency totally disregards any accusation – quite often levelled against Schmitt, regardless of its cogency – of destining politics to an obscure dimension, in which all cows are black and all shirts are brown. Indeed, it is our conviction that to be conclusive, the critique of Schmitt's anti-normativism should give up any normative presupposition *in the first place*. In this sense – that is, by focusing exclusively on the internal consistency of Schmitt's position – the problem of exceptionalist decisionism is twofold. On the one hand, it presupposes an existential and irrational plan (in the sense that we have just clarified) without being able to make sense of how it can subsist as such (that is to say, as a plan that precedes and conditions every form of regulation). On the other hand, exceptionalist decisionism fails to explain how, once it has been established, this plan can be completely 'grasped' and at least in part incorporated by the legal order. To put it another way, the problem is not that there is something that pre-exists the norm. Rather, the problem is that it is impossible to know what it is that exists, why it exists in the way in which it exists and how it can be made compatible with its normative translation – beyond the decisionist spell, which ultimately begs the question of how to explain what it presupposes.

[15] Among the various critiques that take this path, see Heller, 'Bemerkungen zur Staats- und rechtstheoretischen Problematik der Gegenwart'.

INDISCRIMINATE DECISIONS

The accusations of existentialism and political irrationalism were targeted at the risk of an authoritarian slippery slope as critics were concerned about Schmitt's opening the door to the dark maelstrom of an origin of the political that defied any standard of rationality and accountability. Other interpretations, instead, homed in on the fact that such a slippery slope could also be the consequence of another feature of exceptionalist decisionism. According to this complementary critique, the major flaw of Schmitt's theory does not lie in the irrationality of the standard whereby the decision is made. Rather, and more radically, the major flaw lies in the fact that *there is no criterion whatsoever*. As this latter critique goes, what matters for Schmitt is not the content of the decision, but that a decision is made – that is to say, that someone may give effectivity to a decision so as to re-establish the order. After all, Schmitt himself wrote that 'the decision as such is in turn valuable precisely because, as far as the most essential issues are concerned, making a decision is more important than how a decision is made'.[16]

One can get a first clue to this critique in Kuhn's conclusion that exceptionalist decisionism is the flip side of liberalism, as both theories fail to draw the boundaries of the political: 'The liberal individual is decided not to decide .... The existing individual is decided, but not to something, only to the decision in general.'[17] Although one often tends to neglect it, Schmitt's idea of a decision is such that the decision is to prove effective, and this is not a purely formal requirement. However, like 'being' for Aristotle, effectiveness can be said in many ways and can be achieved in even more numerous ones (and one should then ask oneself, classically, who decides on the effectiveness of a given decision, the crucial question *quis iudicabit*, that Schmitt was so passionate about?). Therefore, while the requirement that the decision be effective considerably decreases the range of possible courses of action, the fact remains that Schmitt's exceptionalist decisionism does not provide any standard for deciding which course of action is actually preferable.

On this point, Karl Löwith's critical review – undoubtedly one of the peaks of the literature on (and against) Schmitt – is enlightening; and not only because of the success met by his accusation of 'occasionalism', which left a lasting mark on subsequent interpretations of Schmitt's thinking. To make a long (and richer) story short, Löwith's pitched battle with the Schmittian text can roughly be said to boil down to two main claims. First, exceptionalist

[16] Schmitt, *Political Theology*, 55–6.
[17] Kuhn, 'Carl Schmitt, *Der Begriff des Politischen*', 195.

decisionism appears to be an empty box that can be filled with any content according to the forces and the inertial drives that are at play time by time. Second, because of its polemogenic groundlessness, this paradigm is doomed to an inevitable self-dissolution.

As regards the first claim, it is worth quoting two excerpts from Löwith's text:

> Thus it is not simply occasionally that decision in his sense, which is free-floating because it is self-sustaining and hence sustained by nothing, is in danger of missing the 'stable content' which is to be found even in every great political movement, a danger which is familiar to Schmitt and which arises by 'making the instant pointlike'. On the contrary, decision in this sense is unavoidably, and from the very beginning, subject to such danger at all times, because *occasionalism* is essential to it, though in *unromantic and decisionistic form*. What Schmitt defends is a politics of sovereign decision, but one in which content and aim are merely a product of the accidental *occasio* of the political situation which happens to prevail at the moment.[18]

> Is there, as decisive, a natural distinction here between foreign being and one's own being which makes possible a determination regarding the possibility of war, or is it instead the case that the very distinction between one's own being and foreign being follows only from the fact of an actual decision to enter into war? In other words, does war as the political case of emergency exist because there are essentially different peoples and states or political '*forms* of existence' essentially different in their being; or is it only when a war happens to take place, hence accidentally and occasionally, that even the most extremely tense and purely existential commitments and divisions emerge, which according to Schmitt are the distinctive and essential characteristic of the political?[19]

Also, in the light of the role played by the accusation of occasionalism in Löwith's essay, this first critical remark has been generally understood as meaning to denounce the theoretical echo of a personal trait of Schmitt's as a man even more than as a theorist: his multifarious personality as well as his opportunism when it came in handy. And there is little doubt about this. However, the link between conceptual aspects and biographical details, which is certainly *one* of the threads of Löwith's text, has led many to neglect his primary aim, especially in the junctures quoted above. He wanted to give the lie to Schmitt's claim from the vantage points of genealogy and description. Schmitt's idea of a potentially polemogenic opposition between political entities that are given with no identity other than the one that derives from

[18] Löwith, 'The Occasional Decisionism of Carl Schmitt', 144 (translation revised).
[19] Ibid., 147 (translation revised).

the negation of the other-than-itself gets caught not in one but in two double binds. First, this conception does not account for the pluriverse of states, which unsurprisingly Schmitt was forced to take for granted as if it were a sort of political *a priori*. (If community A is simply defined as non-B, and vice versa, then, one must assume the existence of at least one group of, so to say, original communities – that is, communities that are not included in this identity-building mechanism – lest one lands oneself in a *regressus ad infinitum* ignited by the impossibility of tracing an identity not constituted by opposition.) The second double bind is that Schmitt failed to explain how it is possible, even if one takes such a pluriverse for granted, to explain the fluctuating relations among states and their morphing alliances and enmities. Especially if these changes are supposed to rub off on the constitutive identity of the state community – or, on the contrary, to be grounded in it (this is far from clear). This certainly narrows the scope of a theory that purports to grasp the essence of the political by looking first and foremost at the supra-state level and yet fails to explain why certain inter-state relations are obtained and how these dynamics affect the domestic life of a political community. This is particularly relevant from a descriptive vantage point, on which Löwith seems to place particular emphasis; which is to say, when it comes to vindicating what the features are that make the political what it is.

The second point raised by Löwith has aroused less interest, although we think it is key to understanding the main limit of exceptionalist decisionism. It is that not only does exceptionalist decisionism offer no guarantee against a reckless use of the decision (if only because the decision requires and implies such a use), but, more problematically, it portrays the decision as inescapable. There are two main difficulties with this.

To commence, if one takes seriously the polemical tension undergirding Schmitt's approach, the claim itself that the political stems from the opposition of a friend to an enemy cannot but be a constitutive part of this contrast. This rules out the possibility of identifying this very opposition as the invariable and universal essence of the political. Moreover, it was Schmitt himself who smugly asserted: 'Nothing can escape this logical conclusion of the political.'[20] A few lines later, Schmitt easily made the case that even a pacifist opposition to war, if it is to be an opposition (that is, if it aims to be a polemical challenge), is destined to confirm the logical conclusion of the political (and thus the logical conclusion that war is a real possibility and the gravitational centre of political relations). And yet, there is a more effective test for the

[20] Schmitt, *The Concept of the Political*, 36.

Schmittian perspective. How can Schmitt's idea of the political be shown to be inescapable once it is contested at a theoretical level? Let us assume that someone denounces the ideological character of the political as theorised by Schmitt and describes it as instrumental in the imposition of a political conception (maybe even a political faction) that purports to present itself as universally valid, while – the critic goes on – its arguments are inevitably partial, like all those that face each other in a battleground that is structured according to the Schmittian antithesis. In this case, is there an *argumentative* way out for Schmitt (other than the sheer appeal to the irrationally presupposed and self-founding existence of incompatible, antagonistic, and therefore irreducible political *Weltanschauungen*)? So, the problem does not lie in the stipulative definition of the political, which however at some point becomes so assertive that it ends up being, to say the least, counterintuitive.[21] Rather, it lies in the fact that this presupposition, which finds no justification and, so to say, gets redeemed only as the book goes along, turns out to be self-contradictory. If the reasons for the political are cogent, that is, if the polemical position is actually an inescapable condition for politics, then, the political, understood as a universal category and as a standard for the definition of an invariant logic, can hardly materialise. The political, therefore, seems to saw off the branch it is sitting on.

Second, if the decision can by nature be filled with any contents, it well might be the case that, always on occasion, the order it produces makes the sovereign decision itself utterly inessential. In other words, the decision is not – or might not be – necessary for the attainment of the ends that the new regime proves to be able to attain otherwise. In this frame, the decision is a sort of Wittgenstein's ladder that is used and then thrown away thereafter: 'If a state of political emergency is factically dealt with by a decisive act, then at the same time decisionism as a basic political *concept* becomes unnecessary.'[22]

[21] The charge of circularity regarding the thesis of the autonomy of the political has been raised many times. Schmitt is said to assume what he should explain – that is, that the political is entirely reducible to the friend–enemy antithesis and that this opposition cannot be reduced to oppositions in other fields. However, little attention has been paid to another key aspect: namely, the surreptitious adoption of a dichotomous logic as a defining standard whereby Schmitt could transpose a methodological opposition into a substantive *aut-aut*. The political is not only a dichotomous logic like others governing other spheres of reality. More than this, as a result of a sort of quasi-transcendental move, it informs and reproduces the underlying oppositional logic of all other oppositions. Therefore, the political can present itself to other spheres of reality as homogeneous because these spheres are in turn defined according to an oppositional logic that is not only shared by the political, but which fundamentally *is* the political.

[22] Löwith, 'The Occasional Decisionism of Carl Schmitt', 158.

Still, if the decision, as the inescapable act that brings order to society, is contingent on its own contents, as Löwith's seems to imply, the problem of what, and on the basis of what, one decides returns compellingly to the fore. Contrary to what Schmitt claimed, this is a question that cannot be resolved by simply identifying the one who decides and by piggybacking on the presumed argument that what is really decisive is the bare fact that one decides.

It is true that, *pace* Löwith, Schmitt never advocated an idea of legitimisation that takes the existing order as is, as a pure fatality – if only because the alleged advocate of factual praxis is, in fact, to be counted among those who most convincedly denied the existence of any natural order, especially in politics. Despite this, Löwith's critique did a fine job in pinpointing the weaknesses of exceptionalist decisionism and its ordering potential. These weaknesses are to some extent complementary to those emphasised by the critics mentioned in the previous section. Based on the charges of existentialism and irrationalism, the basic question has to do with the indeterminacy of an extra-normative sphere that is as decisive as it is nebulous. On Löwith's critique, on the contrary, it is the normative sphere that turns out to be indeterminate, open as it is to any contents and political outcomes. For it depends on the occurrence of a facticity that turns out to be truly decisive. In both cases, the fundamental aporia resides in the structural disconnection between facts and norms, between widespread practices and regulatory standards, between internal and external ordering factors. This is a chasm that Schmitt was able to delimit only by attributing demiurgic and at the same time compositional properties to a decision that finally collapses under the weight of an impracticable task.

VICIOUS CIRCLES

The various critiques that we have just explored focused on what exceptionalist decisionism fails to explain and the aporias, or even the contradictions, that it engenders when it is used as a normative device. A different set of problems remains to be considered, ones that inhere in the approach and the inner structure of *Political Theology* and *The Concept of the Political*. In this sense, while the criticisms examined above charged exceptionalist decisionism with epistemic and operational inadequacy, this last section illustrates a few paralogisms that make Schmitt's view conceptually unsound. The main point we shall make can be couched as follows. So far, by discussing a few issues raised by those who first reviewed Schmitt's texts, we have contended that his political proposal is not coherently applicable. From now on, we shall contend that, in the way it is presented in Schmitt's canonical texts, this proposal, at a more fundamental level, does not make a coherent political theory.

The aspects that we are about to consider have been abundantly debated in the Schmittian literature. Their doubtful cogency, as well as Schmitt's blurred treatment of them, should have led interpreters to dispose of exceptionalist decisionism once and for all. However, quite surprisingly, this did not happen. This is surprising because, as we shall see, these conceptual limits compromise the foundations of the idea itself of a deciding sovereign act that is able to create as *ex nihilo* an existential opposition between rival groups (which also are to be created). To repeat: we are not interrogating the potential dangers or the sinister and irresponsible vagueness of an approach to the political that pivots on a radical conception of politics. Rather, our claim is that the series of logical shortcuts that surface here and there in many decisive junctures of Schmitt's texts make it very difficult to reconstruct decisionism as an orderly sequence of argumentative steps, and even more so if one considers the way in which decisionism is supposed to work and to affect reality. In other words, it is the advocate of exceptionalism, much more than the alleged *Kronjurist* of the Reich (who has been duly and justly flogged for some time now), who is accorded an inexplicable credit.

Let us begin again with *Political Theology*, whose main theoretical lines have been explored in Chapter 1. The sovereign is the one who is able to decide when a state of exception obtains, and if the situation truly requires the legal order in force to be suspended. If these circumstances arise, the sovereign is called on to decide on the state of exception in another, complementary sense. For she must suspend the whole legal order and must provide guidance on what conditions should materialise to re-establish the order; which is to say, she must ensure a condition of factual normality and a set of legal provisions that are effectively able to guide social conduct. Despite this, almost at the end of this exposition, Schmitt averred: 'In such a situation it is clear that the state remains, whereas law recedes. Because the exception is different from anarchy and chaos, order in the juristic sense still prevails even if it is not of the ordinary kind.'[23] To begin with, it is far from clear how such a persistence of the state order can be consistent with the option of a sovereign dictatorship (in which the decision does not restore the suspended legal order but creates a new one). Even less clear is the essence of this 'order in the juristic sense' that is still not a legal order.

[23] Schmitt, *Political Theology*, 12.

One may assume that it amounts to that which is left of an order on the verge of collapsing, something endangered but not completely destroyed, a social condition in which legal certainty has been lost but the law's basic pillars are still standing. If that is the case, such an order in the juristic sense can be interpreted as a factual order, the sort of inertial though only partial reiteration of the social relations that were regulated by the former legal order. Yet, given that the legal order is practically ineffective and legally suspended, to such an extent that a state of exception had been declared, based on what can one qualify the extant order as an order from a legal point of view? How can one claim that social relations are substantially left unaltered when it is exactly their alteration that determines the impossibility for the legal order to continue to be in force? If there is no legal norm, and the decision has not yet made its salvaging cut, based on what standards and what principles can that which remains in this intermediate condition be defined as an order? On the other hand, is it not the recognition itself of the state of exception that certifies the collapse of a social structure (stable enough to be defined precisely as a socially structured reality) and calls for an action that exceeds the legal order?

The Concept of the Political, which will be examined in some depth in Chapter 4, is even more problematic when it comes to circumscribing the concept of the enemy: 'The enemy is not merely any competitor or just any partner of a conflict in general. He is also not the private adversary whom one hates. . . . The enemy is solely the public enemy, because everything that has a relationship to such a collectivity of men, particularly to a whole nation, becomes public by virtue of such a relationship.'[24] The circularity of this passage is blatant and repeatedly emphasised. The enemy is what it is only if one refers to a people, but the people is what it is only when it fights a public enemy. The enemy presupposes the existence of the people, and the people presupposes the existence of the enemy. To get out of this circularity, one can drop one of the following options. Either one admits that enmity is destined to become an utterly ubiquitous condition, which even infiltrates the sphere of private relationships. Or one identifies an alternative criterion to account for the formation of such a salient political association as the people – a criterion other than the shared disposition to kill and to be killed to fend off an enemy who is recognised as posing a threat to all the members of a group (and other than the principle of statehood, which would jeopardise the primacy of the political over the state).[25]

[24] Schmitt, *The Concept of the Political*, 28.

[25] This is an objection that has stuck to Schmitt's text like a shadow since its first publication in the book *Probleme der Demokratie* (Berlin-Grunewald, Rothschild, 1928: 1–34). In the essay that

The same circularity haunts the game of mirrors between constituent power and constituted power that animates *Constitutional Theory* (1928),[26] one of the texts that effected a break, though not completely, with exceptionalist decisionism. The constitution is defined as 'the concrete manner of existence that is a given with every political unity'.[27] The concept of political unity conjured in this juncture is to be interpreted as both the (at least) ideal reference that legitimates the non-legal order in force within the state of exception and the substantive form of the people which desperately searches for an identity to oppose to that of the enemy. However, this concept is as key as it is obscure. Schmitt openly reclaimed this aspect: 'This act *constitutes* the form and type of the political unity, the existence of which is presupposed.'[28] In the chapter tellingly entitled 'Legitimacy of a Constitution', Schmitt comes back to this concept: 'The political decision reached regarding the type and form of state existence, which constitutes the substance of the constitution, is valid because the political unity whose constitution is at issue exists and because the subject of the constitution-making power can determine the type and form of this existence.'[29] Based on this, it seems that the constitution is expected to give form (at least a legal form) to something that already has a form (at least a pre-legal form) – and here Schmitt thought he could trade a circular argument for a laconic postulate: 'It is presupposed', 'It exists.' However,

immediately follows Schmitt's, Hermann Heller observed: 'Carl Schmitt is blind to the sphere of unity-formation within the state as politics. Suppose that in fact all political activity could be reduced to the friend-enemy distinction, where the enemy means the one who "in some especially intensive sense is existentially something alien and strange," one who must be fended off and fought, if need be annihilated, for the protection of the form of life appropriate to its essence. It would follow that the establishment and existence of political unity would be something altogether unpolitical' (Heller, 'Political Democracy and Social Homogeneity', 258).

[26] In truth, this is a text that, despite the undisputed centrality of the decision, exhibits the first symptoms of Schmitt's intensifying attention to the life of institutions, particularly the growing importance of a complete, visible and organised structure of the constitutional system. On this point, see Croce and Salvatore, *The Legal Theory of Carl Schmitt*, 71–3. On the problematic relationship between constituent power and constitutional setting, see Arato, 'Multi-Track Constitutionalism Beyond Carl Schmitt'; Kraft-Fuchs, 'Prinzipielle Bemerkungen zu Carl Schmitts Verfassungslehre'; Loughlin, 'The Concept of Constituent Power'; Schupmann, *Carl Schmitt's State and Constitutional Theory*; Vinx, 'The Incoherence of Strong Popular Sovereignty.' Let us note that the English translation of the term *Verfassungslehre* as 'constitutional theory' is somewhat misleading as it fails to grasp the 'foundational' dimension of an approach to public law that provides a fully fledged theory of the constitution both as a legal concept and as an institutional setting.

[27] Schmitt, *Constitutional Theory*, 59.

[28] Ibid., 75.

[29] Ibid., 136.

it is not at all clear what form this something has, let alone who gave it to it or how. Evidently, exceptionalist decisionism is forced to postulate the existence of entities, units and realities that are already formed, well before a normative act gives them a form.[30]

[30] It is our claim that *Constitutional Theory*, and more generally most Schmitt's writing from the late 1920s, embodies a complex and uneasy union of two different and even mutually opposing forces: the potentially ever-changing decision of a permanent constituent power and the actual concreteness of an institutional setting that always remains unstable. On the one hand, there is the interventionism of an extra- and supra-institutional will that orients the political action with no reference to any existing state of affairs other than its own self-constituting concreteness. On the other hand, there is the social foundation of a complex web of institutional contexts meant to shape the normative core of a political identity. Despite its allegedly systematic character, *Constitutional Theory* is the ultimate outcome, both in its inspirations and theorising, of these two opposite tendencies – the immanence of the constitution-making decision and the persistence of institutional continuities – that characterise Schmitt's transitional phase from the former decisionist occasionalism to the far more consistent institutional approach of the early 1930s. Nor does the appeal to a constituent power appear to be capable of overcoming the problem of occasionalism that haunts Schmitt's decisionism. Is the turn from a deciding sovereign to the fundamental decision by the holder of the constituent power an effective and satisfactory solution to the lack of a pivotal criterion that may guide and orient political action over time? The answer, we believe, is negative. The deciding sovereign, as described in *Political Theology*, can only provide extrinsic and unrelated decisions meant to overcome immediate states of exception, without a unifying action able to connect them in a consistent way; likewise, the popular constituent power he sketches in *Constitutional Theory*, presents a unified will that has no political agency other than the inaugural act of a constitutional order with no clear shape. Schmitt is crystal-clear in denying any relationship between the constituent power and everyday politics: 'In times of peaceful order, these types of expression are rare and unnecessary. That no special will is perceivably expressed simply signifies the enduring consent to the existing constitution' (ibid., 132). The critical point of such a radical separation between constitution-giving primordial act by the popular constituent power and constitutional state-building activity by a leader invested with charismatic power is to be viewed in Schmitt's simplistic conception of a constitution that can be both conceived and enacted independently of any ordinary constitutional law-making. In fact, while insisting on the existential dimension of the constitutional order and rejecting the legalistic view of the constitution as a purely normative construction, Schmitt completely ignores the social dimension of the very constitutional order. This approach inevitably leads to a flagrant contradiction. On the one hand, Schmitt laments the abstract essence and the lack of concreteness that affects the constitutional domain, and consequently paves the way to the extraordinary moment of the constituent process. On the other hand, however, he utterly disregards the mutual relationship between constitutional norms and their concrete functioning in the political dimension of social interactions. Legally relevant ordinary activities remain confined to the making of constitutional norms and distinct from what appears to be the only legally relevant moment outside the constitutional field – that is, the agency of the constituent power. No attention is paid to another ordinary moment, still legally relevant: that is, the emergence and maintenance of social interactions that are both structured by, and at the same time structure, the constitutional order. Again, while relentlessly insisting that the constitution is not merely a set of legal norms but a fundamental form of concrete social and political order, Schmitt proves to be actually unable to break with a fundamentally abstract

In this light, a most common criticism against *The Concept of the Political*, relating to the underdetermination of the concept of friendship, turns out to be more important than it appears at first glance. It does not simply blame the undue importance granted to the figure and role of the enemy – as if the latter, short of a clear definition of the way in which social relations *within* the community are imagined and organised, could be more than a phantasmal presence. Nor is it a matter of bellicism, in that Schmitt never claimed – and actually rejected, not only in *The Concept of the Political* – that everything is political, politics is nothing but war, and war is a normatively legitimate option.[31] Rather, what this criticism brings to light is the necessity, and thus the lack, of a *theory of social bond*. Without such a theory, Schmitt can hardly

conception of the functioning of a legal order. In the end, despite Schmitt's stressing the need to ground legal order on concreteness, his constitutional theory remains confined to matters of principles (and to the problem of their balance within the constitutional setting). He neglects the crucial issues of influence of these principles on everyday social life and, consequently, fails to capture social reality in its concrete existence. Despite the effort he put into overcoming the weaknesses of his former decisionism, Schmitt's constitutional thinking offers no viable solution to the problem of how to provide the legal order with a durable institutional foundation. The promised land of a *truly* concrete order is yet to come.

[31] The relevance of this point, and reversely the misleading potential of misunderstanding it, cannot be overstated. Let us shortly substantiate the three tenets mentioned above. (a) From the fact that the political 'can derive its energy from the most varied human endeavours, from the religious, economic, moral, and other antitheses' and that 'does not describe its own substance, but only the intensity of an association or dissociation of human beings' (Schmitt, *The Concept of the Political*, 38), it follows that politics only has to do with a limited set of social relationships – that is, with antitheses (1) of a very particular kind (2). (b) 'It is by no means as though the political signifies nothing but devastating war and every political deed a military action, by no means as though every nation would be uninterruptedly faced with the friend-enemy alternative vis-à-vis every other nation. And, after all, could not the politically reasonable course reside in avoiding war?' (33). (c) 'There exists no rational purpose, no norm no matter how true, no program no matter how exemplary, no social ideal no matter how beautiful, no legitimacy nor legality which could justify men in killing each other for this reason' (49). Still, if Schmitt's arguments do justice to the Schmitt who deserves it, the problem of what politics is, short of the political, gets even more urgent precisely because he himself assumes that the political is only part – the degenerated one – of the more comprehensive domain of politics. If so, again and with increased awareness: what comprises politics in its normal course – that is, when the extraordinary conditions of the political recede? The problem is not the primacy of enmity, but the complete absence of any clue about the formation process of differences and similarities, based on which political divergences and commonalities can be explained. In other words, Schmitt assumes, and never vindicates, the reasons why a given community is a community, to commence with the two basic assumptions he makes in substantiating his own perspective: (i) what explains why the Schmittian community is comprised of different and autonomous domains – morals, economics, aesthetics, and so on – arguably based on some mysteriously shared (and merely dichotomous) set of social meanings; and (ii) based on what reasons, within that very community, should a difference in the degree of intensity be considered as a generally accepted criterion for distinguishing politics from the political?

account for the existing regularities that he presupposes and still claims to be in need of a foundational decision. A previous bond does exist, a previous relationality inscribed in the social world – one that Schmitt was constantly forced to presuppose, and in fact almost always presupposed (sometimes, explicitly theorised, as we have just seen). However, he never cared to justify how this relationality is organised, from what it derives and what determines the consolidation of a series of individual conducts into an organised structure that recognises itself (and is therefore recognisable) as such.

Let us now go back for a moment to the conceptual tenability of *Political Theology*. In the light of that apparently negligible penumbra zone of a non-legal (yet legally relevant) order examined above, it is evident that the exceptionalist decisionism of the 1920s fails to explain where the sovereign comes from, as she is portrayed as a demiurge capable of creating an order out of nothing. Nor does it explain why particular individuals come to recognise themselves as friends (and others as enemies) or how a single original decision draws the boundaries of an order that is at once social and legal. It is not at all clear, and looks indeed inexplicable, why the sovereign is recognised as such, or rather, why her decision, among others actually emerging as potentially alternative decisions, gains support and hence becomes effective. It is not at all clear on what basis a group of individuals come to perceive another group as something other than themselves, or rather, why some individuals recognise themselves as alike and why they come to see a particular group, and not others, as the existential denial of their own way of life. It is not at all clear how the act of exclusion underlying each decision can at the same time give rise to an orderly social context for those who are included, or rather, why individuals continue over time to consider the state of affairs that has been established by the decision as a durable and acceptable condition of normality in and for the future. In sum, a particular decision – even if it is a sovereign one, or rather especially if it is a sovereign one – can establish the conditions for its effectiveness, as Schmitt repeatedly claims, but certainly not the conditions whereby it is accepted and complied with as an effective decision. Viewing something as something (viewing a decision as an effective and thus reliable solution, viewing a person as a friend or an enemy, viewing a given state of affairs as a normal and ordered condition) essentially depends on a pre-existing social commonality, which in its turn depends on a shared set of epistemic beliefs that structure (and are not structured by) our world.

Pace Schmitt and those who believe exceptionalist decisionism is his most convincing position, the capacity of the sovereign decision to bring order is next to nothing. The decision eventuates in an isolated intervention that simply displaces, or puts off, the need to obviate the much more urgent problem of regulating the interactional patterns of a given social context. Moreover, one would be at a loss if one tried to find at least one practical example, historical or otherwise, of how a single sovereign decision succeeded or could have succeeded in establishing a stable or durable system. The kind of nothingness – normative or otherwise – from which the decision is supposed to arise is therefore utterly fictitious. It conceals the actual societal dynamics comprising intersecting social flows – that is, a plurality of competing, overlapping sub-state orders that the sovereign, if anything, is required to make compatible as far as it is possible in practice. Beyond such leeway, which he hardly considered to be that broad, Schmitt came to envisage quite a different logic of intervention for the decision – much less extraordinary and much more effective. It is therefore with the concrete-order and formation thinking, to evoke how Schmitt dubbed his own version of legal institutionalism, that the order revealed itself as something that pre-exists any political decision. And this looks like a complete volte-face with respect to the exceptionalist decisionism of the 1920s.

4

A Fresh Start

Schmitt and State Pluralism

This chapter focuses almost exclusively on one of Schmitt's best-known writings, *The Concept of the Political*. The principal objective of this work is to identify the *criterion* by which one can determine whether a given association (or dissociation) is *political* in nature. In a way that will become clearer as we go along, *The Concept of the Political* depicts the political as an *epistemic device* that measures the degree of intensity of a conflict. However, the political is not only an epistemic device, but also a potential state of affairs. For the political culminates in a concrete condition when the members of a particular group are prepared to sacrifice their lives and take the life of others to salvage their group and the form of life it embodies. This double nature notwithstanding, what is crystal clear is that Schmitt did not conceive the political as a particular field or a practice. Rather, it is a threshold or cut-off point describing a sort of phase change: the transition from a situation in which a group is a *social* group to one in which the group defines itself as a *political* group. Accordingly, the political has to do with a definitional enterprise of utmost importance, one that grounds the ultimate distinction 'to which all action with a specifically political meaning can be traced'.[1] This distinction, as we shall explain in the following pages, allows the state to preserve itself from possible threats posed to the political community that it is called on to protect. The core argument of the present chapter is that Schmitt's take on the political bespeaks an important fracture with his own theorising prior to 1928, the year of the first extended edition of *The Concept of the Political* – a fracture that attests to the end of exceptionalist decisionism and the progressive adherence to an institutional theory of law.

1 Schmitt, *The Concept of the Political*, 45.

This fracture has long been overshadowed by the criterion of the political that Schmitt advocated, namely the notorious 'friend–enemy' antithesis. On his view, if compared to other antitheses such as beautiful vs ugly, good vs evil or profitable vs unprofitable, friend vs enemy is the only one that captures the *extreme degree* of the conflict between societal groups. It should come as no surprise, then, that Schmitt's alluding to the innate, primeval, primitive character of enmity, as well as his conjuring war as the prototypical context of the friend–enemy antithesis, have attracted the bulk of the critical attention.

For many interpreters, Schmitt's extolling the agonal nature of the political in *The Concept of the Political* was the unsurprising counterpart of his exceptionalist decisionism. For a people (here understood as the friend) to come about, an *existential, concrete* enemy is to be presupposed who threatens this people from inside or from outside.[2] Other critics see this antithesis as a vitalist critique of Enlightenment rationalism.[3] Still others deem it to be the manifestation of a mechanism with blatantly fascist connotations that is meant to feed a warlike culture of hatred.[4] With some sympathetic undertones, other scholars have argued that the enemy does refer to a *real* enemy, still not an *absolute* one.[5] On this more charitable view, the enemy is not someone who is to be concretely exterminated, but an entity that gives life to a vital oppositional dialectic. If friendship is what gives meaning to a people's political life, the elimination of the enemy – as the entity that brings the people into life – could eventuate in the disappearance of that very same people (at least as a politically relevant entity). Finally, some scholars have argued that liberal political theory and liberal institutions should take to heart the basic lesson of this antithesis. Denying the existence of concrete threats to democracy is of no aid to democratic institutions. On the contrary, recognising a broad spectrum of distinctions between friends and enemies, which also occur in the political life of liberal democracies, enhances 'the diversity of values and interests within society and enables accommodations to be arranged between them'.[6]

It is out of the scope of this chapter to offer an analysis of the difficult relationship between Schmitt's political theory and liberal democracy.[7] Nor shall we expand on the conservative and reactionary nature of his political

[2] Kennedy, '*Hostis* not *Inimicus*'.
[3] Wolin, 'Carl Schmitt: The Conservative Revolutionary Habitus and the Aesthetics of Horror'.
[4] Neocleous, 'Friend or Enemy? Reading Schmitt Politically'.
[5] Rae, 'The Real Enmity of Carl Schmitt's Concept of the Political'.
[6] Bellamy and Baehr, 'Carl Schmitt and the Contradictions of Liberal Democracy', 183.
[7] Important works are devoted to Schmitt's critique of liberalism and its bearings on democratic politics: e.g. Adair-Toteff, *Carl Schmitt on Law and Liberalism*; Dyzenhaus, *Legality and*

theory. Rather, we shall offer one further interpretation of Schmitt's concept of the political by tracing two intersecting lines of argument that he developed within the frame of his more comprehensive attempt to remedy the deficiencies of exceptionalism. The first line of argument relates to the primarily *epistemic* nature of Schmitt's theoretical enterprise in *The Concept of the Political*. His search for the criterion of the political can be included in the broader search for the cognitive criterion that allows a certain activity to be described as an instance of a particular practice. More specifically, his primary aim was to pinpoint the conceptual base for a people and its state – that is, 'the political status of an organised people in an enclosed territorial unit'[8] – to be correctly described as a people and its state. Such an undertaking teems with pragmatic consequences. Indeed, the second line of argument we shall pinpoint concerns Schmitt's further conceptual objective to explain what a state is required to do if it wants to keep its monopoly on coercive power. These two intersecting lines open the door to a more integral and complete interpretation of Schmitt's thought from the late 1920s to his later works. Based on this, we shall make the case that between 1928 and 1934 Schmitt progressively came to cast doubt on the position advocated in the early 1920s and developed an increasing interest in the questions of social normativity and societal pluralism.

This chapter will commence by discussing two interpretations of *The Concept of the Political* which attempt to clarify a few ambiguities that beset this seminal text. These are two possible readings, not entirely contradictory, and yet not entirely compatible: the *exceptionalist* and the *concretist* reading. As already mentioned in various other junctures of the present book, we believe that the abundant literature available today, most of which inclines towards the exceptionalist reading, fails to account for Schmitt's thinking as a whole.[9] We do not claim that the exceptionalist reading is outright incorrect, in that it does highlight some central concerns present in the text. Among the

Legitimacy, 58–70; Galli, 'Carl Schmitt's Antiliberalism'; Holmes, *The Anatomy of Antiliberalism*, 37–60; McCormick, *Carl Schmitt's Critique of Liberalism*; Richter, 'Carl Schmitt: The Defective Guidance for the Critique of Political Liberalism'. Other works focus on the relationship with liberal constitutionalism: e.g. Gibbs, 'Modern Constitutional Legitimacy and Political Theology'; Hampsher-Monk and Zimmerman, 'Liberal Constitutionalism and Schmitt's Critique'; Scheuerman, 'Carl Schmitt's Critique of Liberal Constitutionalism'; Scheuerman, *Carl Schmitt: The End of Law*; Seitzer, *Comparative History and Legal Theory*.

8 Schmitt, *The Concept of the Political*, 19.

9 As we shall see in Ch. 5, in the last few years, especially within the Anglophone debate, more and more works have cast new light on many aspects that the exceptionalist reading tends to neglect.

most interesting ones are the *formal metamorphosis* of conflicts and the *performative conception* of the enemy. However, in our interpretation, if one looks at these two interesting notions more closely, it becomes easier to see why the exceptionalist reading does not cut deep enough. Drawing from this, the concretist reading we shall advocate attaches particular importance to the link between *The Concept of the Political* and the theoretical developments of the early 1930s and minimises the connection that most interpreters claim exists between *The Concept of the Political* and *Political Theology*.

THE EXCEPTIONALIST READING OF *THE CONCEPT OF THE POLITICAL*

As we have mentioned in the previous chapters, the idea of a continuity, rather than contrast, between *Political Theology*, published in 1922, and *The Concept of the Political*, published six years later, is widespread among Schmitt scholars. On this account, the notion of the political is claimed to represent one of the basic elements shared by these two texts. William Scheuerman puts it this way:

> For Carl Schmitt, the emergency situation constitutes nothing less than the apex of politics. It unleashes the underlying antagonisms and conflicts of the political sphere, freeing them from the antipolitical confusions that may have kept their full significance from view. If politics is ultimately about normatively irresolvable existential friend/foe conflicts, they manifest themselves most completely during a crisis.[10]

David Dyzenhaus's interpretation is even more decided. He writes that the formulation of sovereignty offered in *Political Theology*:

> becomes clearer when paired with Schmitt's claim that the primary distinction of 'the political' is the distinction between friend and enemy. It follows, he supposes, that the political sovereign is the person who is able to make that distinction, is indeed revealed in the making of that distinction, and that he decides both that there is an exception and how best to respond to it.[11]

On this account, *The Concept of the Political* is alleged to complement and complete Schmitt's earlier exceptionalism. Although we definitely refute the exceptionalist reading, especially if applied to writings other than *Political*

[10] Scheuerman, *Between the Norm and the Exception*, 67.
[11] Dyzenhaus, 'Kelsen, Heller and Schmitt', 341.

Theology, it is worth identifying some of its strengths and understanding how it can be linked to the concretist reading we shall advocate below.[12]

While we have discussed exceptionalist decisionism at some length, it is imperative here to understand how it ties to the notion of the political. Positivist theorists – or better, Schmitt's straw man – believed that the legal order was intelligible, and could be merely described, by analysing its formal structure. In particular, according to Kelsen's Pure Theory, legal scientists can hardly understand the unity of the legal order unless they postulate the existence of a basic norm whereby all legal norms can be shown to be connected to one another and to be ultimately anchored to the constitution in force. For Kelsen, the defence of a 'pure' methodology made it possible to expunge all non-legal considerations, especially political and moral ones, from the domain of legal science. The legal scientist needs nothing more than the conceptual toolkit of legal science to produce a sound description of the legal order – one that leaves no room for such extra-legal notions as justice, sovereignty, sovereign will and power; which is to say, all the notions that cannot be reduced to the concepts of 'legal norm' and 'coercion'.

Schmitt rejected the claim that the conceptual toolkit of positivism is self-sufficient. He argued that such an unjustified theoretical assumption obscured the 'situational' nature of law – one that escapes the attention of legal theorists as long as they fail to pay heed to the concrete circumstances of a political community and only keep their eyes on legal norms and procedures. In his view, the main limit of legal positivism is that it only investigates legal 'normality' – that is, the everyday reality of a legal order in force – and believes normality can provide all the answers to the questions concerning law. His main objection to this methodological attitude was that everyday normality, the quotidian workings of a legal order, has little to say about the conditions of possibility for the law. It was Schmitt's firm conviction that legal positivists' exclusive concern with the 'recognisable' betrayed a lack of interest in the less visible, but certainly more important, elements of the life of the law.

Whether one holds an exceptionalist or a juristic reading of *Political Theology*,[13] nobody could afford to turn a blind eye to the key role of the exception in 1922. There Schmitt contended that both the legal order and the underlying social order (which shore up the effectiveness of legal norms in normal conditions) presuppose the 'limiting concept' of the state of exception. This corresponds to a condition in which legal normality is suspended for the

[12] Against this view, and in line with our interpretation, see McCormick, 'From Roman Catholicism to Mechanized Oppression', 396–8.

[13] We detailed and discussed these two readings in Ch. 1.

re-establishment of the order (or the introduction of a new one) when the community is under threat. This is the reason why the state of exception cannot be equated to a condition of crisis or chaos: it is a suspension of the order following the decision of the sovereign, which introduces a new normality. The sovereign herself is not a predefined institutional figure (although she may be formally so in particular circumstances where constitutional laws provide for it). The sovereign is someone who effectively decides on the state of exception, that is, the person who successfully imposes an order after suspending or abolishing the previous one.

In this frame, the connection between *Political Theology* and *The Concept of the Political* might appear quite strong: the sovereign's decision is the one that identifies the enemy, and thereby creates the friend. The content of the decision is nothing other than the identification of the enemy. On this reading, in *The Concept of the Political* the enemy turns out to be the condition of existence of the friend by virtue of a *polemical* and *polemogenic* process that is necessary for the creation of an order *ex nihilo*. This is the analogue of the divine miracle in the field of legal theory. The creation of an order presupposes the intervention of a supreme entity that carries out this creative activity by identifying an 'existential' threat – that is, one that puts the life of the political community at risk, as Schmitt emphasised. The decision mobilises the people's will to gather together in order to fend off the threat embodied by there being an enemy. On the one hand, the sovereign fulfils her duty only to the extent that she convinces the friends that the enemy is posing a lethal threat to their form of life. On the other hand, the friends come to form a self-conscious political entity and to acquire awareness of their own political nature only to the extent that they are willing, under extreme conditions, to give their own life and take the life of the enemy.

In the light of the connection between these two key Schmitt's texts, an exceptionalist reading vindicates two notions that are in no way incompatible with the alternative reading we shall advance below: the *formal metamorphosis* of non-political conflicts and the *performative conception* of enmity. As we pointed out at the very outset, in *The Concept of the Political* Schmitt makes it clear that the political is not a field or domain (such as morality, economics or aesthetics), but denotes 'the utmost degree of intensity of a union or separation, of an association or dissociation'.[14] This means that any opposition, regardless of the sphere in which it initially takes shape, can turn into a political conflict. It is precisely from that moment – when the conflict turns

[14] Schmitt, *The Concept of the Political*, 26.

into a political conflict – that the political becomes the dominant feature of an association or a dissociation. In other words, any opposition divests itself of its moral, religious or economic nature to become genuinely *political*. The opposition should no longer be described as moral, religious or economic, but as political. If this is the case, the distinctive feature of a political opposition is not what is at stake, but the conflict itself insofar as it takes a new and extreme form. Regardless of the nature of the stake, the conflict becomes political *because* some individuals associate among themselves *as members of a uniform group*. They make their personal identity conditional on the identity of the group to such a degree that they are willing to kill and be killed if the existence of the group is in jeopardy. This metamorphosis can be defined as *formal* because the content of the conflict may well stay the same, while the group members' disposition to fight for it changes to the extent that sacrificing their own lives and those of others is on the table.

At this stage, two alternative interpretations of the political can be juxtaposed. On the one hand, it could be interpreted as a typical trait of human nature, a sort of conflict-based identity dynamics. The idea that conflict is the hallmark of human beings as antisocial animals with a natural proclivity for war resonates with the style and the arguments of *Political Theology*. Here the exception, the extreme case, which in *The Concept of the Political* corresponds to war, is that which allows defining the situation of normality. No doubt, Schmitt's reference to the philosophical anthropology of Helmuth Plessner and his conception of the human being as an undetermined being seems to square with the interpretation of the political as an intrinsic feature of human nature. However, our interpretation of the political goes down a different path. It is not an essential property of the human animal, but a measure, a *gradient of intensity*. In this sense, the friend–enemy distinction enables one to assess the (constantly variable) political degree of human practices – that is, of those activities that are neither political nor apolitical by nature. So conceived, the political is a criterion whereby one can measure the intensification and de-intensification of antagonisms, an *epistemic* criterion to assess the intensity of a conflict. A group or a population becomes the 'friend' when the opposition to the 'enemy' does not exclude, at least hypothetically, the use of weapons, whatever the motives of the conflict may be.

The idea of a formal metamorphosis coupled with the idea of the political as a gradient of intensity leads to the second notion mentioned above. In effect, if the political is the utmost degree of intensity, and not a socially observable field or a particular type of conflict, it is arguable that it serves as the *performative* condition for a group to come into life. The formal metamorphosis of a conflict urges the members of a group to conceive of themselves as parties to the same entity. In a way, this could be likened to an activity of 'performative citation' whereby the talk over something brings this something into existence by dint of being mentioned as something.[15] In this light, the degree of intensity that the political marks prompts people to verbalise their condition in such a way that a new entity becomes the pivot of their verbalisations. This citational performance parallels the creational activity Schmitt mulls over in *Political Theology*, whereby one's pointing the finger at the menace posed by the enemy performatively constitutes the group of friends as the latter look at the situation as a group and conceive of themselves as such.[16]

If this is the case, much as Schmitt insisted on the *concrete* and *existential* nature of conflict, the friend–enemy antithesis is more of a conceptual device than a real opposition. The threat is existential not so much because it marks an irremediable fact of the human condition, but because political escalation brings about a condition in which individual life and the existence of the group as a group are at stake. Put otherwise, this antithesis is essentially marked by the *virtual possibility* of an existential conflict. *Virtuality* here is more important than the happenstance of a concrete clash. For the virtual possibility is what triggers the mechanism of formal metamorphosis and primes the process of self-recognition of the group as a group. What matters, therefore, is not so much the conflict itself, as its *thinkability*, the mere fact of its possibility – that is, the very idea that a conflict can arise.

On this account, far more than the *polemical* aspect, the key to the process of political escalation is the *polemogenic potential* – that is, the possibility itself of giving rise to a potentially lethal confrontation. It is the mere possibility of a mortal conflict that matters in the first place. The trigger of the political mechanism lies in the friends' acquired awareness of a dynamic that requires their willingness to kill and be killed, one that transforms a conflict of any kind into a *political* conflict. At first sight, this reading could be taken to account

15 This important theory was developed by David Bloor with reference to the late Wittgenstein and Barry Barnes's bootstrapping paradigm (see Barnes, 'Social Life as Bootstrapped Induction'). Bloor argues that standards to understand and criticise practices emerge out of a self-referring activity – that is, an activity of citing whereby a given performance becoming a standard is determined by one's 'commenting on the performances of others, and of one's self' (Bloor, *Wittgenstein, Rules and Institutions*, 33). Such a creational activity is thoroughly resolved into the practice itself when people draw their attention to a given performance and provide it with a stable, objectified, and transmissible description of it. See also Croce, 'Governing Through Normality'.

16 As Martin Loughlin suggests, the concept of the political is constituted by the criteria that enable one to identify a group as a group, as an organised political entity. See Loughlin, 'Politonomy'.

even better for the possible link with *Political Theology*. The sovereign decision paves the way for a polemogenic – in the sense that it stimulates people's willingness to engage in battle – recognition of the specific intensity of a conflict. The sovereign decision transforms any grouping into a political structure by virtue of a new awareness on the part of its members of their identity as well as the identity of the grouping they must oppose. This is Lars Vinx's interpretation of the way in which, in *Constitutional Theory*, a people come about:

> The 'political existence' of a people is manifested in its will to assert itself . . . . Indeed, the unified will of the people exists only to the extent that it is ready to make (or rather support) genuinely political decisions; decisions on the exception that constitutes the political community, in an extra-legal space, through the creation of a line between friend and foe.[17]

Therefore, a careful reading of the link between *Political Theology* and *The Concept of the Political* – a link that does exist, although we shall narrow it down – leads to an epistemic conception of the political. Just as *Political Theology* seeks to refute positivism as an effective approach to the knowledge of the legal order, so does *The Concept of the Political* seek to explain the way in which a group or a population or a people or a community emerges. When it comes to the legal order, understanding its generative dynamics requires going beyond the constitution in force and investigating the creational moment at which the order is established. When it comes to the political community, it is again the analysis of the creational moment that points to the generative dynamics triggering the performative mechanism whereby individuals come to conceive of themselves as members of a group opposed to other groups in a (virtually) fatal conflict.

THE CONCRETIST READING OF *THE CONCEPT OF THE POLITICAL*

But why is a purely exceptionalist reading of *The Concept of the Political* not enough? Why insist on the political as a gradient of intensity relating to a performative mechanism? There are many clues that, by the end of the 1920s, Schmitt was dubious of the paradigm he had defended in *Political Theology*. As early as 1927, when Schmitt wrote *The Concept of the Political*, the evocative scenario he had painted in 1922 seemed no longer tenable to him for two main reasons. First, the notion of exception obfuscated the historical, material nature of the institutional life of a community. He came to think that

[17] Vinx, 'Introduction', 15.

the decision should be anchored to a consolidated form of life, which imposed limits on the sovereign's freedom to decide whatever she wants. Second, the 'miraculous' mechanism of decision failed to account for something that at the end of the 1920s Schmitt thought to be central to human societies – that is, a *natural tendency to self-differentiation*. In this sense, the social-theoretical background of the early 1920s was too artificial and abstract to take issue with this phenomenon in that it painted a scenario in which everything is (politically) possible and social groups are formed based on a decision out of nowhere. When he pondered on these two basic flaws, Schmitt gradually began to amend his own conception.

For our analysis to get off the ground, it is important to recall that *The Concept of the Political* was first published in 1927, in the form of a lecture given in Berlin in May at the Deutsche Hochschule für Politik. In 1928, it was printed as a book, then reworked and republished in 1932. More than thirty years later, in 1963, it was republished with a new Foreword and some new comments, accompanied by three 'corollaries', respectively dated 1931, 1938 and 1950. This chronology is particularly important because 1928 is the year in which Schmitt published *Constitutional Theory*, in which he considerably changed the conceptual framework of the sovereign decision. All this supports the claim that, at the end of the 1920s, Schmitt intended to revise the concept of decision in the light of the idea of constituent power. In this new frame, the fundamental decision is made by a people as they establish their own form of political life and, in doing so, affirm their existence as a community.

Schmitt had always held the idea that the constitutional order does not correspond to a mere set of constitutional laws contained in a written-down text.[18] However, in *Constitutional Theory* he developed the stronger claim – which had emerged but was underdeveloped in earlier writings (see Chapter 2 of this book) – that such an order cannot result from a sovereign decision, especially from an *ex nihilo* decision. A constitution is first and foremost a concrete social order, a positive constitution. According to the absolute and concrete concept of a constitution,[19] an 'order' is a manifold device that brings about the public life of a community. Only a small part of it can be rendered into codified rules and principles. The constitutional order is created through the exercise of constituent power, but in such a way that it can encompass the set of norms, principles, values and practices that constitute the essential core

[18] On Schmitt's 'materialist' understanding of the constitution, see Croce, 'What Matter(s)? A Processual View of the Material Constitution'.

[19] Schmitt, *Constitutional Theory*, 59–66.

of the underlying social order. Fundamentally, the written constitution is nothing more than an attempt to codify an underlying social order, to which the constituent decision of popular sovereignty confers legal effectiveness.

Doubtless, Schmitt was always concerned with the concreteness of social practices as that which makes legal norms effective. However, it was not until the end of the 1920s and the beginning of the following decade that he rooted the element of concreteness in an institutionalist thinking, in the light of his renewed interest in the work of Maurice Hauriou and Santi Romano, the pioneers of legal institutionalism. As we shall show in the next two chapters, and particularly in Chapter 6, between 1933 and 1934 Schmitt drew from the theory of these two authors to develop what he named 'concrete-order and formation' thinking. He realised that decisionism, like normativism, fails to make room for key elements of social life and their role in the production of a legal order. However, before embarking on a closer inspection of the works of the early 1930s, it is worth examining the transition that led Schmitt from the rejection of exceptionalism to the notion of a concrete order.

In the 1963 Preface to *The Concept of the Political*, Schmitt took issue with the criticisms of those who, in his view, had overemphasised the concept of enmity and undervalued that of friendship. He saw this as a prejudiced reading neglecting 'that every movement of a legal concept emerges with dialectical necessity from negation. In the living law as well as in legal theory, the inclusion of negation is anything but a "primacy" of that which is negated.'[20] Then he went on to say that in criminal law the concept of punishment presupposes wrongdoings, but this hardly implies that criminal law extols the latter. While also in this case enmity is presented as a conceptual condition of possibility for the constitution of the friend (just as the crime is a conceptual presupposition of criminal law), what matters here is that enmity is portrayed as *a threat to a stable order*. The offence is not a mere conduct backed up by coercion and included in a proposition of the criminal code, but a threat to the underlying order. This consideration provides the key to an alternative reading of *The Concept of the Political*, which helps unpack the kind of threat Schmitt was thinking of between 1928 and 1932.

An even more decisive clue, because it is clearly not a late afterthought (as one might think the 1963 Preface was), but dates back to 1931, is to be found in the first of the three corollaries mentioned above. Here Schmitt introduced four alternative meanings of the term 'neutrality' and dwelled on the fourth, namely 'neutrality as equality' – that is, the state granting equal consideration

[20] Schmitt, *Der Begriff des Politischen*, 44.

and equal opportunities to the various sub-state groups. In this passage Schmitt concerned himself with social, cultural and religious pluralism and tackled the question of whether the state can really be neutral when it comes to this key issue. This raises a thorny dilemma as to the very nature of the state and the political community it embodies – namely, what groups that are to be considered for the purposes of equality. His conviction is that this type of neutrality is:

> practically feasible with respect to a relatively small number of legitimised groups and only if there is a relatively undisputed allocation of power and influence among equally legitimised partners. An excessive number of groups claiming to be treated equally, or even an excessive uncertainty in the assessment of their power and relevance, that is, uncertainty in determining the share to which they are entitled, hinders both the implementation of the principle of equality and the evidence of the principle on which it is based.[21]

In other words, the state is tasked with determining what groups are to be considered eligible. It behoves the state to identify a criterion for selecting some of them and selecting out others. This is the entry point to a reconsideration of the socio-ontological background of Schmitt's argument. In 1927–8 he espoused a degree of sociological realism that was much broader and much more refined than the vague allusions to the demiurgic miracle of *Political Theology*. This element acquired prominence in a pivotal essay dated 1930, in the middle of the transition we are homing in on, titled 'State Ethics and the Pluralist State', which appeared in *Kant-Studien*. Here Schmitt rejected the Hobbesian ontology of a civil society made up of atomised individuals who have a direct relation to the state and recognised the plurality of social groups as a structural and permanent condition of complex societies. With reference to a few key thinkers in the Western tradition, from Aristotle to Hegel, Schmitt acknowledged that the social fabric teems with semi-autonomous groups and associations. No political government, however centralised and powerful it may be, can (or even should) assimilate and homogenise them.

Such an underlying social ontology, together with Schmitt's comments on the most debated coeval theories of pluralism (such as those of Léon Duguit, G. D. H. Cole and Harold Laski[22]), is indicative of how Schmitt's thought at the time revolved around a fundamental axis: the pluralism of life forms and

[21] Schmitt, *Der Begriff des Politischen*, 263.

[22] A very well-documented and instructive work on pluralist theories of the state in the English context is Runciman, *Pluralism and the Personality of the State*. See also Eisenberg, 'Pluralism and Method at the Turn of the Century'; Laborde, *Pluralist Thought and the State in Britain and France, 1900–25*; Nicholls, *The Pluralist State*; Stears, 'Guild Socialism'.

its complicated relation to the state. For him, there is no easy way to govern the plurality of social life. The conflict between groups and the state is not only primeval but also inescapable. The state extracts its symbolic and material resources from the rich tapestry of the normative life of sub-state groups. It would then be unwise and counterproductive of the state government to exert a coercive power that may endanger their internal life and disrupt their inner normative orders. Unsurprisingly, though, this consideration does not betray any conversion to a pluralist theory. Schmitt held onto the view that unrestrained pluralism is conducive to dangerous dynamics of fragmentation and is incompatible with the existence of the state as the supreme political entity. This theoretical oscillation is a pointer to Schmitt's teetering between two needs that are to be reconciled. On the one hand, he did bring himself to embrace a more concrete conception of society that did justice to the inner plurality of social life. On the other hand, however, he did so with a view to devising effective means for domesticating pluralism. He wanted to strike a difficult balance between (theoretical) pluralism and (pragmatic) homogeneity – to the detriment of the former, as we shall see in Chapter 6.

THE ROLE OF THE STATE VIS-À-VIS PLURALISM

With this in mind, let us now look at the famous incipit of *The Concept of the Political*: 'The concept of the state presupposes the concept of the political.'[23] In the first decades of the twentieth century, this must have come across as a disconcerting statement. Schmitt's contention was that modern statehood was contingent on the concept of the political and not the other way round. Between the last decades of the nineteenth century and the first three decades of the twentieth century, most theories of law in Germany and other European states had striven to portray the state as the sole source of sociality and legality.[24] The state was celebrated as the existence condition for the political community and more in general any instance of social life. The common view was that the state was not only the cradle of politics, but also its immutable destiny. The political, according to this view, hinged on the state as the supreme law-making entity, short of which social life cannot germinate.

Schmitt thought this perspective was both naïve and dangerous. It postulated a trans-historical connection between the state as a *political form* and the political as a *conceptual category*, and thus concealed the transient nature of

[23] Schmitt, *The Concept of the Political*, 19.

[24] For a general outline of this debate and its consequence on the role of jurisprudence, see Croce and Goldoni, *The Legacy of Pluralism*, 11–50.

the state. The latter is a context-specific, tradition-bound political structure that gained the monopoly of the *jus belli* – that is, the right to use force when confronting an internal enemy or fighting an external one. But the state, according to Schmitt, remained a transitory configuration of the political, which had a beginning and will come to an end. It is doomed to disappear the very moment it lets go of the monopoly on the *jus belli* and *a fortiori* its ability to inhibit the formal metamorphosis of non-political conflicts. At that point, the state will no longer be able to prevent internal social conflicts of any nature from crossing the threshold of the political.

In short, Schmitt's thinking was that if the state were to lose this crucial prerogative, its position as the supreme political entity would *ipso facto* be lost. Similarly, if the members of any group were to decide on their own that a conflict in which they are involved requires them to kill and be killed, this group would *ipso facto* become a *political* group. Whether deliberately or otherwise, this group would be raising a claim to the *jus belli*. Such a performative activity would cause an unprecedented rupture in the traditional political landscape dominated by the state. The political stance of a group, originating from this group's decision that the conflict is *political* in nature, would dangerously challenge the state as the supreme political structure. The mere *possibility* of a particular group conceiving itself as involved in a political conflict would trigger the collapse of the state as the fundamental political entity. This explains why, in Schmitt's view, control over pluralism cannot but presuppose the control over the conceptual grid through which sub-state groups conceive of themselves and their autonomy.[25]

On this account, the main concern of *The Concept of the Political* is not so much with explaining how a political community arises when it confronts a threat posed by an enemy. Rather, its main concern is with explaining the risks a state must minimise if it wants to preserve its monopoly on the political. This is the main disagreement between an exceptionalist reading of this key essay and the concretist reading we are advancing here. An exceptionalist reading glues together *Political Theology* and *The Concept of the Political* in such a way that the friend–enemy antithesis turns out to be a condition that the state must favour to create the group of friends. Quite the contrary, the concretist reading posits that Schmitt's concerns in 1922 were quite different from his concerns in 1927–8, so much so that *The Concept of the Political* should be regarded as a break with *Political Theology*. Based on this, the friend–enemy antithesis should be interpreted in a dual sense. From a theoretical point of

[25] In this respect, Croce and Salvatore, 'Normality as Social Semantics' explores a few significant convergences with Pierre Bourdieu's social theory.

view, it is a conceptual device that allows identifying what the political unit is. From a pragmatic point of view, it is a potential condition of conflict that the state should strive to inhibit.

While we have already expanded on the epistemic role of the antithesis in question, at this stage it is the pragmatic aspect that becomes salient. Unlike the sovereign of Schmitt's exceptionalist period, who suspends the order and quashes normality, the state in *The Concept of the Political* is tasked with guarding against the actualisation of a virtual possibility – the *political* conflict – which would draw the state's political community to destruction. The criterion of the political, as a conceptual device, enables one to measure the extent of a pragmatic risk – which is to say, the risk that a growing political pluralism may call into question the loyalty and allegiance of the various sub-state groups to the state. The most insidious danger to the life of the state is an internal erosion due to the balkanisation of society. At a certain moment in history the state emerged as the supreme political entity by virtue of its monopoly on the political, but this position could be undermined by the proliferation of groups that the state cannot eradicate but must keep at bay. The state must guard against the risk that a political escalation of a conflict may give rise to entities endowed with a *political* nature – entities that could lay a claim to the right to engage in armed conflict. For this reason, in the concreteness of ordinary politics, the friend–enemy antithesis should never materialise, in that the formal metamorphosis of a conflict could bring about a state of affairs that could radically change the configuration of the political.

In summary, there is a clear break between 1922 and 1927–8. *Political Theology* portrays the state of exception as the original moment in which the conditions for the ordinary functioning of a society are set. *The Concept of the Political* portrays the opposition between friend and enemy as a harmful condition that the state must prevent by any means. While in *Political Theology* normality is the by-product of sovereign decision, in *The Concept of the Political* it is a basic, pre-existing condition for the constitutional order. Therefore, in our concretist interpretation, the central focus of Schmitt's analysis in *The Concept of the Political* is how to preserve friendship and the normality it embodies, rather than how to produce enmity. This is also Ernst-Wolfgang Böckenförde's conclusion as he examines Schmitt's constitutional doctrine. He explains that the objective of *The Concept of the Political* is to show how the state's main task – what makes the state the fundamental political entity – is to pacify internal politics:

> In the light of Schmitt's idea of the political, the state as a *political unity* means a pacified unity encompassing the political. While fencing itself off

> against other external political unities, its domestic distinctions, antagonisms, and conflicts remain *below* the level of friend–enemy-groupings. This is to say that all these domestic relationships are embraced by the relative homogeneity of the people held together by some sense of solidarity (i.e. friendship). Domestic conflict can thus be integrated into a peaceful order guaranteed by the state's monopoly of coercive power. This in turn means that, as Carl Schmitt himself pointed out, unlike foreign politics, politics within the state is 'political' only in a secondary degree. Domestic politics in its classical sense aims at good order within the community by trying to keep conflicts and debates within the framework of peaceful coexistence.[26]

Needless to say, we are conscious that this understanding of domestic politics does not fit an idea of political institutions as based on democratic deliberation and fair co-operation. The ultra-conservative aspects of this conception of politics are conspicuous. However, what counts for our interpretative purposes here is that in 1927–8 Schmitt thought the state should be able to *inhibit the possibility* that one or more components of civil society feel and feed the desire to intensify their opposition to the state or to other sub-state groups. If the state were to fall short of this foundational task, the result would be the self-constitution of autonomous political groupings which could fatally jeopardise the unity of the state.

We interpret this change of interest as indicative of a comprehensive revision of the concept of decision that is no longer hospitable to the notion of exception. At the end of the 1920s Schmitt's concern with political and legal pluralism was evidently on the rise. This novel concern was about to produce a radical transformation in his conception of politics and the role of the state. It is no coincidence that he paid more and more attention to the pluralist theories of the state. He had mixed feelings about them. On the one hand, he found them enlightening, and especially their conception of the social, for it unveiled the historical, unstable nature of the state:

> The juridic formulas of the omnipotence of the state are, in fact, only superficial secularizations of theological formulas of the omnipotence of God. Also, the nineteenth-century German doctrine of the personality of the state is important here because it was in part a polemical antithesis to the personality of the absolute prince, and in part to a state considered as a higher third (vis-à-vis all other social groups) with the aim of evading the dilemma of monarchical or popular sovereignty.[27]

26 Böckenförde, 'The Concept of the Political', 6–7.

27 Schmitt, *The Concept of the Political*, 43.

On the other hand, however, he was clearly of the opinion that the advocates of pluralism, and in particular Cole and Laski, underestimated the lethal danger intrinsic in the political scenario they envisaged. The origin of this faulty conception, Schmitt suggested, was Otto von Gierke's idea that the state is the 'association of associations'. In fact, it is from this conception of the state as being on a par with other associations (at least conceptually) that all the pluralist theories of the late nineteenth and the early twentieth centuries took their cue. Gierke's monumental theory was a decisive step towards a pluralist conception of the state, in which the latter is portrayed as nothing other than the guarantor of the social existence of groups. According to Schmitt, pluralist theories favoured a complete devaluation of the state, which was reduced to a neutral, mechanical apparatus – one that oversees the peaceful relations between largely autonomous entities. To give an example, while taking issue with Léon Duguit's pluralist theory of law, Schmitt recognises that Duguit rightly unmasked the sophistications typical of the metaphysics of sovereignty. However, he continues, just like Cole and Laski, Duguit downplayed the key question of the decision in the 'extreme case'. Yet, unlike *Political Theology*, this type of decision has nothing to do with the suspension of the legal order. Rather, the decision Schmitt talks about in *The Concept of the Political* relates to the problem of how to make sure that associations may not endanger the citizens' loyalty to the state. Put otherwise, the decision relates to how to prevent the materialisation of the extreme case:

> Their pluralism consists in denying the sovereignty of political entity by stressing time and again that the individual lives in numerous different social entities and associations. He is a member of a religious institution, nation, labor union, family, sports club, and many other associations. These control him in differing degrees from case to case, and impose on him a cluster of obligations in such a way that no one of these associations can be said to be decisive and sovereign. On the contrary, each one in a different field may prove to be the strongest, and then the conflict of loyalties can only be resolved from case to case.[28]

While Schmitt unambiguously recognised that the state is an association of associations – and *a fortiori* that associations exist and cannot be annihilated – he also insisted that the state must remain the association to which people lend firm and permanent loyalty and allegiance. A situation of political conflict between associations and the state must remain inconceivable. Unlike *Political Theology*, in *The Concept of the Political* the extreme case

[28] Schmitt, *The Concept of the Political*, 41.

is something to be avoided. The state is no longer a political structure that depends on someone who makes a fundamental decision. Rather, state politics is, and should persist as, a pacified condition in which the members of the political community owe their full loyalty and allegiance to the state authority. The state political structure must preserve its superiority over all other groups and associations in ordinary life, in the normality of the existing order, to inhibit the lethal dangers naturally associated with pluralism.

Although the issues discussed in *The Concept of the Political* are several, what we have so far concerned ourselves with is the shift in Schmitt's thinking on the extreme case. We think this shift bespeaks a major fracture between the works prior to 1928 and those reflections that Schmitt drew from pluralist theories of the state and from institutional theories of law.[29] However, his yielding to such an ambivalent attitude to pluralism led him to an even more resolute defence of political homogeneity, which will be the crux of the following chapter. We shall describe Schmitt's adherence to an institutional paradigm based on a few decisive misappropriations of institutionalism that turned it into a highly conservative theory.

[29] Institutional theories of law will be discussed in Ch. 6 of this book.

5

Out of the Exceptionalist Quagmire

The Notion of Institution in Schmitt's Thinking

The previous chapter provided the ground for holding that at the end of the 1920s Schmitt began to move away from his earlier exceptionalist decisionism. His interest in the exception, the foundation of the law laden with numinous reminiscences, had distracted him from the concreteness of everyday life – the life in which the material and symbolic resources for the subsistence of a political community are produced. As we anticipated, in the early 1930s second thoughts became complete awareness. Schmitt realised that decisionism, especially in the exceptionalist key, failed to account for how the law works in ordinary life, the broader and arguably the most significant part of the existence of a community. In the following pages we shall trace the stages of this theoretical shift and discuss its strengths and weaknesses.

A central stage in this interpretative journey will be the analysis of the main features of Schmitt's notion of institution. For it is the mainstay of a far-reaching revision of his own theory that is most often neglected in the literature – not only the literature that deems *Political Theology* to be the acme of Schmitt's thinking, but also the more recent one that emphasises his constant fascination with the issue of institutions. We shall begin with a discussion of a 'resolute' reading of Schmitt's work that makes exceptionalism altogether liminal. According to this resolute reading, Schmitt was always a committed advocate of institutionalism, whereas the degree of his conservatism intensified over time. In our opinion, such an interpretation is certainly more tenable than the exceptionalist one. Still, it is too resolute in that it minimises theoretical innovations that between the late 1920s and the early 1930s effected a clear break in Schmitt's thinking about institutions. Therefore, if it is true that exceptionalist decisionism must be contextualised and narrowed down, it is just as true that it cannot be reduced to a momentary distraction from his enduring institutionalism – if only because it fails to appreciate why and to what extent Schmitt changed his mind.

An unquestionable strength of the reading that we see as too resolute is that it highlights aspects that most often are underestimated by Schmitt scholars. Its weakness, on the contrary, is that it does so by imposing homogeneity on Schmitt's oeuvre – one that is at variance with his occasionalism. Thus, this resolute reading gives the lie to the exceptionalist reading and points to significant omissions in the literature of the second half of the twentieth century. Yet, the exegetical price it has to pay is too high, in that it obfuscates the various changes that Schmitt's concept of institution underwent between the 1920s and the 1930s – changes that reverberated on the whole theoretical edifice of his thought. This transition will be the core of our analysis in the remainder of this chapter focused on the institutionalist theory with which Schmitt believed he could solve the theoretical problems that beset the exceptionalist decisionism of the early 1920s.

THE PAN-INSTITUTIONALIST READING

'Schmitt was an institutionalist from inception', writes Jens Meierhenrich, one of the authors who have recently placed emphasis on what we might call Schmitt's 'pan-institutionalism'.[1] We named it 'pan-institutionalism' in the sense that the Schmittian literary corpus as a whole is interpreted under the banner of the institution. One of Meierhenrich's starting points is his criticism of a thesis that we put forward in 2013 in a book devoted to Schmitt's legal theory.[2] As we shall explain at some length below, our claim is that it makes sense to speak of an *institutional turn* of Schmitt between 1928 and 1934. Meierhenrich believes that the idea of a turn is wrong twice over. First, it buys into what we called the exceptionalist reading, while the exceptionalism of the early 1920s, in Meierhenrich's view, was nothing but a deformation of Schmitt's preceding institutionalism. Second, it obscures Schmitt's most interesting (and less deplorable) works – that is, those that precede *Political Theology*, along with some other writings of the early 1920s, where he was still sensitive to the issue of the constitutional limits of the government. In reply to these concerns, we shall argue that the basic flaw of the pan-institutional perspective is that it homogenises Schmitt's conception of the institution, as the way he conceptualised such a pivotal notion significantly changed over time. But let us first give an account of the pan-institutional reading.

Its basic premise is sound. Schmitt always placed at the heart of his reflection the theme of social order and how it should be secured by political and

1 Meierhenrich, 'Fearing the Disorder of Things', 179.
2 Croce and Salvatore, *The Legal Theory of Carl Schmitt*.

legal institutions. It should be noted, however, that in the pan-institutional reading, 'institution' is attributed, as it were, a 'thinner' meaning than the 'thick' one we shall discuss below. Such a thin notion signifies an agency or public body (e.g. the state or the Church) endowed with organisational power – in other words, collective bodies that oversee specific social functions. We do not think this was the concept of institution that marked the turning point of the years 1928–34. But it is precisely in the light of this thin conception that Meierhenrich accounts for the gradual transformation from (what he dubs) 'pragmatist institutionalism' to 'extremist institutionalism'. He divides Schmitt's work into three main phases. From the 1910s to the early 1930s, his institutionalism was 'pragmatic'. From the time he joined the Nazi Party until his break with the party cadres, he took a 'racial' turn. From 1938 to his later publications, institutionalism finally took on 'extremist' overtones. In short, Meierhenrich envisages a progressive corruption of the institutionalism of the early days. Schmitt, a conservative thinker always on the lookout for stability, relied from the very outset on robust institutions legitimised by the people's consensus. Still, as the years passed, he inclined towards an authoritarian kind of institutionalism that exalted the figure of a leader freed from constitutional limits.[3]

Meierhenrich defines Schmitt's early institutionalism as *pragmatist* in the sense that it treated institutions as fallible instruments to tackle circumstantial problems. Their effects should be measured against the task assigned to them in the first place. Schmitt was still far from the conception of a sovereign decider who introduces a state of exception for the establishment of a new order. As William Scheuerman also points out,[4] in *Die Einwirkungen des Kriegszustandes auf das ordentliche strafprozessuale Verfahren* (The Impact of the State of War on Ordinary Criminal Law Procedure), published in 1917, Schmitt advocated a pretty conventional conception of the effects of the state of war on criminal law. While in a state of siege military authorities are put in charge of the administrative system and are thus entitled to abrogate civil liberties and fundamental protections, Schmitt recommended a modicum of independence for the judicial system. The institutions of criminal justice should be able to prevent the dismantling of the normal order of ordinary times despite the extensive alteration of ordinary procedures.

Two themes seem to support this pan-institutionalist hypothesis: the protection of institutions that the state of siege must safeguard, not eliminate, and the

3 The formulation of this hypothesis owes much to Bates, 'Political Theology and the Nazi State'.

4 See Scheuerman, 'States of Emergency'.

pivotal role played by the judicial system. In other words, in his early writings, Schmitt exhibited a sharp interest in the institutional apparatus and the judiciary as the protector of ordinary life. Even in the 1921 edition of *Dictatorship*, according to Meierhenrich, Schmitt offered an institutional perspective of the legal concept in question. And indeed, as we pointed out in Chapter 2, frictions are manifest between *Dictatorship* and *Political Theology*. Meierhenrich teases them out to highlight Schmitt's defence of the commissarial dictatorship as opposed to the sovereign one. In the former, the dictator has the specific and limited task of restoring order in exceptional times of crisis, but is in no way, as happens in the latter, the bearer of a sovereign decisional power.

However, between the two editions of *The Dictatorship*, 1921 and 1928, a visible shift occurred towards sovereign dictatorship. In his keynote address to the 1924 convention of the Vereinigung der Deutschen Staatsrechtslehrer (Association of German Public Law Professors) in Jena, Schmitt stated that Article 48 of the Weimar Constitution did not prevent the Reich president from derogating from constitutional provisions other than those explicitly mentioned in the article, such as the creation of 'exceptional courts' to deal with enemies of the Reich in 1920, which violated Article 105 explicitly prohibiting such courts. Schmitt's notorious position was that Article 48, concerning the powers of the Reich President in an emergency, was, both in spirit and in letter, incompatible with the restriction of those powers. The president, in Schmitt's view, had two powers. First, he was entitled to introduce measures that derogated from the rules valid in ordinary times. Second, he was entitled to suspend their effects. The 'suspension' entailed by this second power conferred on the Reich president a more general legitimacy to deviate from constitutional provisions.

On the pan-institutionalist reading, this is a period of transition. This explains why Schmitt teetered between commissarial and sovereign dictatorship: even in the least restrictive interpretation, he observed, presidential dictatorship knows three limits. First, the purpose of the Reich president is to restore order, as embodied in the very constitution that gives him commissarial powers. Second, the transitional dictatorial order cannot uproot a minimum, basic order, regulating at least the agencies of the presidency, the government, and the Reichstag. Third, presidential measures only apply to extreme circumstances. For example, they can suspend the effects of a code, but cannot introduce a new code.[5] Nevertheless, unlike preceding texts, Schmitt's analysis in this keynote address betrays a shift towards sovereign

[5] For a careful analysis of the Schmittian text and, more generally, of the debate that took place in 1924 in Jena, see de Wilde, 'The State of Emergency in the Weimar Republic Legal Disputes over Article 48 of the Weimar Constitution'.

dictatorship, especially as he highlighted the inconsistencies of constitutional norms on the matter. As Scheuerman notes, although Schmitt reiterated that Article 48 of the Weimar Constitution allows a commissarial dictatorship, he pointed out that the vagueness and incompleteness of some junctures open the door to possible transitions towards a dictatorship that is far less limited by pre-existing constitutional provisions.[6]

According to the pan-institutionalist hypothesis, the symptoms of the theoretical transition are to be found in this slow but gradual inclination towards the notion of a sovereignty that is less and less bound to the norms of the legal order in force. In the 1910s up to 1921, Schmitt believed that dictatorship was an institution destined to abolish itself once it had achieved the task it was designed to serve. Over the course of the 1920s, however, he granted more and more space to a kind of sovereignty that could not only suspend the order to restore it but could also create a brand-new order. It is the spirit of *Political Theology* that takes over. In the pan-institutionalist interpretative frame, this is to be considered as indicative of a gradual corruption of Schmitt's early (more genuine) institutionalism. At the beginning of the 1920s, an institution – the dictatorship – figured prominently at the centre of his analysis, but this institution was treated in such a way that Schmitt's theory could not be said to be exceptionalist, conservative though it might be. As he made his way into the 1920s, the dictatorship became less and less regulated, independent of the order that, at least originally, allows and controls it.

In this interpretative key, which describes a slippery slope, a less explicable aspect of Schmitt's thinking at the time is *Roman Catholicism and Political Form* (1923). In the pan-institutionalist reading, this text, too, is alleged to betray Schmitt's misgivings about his recent exceptionalist inclination. In Chapter 2 of the present book, we also described *Roman Catholicism and Political Form* as in fact much more than a *détour* from the exceptionalist framework. However, there is one main difference between our interpretation and the pan-institutionalist one. While in *Roman Catholicism and Political Form* we detect traces of a theoretical interest that would explode a few years later, the pan-institutionalist reading interprets this writing as the reflection of a basic friction between Schmitt's early (conservative but genuine) institutionalism and the adherence to a substantive conception of the political community – one that comes across as the combination of Schmitt's theory of exceptional sovereignty and his growing, Janus-faced interest in what could be called the 'substance' of a political community – that is, a particular set of

6 See Scheuerman, 'States of Emergency', 556–7.

tradition-bound principles, practices and values, shared by the members of a historical community.

We used the expression 'Janus-faced' because the pan-institutional reading correctly emphasises that Schmitt's interest in the substantive background of social institutions is paired with a fundamental agnosticism regarding the actual contents of this background. Put simply, the pan-institutionalist reading recognises that Schmitt never thought of the sovereign as someone who can decide whatever she wants. The sovereign must pick out some particular contents, some particular products of a historical and cultural tradition, to make them the distinctive features of the political community. However, what counts for Schmitt is not so much what these contents are, as it is the mere fact that these contents exist and that they result from a selection on the sovereign's part. It is in this light that Meierhenrich traces the route from Schmitt's early pragmatism to his hideous defence of the Nazi racial order in between 1934 and 1938. Meierhenrich notes that Schmitt did not wholeheartedly espouse the idea of a totalising fusion of state, party and society; still, Meierhenrich underlines, there is no longer any sign of Schmitt's earlier insistence on the independence of the judiciary.

The pan-institutionalist reading draws particular attention to the 1933 essay, *State, Movement, People*, which not even Schmitt's most sympathetic readers would ever defend from the allegations of unabashed racism. Instead, the essay on which we shall focus on the rest of this chapter, *On the Three Types of Juristic Thought* (1934), is straightforwardly treated as an attempt to flatter the rising regime. According to Meierhenrich, these Schmitt texts led to an intensification of the extremist character of his institutionalism (which we need not analyse in this context), which even came to pollute his theory of international law. Even in later years, from the post-World War Two era onwards, the basic structure of Schmitt's institutionalism proved unable to purge itself of the racial and nationalist elements that it had taken on in the 1930s:

> Despite the apparent conceptual distance separating *Großraum* and *Lebensraum* the relationship between them is nonetheless tricky to disentangle. Schmitt developed his ideas in support of the Nazis' genocidal imperial expansion and, even if he did not adopt the crude biological reductionism of the Party line, he was happy to single out the Jews as a separate 'racially alien' group who stood outside a new European order of 'national groups.'[7]

[7] Minca and Rowan, *On Schmitt and Space*, 173.

Leaving aside the sickening racist connotations of Schmitt's positions in the 1930s,[8] it is interesting to underline once again that Meierhenrich's objective is to trace the trajectory of a theory that revolves around a main theme: the role of institutions. This comprises, initially, the judiciary with its modicum of independence; then, the dictatorial power of a sovereign who brings about the legal order; then again, the Führer with his vision of the German nation and its essential traits; subsequently, the *Großraum*, nation-based large spaces; finally, the *nomos*, the order of the earth. While the institution was the persisting linchpin of Schmitt's theorising, what changed over time were the types of institution he focused on – although, in his more mature writings, the large spaces and the *nomos* are the seedbed of new institutions rather than institutions of their own.

Paradoxically, the vice of the pan-institutionalist reading lies precisely in its fundamental virtue – that is, the attention it pays to Schmitt's use of the notion of institution, to which, however, it assigns a stable, homogeneous meaning throughout Schmitt's intellectual biography. An institution is regarded as an organisation that accomplishes public tasks. As we shall argue in the following pages, the real turning point came in the early 1930s, when Schmitt espoused a perspective that goes beyond the idea of an institution as a collective agency tasked with public functions and gave it a thicker meaning as the origin of the legal phenomenon.

TOWARDS A THICKER NOTION OF INSTITUTION

Let us return to the conclusion of the previous chapter. Based on a concretist reading of *The Concept of the Political* (1928), we made the claim that Schmitt's major concern at the end of the 1920s was the intensifying pluralism of early twentieth-century societies, composed of increasingly autonomous groups and associations. We believe that *Constitutional Theory* (1928) should be read through this prism, where Schmitt put forward a very different concept

8 There is a voluminous literature on this issue. See e.g. Bendersky, *Carl Schmitt: Theorist for the Reich*, and Rüthers, *Carl Schmitt im Dritten Reich*. A pithy analysis of the literature of the late twentieth century is offered in Scheuerman, 'Carl Schmitt and the Nazis', which takes Rüthers's book as its starting point. See also two recent articles, Ohana, 'Carl Schmitt's Legal Fascism, Politics, Religion & Ideology', and Suuronen, 'Carl Schmitt as a Theorist of the 1933 Nazi Revolution'. We would like to note in passing that one of Suuronen's aims is to demonstrate the link between Schmitt's Nazism and his institutional turn. As we emphasised, the idea that the institutional turn is contingent on Schmitt's espousal of the Nazi ideology is a claim that the present book aims to debunk – obviously, without questioning the Nazi nuances of his writings at the time.

of decision vis-à-vis its use in *Political Theology* (1922) – as we already mentioned in Chapter 2. In the concretist reading, the prevailing concern of the 1928 texts is pluralist parliamentarianism, which for Schmitt was unable to ensure the homogeneity of the political community. Contrary to the exceptionalist intimations of *Political Theology*, in 1928 Schmitt thought that, in the face of the intensifying differentiation of forms of loyalty and alliance, homogeneity cannot be produced by miraculous, demiurgic decisions. Homogeneity must be obtained from the concrete dynamics of associative life. The latter, therefore, is a resource that must be identified in specific social sites, then extracted, governed and used wisely.

Despite his still wavering ideas on how homogeneity is produced, in *Constitutional Theory* Schmitt considered parliamentary majorities to be anything but instrumental in the cohesion of political communities. For they act in the light of self-interested goals and pursue partisan politics. Notwithstanding the exponential growth in the prerogatives of the state, his concern was that the government was in the hands of small sections of society that could hardly represent the people as a whole. Faced with the danger of social disintegration, the constitution is the ultimate support for a foundational (even more than fundamental) and genuinely collective decision – a positive constitution that reflects and embodies a concrete form of life. The decision incarnated by such a constitution gives tangible form to a pre-existing order, to the full development of which constitutional norms are deputed. The will of the people finds unity in the exercise of the constituent power, which expresses the unifying force of the self-affirmation of a community as a community of destiny.

As Schmitt would later argue in his debate with Hans Kelsen on *The Guardian of the Constitution* (1931), the Reich president's broad powers are justified by the need to curb the social divisions typical of parliamentary politics. The supreme task of the guardian of the constitution is to preserve normality, which is indispensable for the proper functioning of public institutions and the legal system. Even beyond times of crisis – and this marks a further departure from exceptionalism – a strong presidency ought to be a permanent feature of parliamentary constitutional democracy, given that:

> the real boundary of the extraordinary competences of the president of the *Reich* and the real protection against an abuse of his power is provided by the *Reichstag's* powers of control, not by normativisms or restraints in judicial form. A *Reichstag* that is capable of forming a majority and of acting will have no great difficulty to make its opinion count, against the president of the Reich and the government of the *Reich*, through the demand for a suspension of the dictatorial measures or, if necessary, through an explicit vote of no confidence. The current constitution of the *Reich* provides a *Reichstag* that is

> capable of forming a majority and of acting with all the rights and opportunities that a parliament may need to establish itself as the decisive factor in the formation of the will of the state. If a parliament that has become a stage for the pluralistic system is no longer able to do this, then it does not have the right to demand that all other responsible authorities become equally incapable of action.[9]

If we jump to 1933, the year of Schmitt's reckless adhesion to the Nazi political platform, one can see how the idea of a continuity of institutionalist thought turns out to be fragile. On the other hand, precisely in those years an obvious contradiction materialised in Schmitt's theorising. If it is partly true that, as John McCormick insists,[10] Schmitt believed that the Nazi rise – which he initially opposed – could represent a handy solution to the pluralisation of society, this unfortunate conviction is, for the purposes of our interpretation, less important than the way in which he came to conceive of, and deal with, pluralism and its social origin: a real conceptual shift, albeit obscured by the ill-fated and opportunistic adhesion to Nazism.

In November 1933, eleven years after its first publication, Schmitt wrote a new Preface to the second edition of *Political Theology*. As we pointed out in Chapter 1, in the original 1922 edition, he had introduced two types of juristic thought, *normativism* and *decisionism*. Hobbes, Schmitt averred, is the iconic representative of decisionist thinking, as he insisted that authority is the sole source of law, while 'authority' is to be understood as a limitless power. Normativism, on the other hand, tends to conceal such a limitless source to look only at the formal structure of the legal order. We shall have to return to this distinction. What matters at this stage is that in his new Preface Schmitt 'supplemented' it with the introduction of a third juristic type:

> I now distinguish not two but *three* types of legal thinking; in addition to the normativist and the decisionist types there is the institutional one. I have come to this conclusion as a result of discussions of my notion of 'institutional guarantees' in German jurisprudence and my own studies of the profound and meaningful theory of institutions formulated by Maurice Hauriou.[11]

9 Schmitt, *Der Hüter der Verfassung*, translated in Vinx, *The Guardian of the Constitution*, 149–50. On the relationship between this conception of the constitution and the (more or less truthful) defence of the democratic system of the Weimar Republic before 1933, see Berthold, *Carl Schmitt und der Staatsnotstandsplan am Ende der Weimarer Republik* and Kennedy, *Constitutional Failure*. On the contiguity between Schmitt's conception of democracy and the rise of the Third Reich, see McCormick, 'Teaching in Vain'.

10 McCormick, 'Teaching in Vain'.

11 Schmitt, *Political Theology*, 2–3.

We shall dwell on the theoretical acquisition one can elicit from these lines later on. Yet it is worth stressing that the change that took place in those years is by no means circumstantial. The encounter with legal institutionalism had such an impact that Schmitt was driven to introduce a third type of juristic thought. It is a jurisprudential line that he arrived at while studying Maurice Hauriou's legal thought (and Santi Romano's, whom he mentioned, again in 1933, in *State, Movement, People*).

Given that Schmitt explicitly referred to it, it is worth briefly mentioning his novel conception of the institutional guarantees. In *Constitutional Theory* (1928), Schmitt made important modifications to his conception of the sovereign decision as the source of the legal order. These modifications were instrumental in a plebiscitary, identity-based notion of the constitutional order founded on the decision of the people who yield a positive constitution. In this sense, against formal understandings of the constitution, Schmitt insisted that the constitutional order is something that shapes and protects a concrete form of life. This is no longer the concreteness of an order grounded on the exceptional case, but a substantive concreteness,[12] one that feeds off existing social practices produced within traditional institutional settings. Evidently, as early as 1928 Schmitt attached more importance to institutions as socio-historically produced patterns of conduct within organised social sites that are to be protected through institutional guarantees *qua* constitutional provisions that grant 'particular institutions special protection' so as to prevent their elimination 'by way of simple legislation'.[13]

In *Constitutional Theory*, though, institutional guarantees form part of the more comprehensive set of constitutional guarantees. Soon after 1928, Schmitt made the role of institutional guarantees more prominent, as he claimed that they are more important than such basic rights as equality before the law, freedom of the person, privacy of mail, freedom of opinion, freedom of belief and conscience, freedom of assembly and association, private property, and others. With respect to these rights, Schmitt reasoned that institutional guarantees have a higher legal status than basic rights because a simple majority cannot modify them, and a two-thirds majority is required. In 1931 he wrote the essay *Freiheitsrechte und institutionelle Garantien der Reichsverfassung* (The Rights of Liberty and Institutional Guarantees of the Reich Constitution), where he distinguished more clearly between *individual rights*, which he called 'rights of freedom' (*Freiheitsrechte*), and the *guarantees*

[12] See Chapter 1 of this book, where we put stress on the difference between the concreteness of *Political Theology* and Schmitt's later notion of the concrete order.

[13] Schmitt, *Constitutional Theory*, 209.

(*Sicherungen*). Guarantees have legal priority over individual rights, because they represent more comprehensive and reliable guarantees for the freedom of individuals.[14] Schmitt was trying to strike a balance between the state being a juridically 'higher' institution, 'the institution of institutions', and there being positive limitations on the legislator's ability to interfere with the inner normative life of institutions.[15] However, his interest in institutional guarantees is not suggestive of any new passion for the protection of basic rights against the tyranny of unqualified majorities. Rather, he was concerned with the danger that the emergence of new institutional forms, favoured by legislative measures, might jeopardise the traditional institutional fabric.[16] Imposing restrictions on parliamentary legislation entailed shielding the political unity and identity of the people that had produced a particular type of social and political order in the form of a substantive constitution.

It was in this conceptual frame that he introduced the further distinction between institutional guarantees (*institutionelle Garantien*), which are guarantees of public law nature, and guarantees of institutions (*Institutsgarantien*), which are of a private law nature. Institutional guarantees are logically prior to the guarantees of institutions in that every institution presupposes organisational forms of a public nature. Institutional guarantees belong to public law and are understood as constitutional guarantees of any institution with public relevance, whereas institutional guarantees are private in nature and are defined as constitutional guarantees of legal institutions, understood as a set of sedimented norms and legal relations. Institutional guarantees apply to pre-existing institutions, already up and running, and organised in traditional forms of their own. The constitution is required to protect these forms against the legislative that could put them in jeopardy via ordinary statutory law.

One of the most significant consequences of this conception is that the protection of individual freedoms comes to coincide with the protection of the status of a member of a given institution. Individual rights are subsumed into institutional guarantees, which protect institutions and make a substantive feature of the constitution. In *Constitutional Theory* Schmitt referred to principles and values that could be abstracted from social practices or social relations, such as marriage as the foundation of family life, holidays, the legal status of state servants and so on. Although in *Constitutional Theory* they are

14 We analysed Schmitt's revision of the notion of institutional guarantees in Croce and Salvatore, *The Legal Theory of Carl Schmitt*, 26–9. See also Schupmann, *Carl Schmitt's Constitutional and State Theory*, 185–9, and Vinx, 'Carl Schmitt and the Problem of Constitutional Guardianship'.

15 See Schupmann, *Carl Schmitt's Constitutional and State Theory*, 189.

16 See Vinx, 'Carl Schmitt and the Problem of Constitutional Guardianship', 42–3.

claimed not to possess a constitutional character, they are in one way or another to be incorporated into the constitution. *Freiheitsrechte und institutionelle Garantien der Reichsverfassung* took a different path. Unlike *Constitutional Theory*, concrete institutions are claimed to form the substance of the social context and to identify the distinctive features of the constitution of the political community. Clear examples are the independence of the administrative justice system, state officials, religious corporations with public law significance, freedom of education, state supervision of the school system and others. This had remarkable consequences on the conception itself of the state's structures. As Schmitt commented in *Legality and Legitimacy* (1932),[17] when the constitution incorporates substantive contents that are protected against ordinary statute law, the organisational structure of the state can no longer claim to be neutral vis-à-vis the various social groups. Therefore, what he called the 'value-free functionalism' of a positivist interpretation of the constitution should give way to a content-laden understanding that grants privilege to some institutions to the detriment of others.

As Schmitt himself mentioned in the 1933 Preface to *Political Theology*, his revised notion of institutional guarantees was a decisive step towards a new and broader conception of institutions. In *Legality and Legitimacy*, he explicitly mentions his institutional inspirer, 'outstanding French public law specialist, Maurice Hauriou',[18] and specifically the notion of *superlegality*. On Schmitt's account, the existence itself of substantive legal contents that get incorporated into the constitution and that cannot be amended by statutory law had put an end to the parliamentary legislative state proclaimed in Article 68 of the Weimar Constitution[19] and had led to a constitutional organisational system fundamentally based on extensive entrenchments and guarantees. This new conception culminated in the 1934 essay, *On the Three Types of Juristic Thought*, in which the issue of institutions as the substantive source of any legal order took centre stage. Two lectures given by Schmitt in 1934 were pieced together in this essay. This could seem to support a *tactical* interpretation of his political positioning: this essay was part and parcel of Schmitt's

17 See e.g. Schmitt, *Legality and Legitimacy*, 49–58.

18 Schmitt, *Legality and Legitimacy*, 57.

19 Art. 68 reads: '1. Proposed statutes are introduced by the *Reich* government or by the membership of the *Reichstag*. 2. *Reich* statutes are concluded by the *Reichstag*.' In *Legality and Legitimacy*, Schmitt argued that the type of parliamentary constitutional regime that this article aspires to bring about is at variance with three main features of this very constitution – namely, the already mentioned superlegality of institutional guarantees, the plebiscitary nature of referenda (Art. 73) and the extraordinary measures on the *Reich* president's part authorised by Art. 48.

strategy to strengthen his ties with the Nazi regime.[20] Such a tactical interpretation is not entirely inaccurate. As early as 1933, in *State, Movement, People*, Schmitt had made overt efforts to highlight his (recent) change of attitude about the formation of the National Socialist state. Infamously, on 24 March 1933 the Enabling Act gave Hitler plenary powers. He could declare a state of emergency and initiate the dictatorial regime via legal means. Schmitt stated that in this act he could see the recognition of the will of the German people who had chosen Hitler as their political leader. In his reading, it was not an amendment to the existing constitution, but the establishment of a new constitutional regime for the new Germany.

From a 'political' vantage point, *State, Movement, People* and *The Three Types of Juristic Thought* are saturated with political (mostly self-interested) intentions. Schmitt censured the liberal conception of the state and the positivist conception of law. He excoriated the bifurcations typical of liberal democratic regimes, which both liberalism and positivism had nurtured: the state vs the individual, state power vs individual freedom, state vs civil society and the public vs the private spheres. For Schmitt, these distinctions did not reflect any concrete entity, because society was no longer composed of single individuals endowed with the same set of rights and freedoms. Liberal society at the beginning of the twentieth century, he thought, had become a field of competition among a small number of economically influential social groups that, behind the diaphanous veil of constitutional democracy, engaged in continuing struggle to gain the power to influence parliamentary life.

The delusions of liberal democracy, Schmitt argued, ended up reinforcing the tyranny of a few social parties over the others. Organised groups of various kinds, from freemasonry to the proletariat, influenced the state to their own advantage, while exercising a kind of leadership that could not help but harm society as a whole, given the partial and self-interested nature of the aims they pursued. In Schmitt's view, constitutional law (in the way liberal and positivist thinkers understood it) was the most effective weapon for taking advantage of party politics. It is for this reason that, both in *State, Movement, People* and in *The Three Types of Juristic Thought*, Schmitt condemned the constitutional law in force as being subservient to the interests of a mercantile and bourgeois society. Legal norms turned out to be pure instruments for co-ordinating the conduct of selfish individuals who sought to maximise profit at the expense of others.

The main thing responsible for this, according to Schmitt, was legal positivism. Positivist scholars had long nourished the illusion of a liberal state

[20] See Maus, 'The 1933 "Break" in Carl Schmitt's Theory'.

able to promote equality and freedom, while liberalism kept increasing the power of few social groups. He thus compared such fragmented, competitive and fundamentally unfair social conditions with that which he presented as a new hope for the German people: the ethical and ethnic identity between the people and their Führer. Along these lines, the conclusion of *State, Movement, People* is a heartfelt call for a brand-new way of understanding the law as the product of a homogeneous community. A truly fair and just legal system can only result from the expression of a common ethnic identity (a theme to which we shall have to return in the subsequent chapter).

There is no shred of doubt that the common elements of *State, Movement, People* and *The Three Types of Juristic Thought* can lead one to see these two texts as motivated by the same objective albeit addressed to different audiences – a broader one in the former case and one composed of legal specialists in the latter. And in the end, it would be foolish to strip a work of its historical connotations: the context of the production of these two essays is that of Schmitt's progressive (more or less committed, but certainly explicit) adhesion to Nazi politics. Nevertheless, beyond this tactical reading of his political position-taking, there is an alternative interpretation of *On the Three Types of Juristic Thought*, which also brings out genuine theoretical reasons that inspired Schmitt's institutional turn.

Our claim is that, beyond the undeniable attempt to pander to the regime, *On the Three Types of Juristic Thought* pursued a theoretical objective, as it intended to elaborate on a new conception of law. Schmitt's objective went beyond the modest intentions of censuring positivism and discrediting the liberal conception of politics. His main goal was to overcome the shortcomings of exceptionalist decisionism. The unsystematic and unorganised nature of the work notwithstanding, a homogeneous line of reasoning can be detected – one that was aimed at identifying the nature of law and its relationship with society. This line of reasoning represented a real change with respect to his previous works. It can be summarised as follows. *Decision*, *norms* and *institutions* are equally vital to there being a legal order. Just as no legal order could exist without one of them, so jurisprudence cannot afford to dispense with any of them. Although, in a given geo-historical context, one element may prevail over the others to the point that it comes to characterise a certain way of conceiving the legal phenomenon, the types of juristic thinking that create too great an imbalance between them (as is the case with decisionism and normativism) are incomplete by nature. In a full and thorough conception of law, norms and decisions must be regarded not as technical instruments in the hands of public agencies, but as something that has to do with social practices, or rather, with an underlying social order – a concrete order – which enlivens and feeds the official legal order.

There is a distinct element in this image, as we shall see in more detail in the following section – an idea of law as the guardianship of institutional life, institutions being the symbolic resource pool for the existence and persistence of the political community. This is the conception that Schmitt baptised as *konkrete Ordnungs- und Gestaltungsdenken* (concrete-order and formation thinking). Concrete-order thinking successfully overhauled and reabsorbed his previous decisionism, purged of the exceptionalist character of *Political Theology*, by assimilating a few central features – suitably reinterpreted, or even intentionally misinterpreted – of Hauriou's and Romano's institutionalist theories.

NORMALITY AND ITS CONTENTS

On the Three Types of Juristic Thought revolves around Schmitt's misgivings about the pre-eminence of the jurisprudential approach that considers norms as the distinguishing mark of law. This might seem to be but an extension of the anti-normativism of the 1920s that we discussed in the previous chapters of this work. However, a closer inspection reveals that something had changed. As Schmitt insists that norms constitute one of the three decisive aspects of any legal order, the target of his critique is not so much legal norms as such as it is *a specific way of describing the nature of norms* – one that isolates norms from the other two aspects – namely, the decision and the concrete order. It is our contention that this different conception of the nature of norms, as well as the different type of critique that Schmitt levelled at normativism, casts an interesting light on the broad scope of his institutionalist turn. After all, it is precisely to defend a sounder idea of the legal norms within the legal order that Schmitt confronted those theories that, in his opinion, propounded a disfigured image of norms.

The theoretical shift brought about by the introduction of his renewed concept of institution is so remarkable that Schmitt thought he should adopt a term that might temper its disruptive effect. A far cry from the continuity advocated by the pan-institutionalist reading. He felt the need to dodge the charge of smuggling a non-German product into the hyper-nationalist field of the developing German jurisprudence. He thought he could not speak of institutional theory – a theory with a French and Italian pedigree – and should rather pass it off for the fruit of a shrewd investigation of the German tradition. This explains the opportunistic dismissal of the term 'institutionalism', which would have been hardly palatable to the Nazi cadres.

In the third section of the second chapter of *On the Three Types of Juristic Thought*, Schmitt dwells on the subject to explain that 'for us Germans, the word "institution" [*Institution*] has all the disadvantages and few of the advantages of a foreign word'.[21] In his view, no German word could be squared with the way the term was utilised in other languages. Neither 'organisation', 'association' nor 'organism', he stated, are reliable translations. Such a shortage of semantic counterparts, Schmitt insisted, was mainly due to the symbolic implications of the various candidates. 'Organisation' was something that could be regarded as the precipitate of an institutional activity. 'Association', in the German culture of his time, had acquired a polemical connotation in relation to the concept of corporation. 'Organism' evoked the opposition to the idea of mechanism.[22]

Whether or not these considerations withstand scrutiny – and one could easily doubt Schmitt was really interested in such semantic subtleties – it is evident that he shied away from the label 'institutionalism' because it did not fit with the Nazi ideology. As we shall see, most implications of legal institutionalism were not reconcilable with Schmitt's political-theoretical project, let alone with the Nazi's political platform. As early as 1933, in the new Preface to the second edition of *Political Theology*, he had censured (what he regarded as) the hazardous inclination of institutional thinkers to put all normative orders on an equal footing, regardless of their relationship to the state. He concluded that 'an isolated institutional thinking leads to the pluralism characteristic of a feudal-corporate growth that is devoid of sovereignty'.[23] It is undoubtedly because of this penchant for pluralism that Schmitt discarded such a compromising label and thought he had found an

[21] Schmitt, *On the Three Types of Juristic Thought*, 89.

[22] This is Schmitt's full quote: 'For us Germans, the word "institution" has all of the disadvantages and few of the advantages of a foreign word. It can be translated neither as *Einrichtung* (establishment), nor as *Anstalt* (institution), nor as "organism", although it embodies something from each of these concepts. The word *Einrichtung* is too general and only permits the factual-external organisational side to protrude. *Anstalt* has become unusable because in the nineteenth century it had acquired a political-polemical meaning as a counter-concept against *Genossenschaft*, which binds it to the situation of the domestic political struggles of the nineteenth century. Finally, the word "organism" is burdened greatly by the now rather commonplace antithesis against "mechanism". That foreign Latin word, however, like many other relationships of Latin derivation, perhaps unconsciously directs us towards a fixation and rigidity. As a result, the coinage "institutional thinking" became overly identified merely as the hallmark of a conservative reaction against nominalism, decisionism, and the positivism of the last century, which was composed of both. And this gave rise to misinterpretations and far-too-many cheap objections' (ibid., 89).

[23] Schmitt, *Political Theology*, 3.

adequate replacement in the convoluted expression 'concrete-order and formation thinking'.

However, this terminological makeshift does not conceal Schmitt's intention to avail himself of the conceptual framework of institutionalism after purging it of its proclivity for legal pluralism. In his interpretation, French and Italian institutionalism detected the deep link between social practices, which give substance to the historical institutions of a community, and the state legal order, which has the task of incorporating and preserving the former. In a move that combines careless exegetical liberality with an admirable conceptual rapacity, Schmitt overturned the conception of normality that he had defended in *Political Theology* and became the advocate of normal life and its political potential. In 1934, the quotidian reproduction of normal life became the condition for social stability whereby norms can be complied with and in which state citizens conduct their life within the framework of established traditional institutions.

It is therefore particularly instructive to understand how his critique of normativism changed. While in *Political Theology* positivism was charged with being blind to the origin of law (that is, the decision on the state of exception), *On the Three Types of Juristic Thought* focuses instead on two main assumptions. As we shall see, they flip over the critical frame of the exceptionalist period.

First, positivism does not grasp the *ontogenetic link* between legal norms and social reality, to the extent that they are located in two distinct realms. Legal norms are put into the field of normativity and are deemed to be independent of what happens in concrete practice – in other words, as we underlined in Chapter 1, legal norms remain valid even when no one happens to follow them. Second, legal norms are used by state officials, and especially by judges, to describe social reality in a language that is quite different from the way ordinary language describes it.[24] Norms and procedures create a sort of metalanguage, which makes it possible to account for what happens in social life in a very special way – that is, in the light of the legal categories produced by the legislator and thus with the legal effects associated with those categories. While in *Political Theology* Schmitt was interested above all in the question of the origin of law, which positivism deliberately ignored, in 1934 the target of his new critique of positivist scholarship was the impoverished image of the relation between legal norms and social reality. Schmitt

[24] Our discussion of Schmitt's novel critique of positivism in *On the Three Types of Juristic Thought* will be cursory because we explored it in some depth in Croce and Salvatore, *The Legal Theory of Carl Schmitt*, 34–9.

gnawed at the normativism of positivist thinkers as they depicted the law as no more than a technique for individuals to calculate and predict the conduct of their fellow citizens and for officials to impose the sanctions that are established by the norm. The law, Schmitt reasoned, is reduced to a co-ordination mechanism, like 'scheduled railroad traffic'.[25]

In short, in stark contrast to *Political Theology*, the critical analysis offered in *On the Three Types of Juristic Thought* praises the ordinary aspect of legal norms. On a positivist account, Schmitt claims, norms are degraded and disfigured into technical instruments detached from social life. In the hands of officials, they are means of describing reality; in the hands of citizens, they are instruments for predicting the behaviour of the other citizens. In doing so, *On the Three Types of Juristic Thought* made the case that the origin of this misrepresentation is positivists' blindness to the relationship between norm and normality. In stark contrast to positivist scholarship, he writes, norms are to be understood as behavioural standards that emerge out of a dynamic relation to the practices they are meant to regulate. Says Schmitt:

> A general rule should certainly be independent from the concrete individual case and elevate itself above the individual case, because it must regulate many cases and not only one individual case; but it elevates itself over the concrete situation only to a very limited extent, only in a completely defined sphere, and only to a certain modest level. If it exceeds this limit, it no longer affects or concerns the case which it is supposed to regulate. It becomes senseless and unconnected. The rule follows the changing situation for which it is determined. Even if a new is as inviolable as one wants to make it, it controls a situation only so far as the situation has not become completely abnormal and so long as the normal presupposed concrete type has not disappeared. The normalcy of the concrete situation regulated by the norm and the concrete type presupposed by it are therefore not merely an external, jurisprudentially disregarded presupposition of the norm, but an inherent, characteristic juristic feature of the norm's effectiveness and a normative determination of the norm itself.[26]

This long quotation is the key to the paradigm shift, a genuine 'turn', made by Schmitt between the end of the 1920s and the beginning of the following decade. The norm incorporates and crystallises sedimented social practices that have come to be followed by the bulk of the population and therefore deserve a place within the legal order to obtain stable permanence over time. In this way, they become *typical* of a specific historical tradition: 'The

[25] Schmitt, *On the Three Types of Juristic Thought*, 53.
[26] Ibid., 56–7.

cohabitation of spouses in a marriage, family members in a family, kin in a clan, peers in a *Stand*, officials in a state, clergy in a church, comrades in a work camp, and soldiers in an army can be reduced neither to the functionalism of predetermined laws nor to contractual regulations.'[27] These are examples of complex practices that cannot be encapsulated by legal definitions or primary legal norms prohibiting conduct. Institutions such as the family, the Church, and the army are substantive features of the concrete order of a socio-historical civilisation.

Based on this conception, Schmitt fully revised the role of the institutional practices that embody and express the 'normality' of ordinary life. Much more than regularities with statistical prevalence, institutional practices are conduct conforming to, and materialising, the 'concrete types' that the law isolates as *exemplary models*. The repetition of certain practices produces those typical cases that the legal order must protect insofar as it aims to preserve the identity of the political community. Legal norms, therefore, are first and foremost tasked with safeguarding normality as the cradle of concrete types, absorbed and crystallised within the legal order. Concrete types offer guidance for conduct to all those who are included in the kind of activities to which they refer. Effective legal norms, Schmitt reasoned, offer genuine *guiding figures* (such as the good family man, the brave soldier, the faithful official) that provide models of conduct which can be replicated within the institutional contexts where they have emerged. These guiding figures are not merely technical instruments, in that they possess ethical and civic value of their own: as the community members conform to them, they guarantee the stable continuation of social life. Consequently, infringement of them poses a threat to the subsistence of the political community.

On this view, the codes of a legal order do not simply impose limits on individual action plans, nor do they merely provide protection against the despotic will of the legislator. Rather, they condense guidelines whose prevailing observance leads the community members to internalise and reproduce specific concrete types. At the same time, no code can detail all the elements constituting these guiding figures. No rule or set of rules can exactly specify each and every essential trait of, say, the good family man, the brave soldier, the conscientious official. For this reason, legal norms must be complemented with 'general clauses' (*Generalklausen*) whereby state officials, and judges in particular, can determine, case by case, the applicable concrete types and their relevant features:

[27] Ibid., 54.

> From all sides and in all areas of legal life, so-called general clauses surge forward in a way that wipes out every positivistic 'certainty': these include indeterminate concepts of all kinds, references to extra-legal criteria, and notions such as common decency, good faith, reasonable and unreasonable demands, important reason, and so on. … Neither legislation nor the administration of justice could dispense with them today.[28]

In the debate that ensued from the introduction of the German Civil Code, the Bürgerliches Gesetzbuch, in 1900, after a gestation period of more than ten years, general clauses met with scepticism. Critics considered them to be intrinsically vague, a source of further vagueness within the legal order, and a potential pretext for judicial activism.[29] On the contrary, Schmitt wanted to rehabilitate general clauses as legal devices that allow 'changing the entire *Recht* … without it being necessary to change a single "positive" law'.[30] On Schmitt's account, they opened up to new interpretations of existing laws for them to be more porous to the inner normative life of the institutional contexts protected by the legal order. While we shall later argue that the rehabilitation of general clauses was coupled with the devaluation of the role of the judiciary,[31] for present purposes it is important to insist on Schmitt's new understanding of the link between legal norms and the normality of social life. Norms crystallise and support institutional models of conduct and open-textured practical guidelines, which are legally translated into guiding figures and general clauses. Their exemplarity is endowed with legal-technical value as well as ethical force, and thus moulds both social practices and judicial procedures – though they can never be entirely converted into statutory norms or legal definitions. The settlement of legal cases and the production of new statutes can count on the ample leeway of these deliberately vague devices obtained from the concrete life of (recognised) social institutions.

Evidently, *On the Three Types of Juristic Thought* centres entirely on the interplay of norms, which consolidate normality, and the concrete order, to which norms contribute legal consistency. While there is obviously no room for the exception, decisionism remains a constitutive feature of the legal order, although it is treated with astounding superficiality. Schmitt seems to suggest

28 Ibid., 90.

29 On the controversy surrounding general clauses and, more generally, the debate around German codification, see Krebs, *Restitution at the Crossroads*.

30 Schmitt, *On the Three Types of Juristic Thought*, 91.

31 See Ch. 6 of this book.

that the decisionist type of juristic thinking easily lapses into an exceptionalist view, which he now regards as a fallacy. With reference to Hobbes, the highest representative of decisionist thought, he writes: 'pure decisionism presupposes a disorder that can only be brought into order by *actually* making a decision (not by *how* a decision is to be made). The deciding sovereign surely does not have jurisdiction for the decision on the basis of an already-established order.'[32] Schmitt's critique is staggering if one juxtaposes it with the exceptionalist view of *Political Theology*. In 1934 he came to the conclusion that decisionism overemphasises the 'who' of the decision and neglects the 'how'. The erstwhile advocate of exceptionalist decisionism made amends: the decision is not a free-floating irruption into normality but is inevitably contingent on 'an already-established order'. Paradoxically, Schmitt charged positivist scholarship with decisionism, in that, he continues, positivism is a hybrid mixture of decisionism and normativism. Positivism exalts the will of the legislator as the sole source of law, grounded on no normative antecedent, but then translates this will into the alleged impersonality of the law. In doing so, positivism picks up the legacy of decisionism but then sweeps it under the carpet of the legal form and keeps from view the arbitrary nature of a legal order that only depends on the will of its creator.[33]

In this way, Schmitt overturned the ontogenetic relation between norm and normality that he had envisaged in *Political Theology*. While in 1922 he stated that the 'exception is more interesting than the rule. The rule proves nothing; the exception proves everything',[34] in 1934 the exception is demoted to an utterly exceptional case, of little importance to the overall history of a political community. Exceptionalist decisionism captures historical moments that are as extraordinary as they are rare. Contrary to *Political Theology*, the exception hardly produces the normal case, while the latter is the seedbed of legal normativity. Nonetheless, despite the expulsion of the exception from Schmitt's new theoretical framework, the institutionalism of the concrete order, as we shall see in the following chapter, reveals unmistakable traces

[32] Schmitt, *On the Three Types of Juristic Thought*, 62.

[33] Schmitt made a similar claim in *Legality and Legitimacy* while discussing the form of state that he called 'legislative state' and its system of legality. Here he writes that an 'unconditional equivalence of law with the results of any particular formal process ... would only be blind subordination to the pure decision of the offices entrusted with lawmaking .... It would be *sic volo sic jubeo* in its most naive form .... One can term that "positivism", just as one can designate uncritically every type of decisionism as positivism' (Schmitt, *Legality and Legitimacy*, 21).

[34] Schmitt, *Political Theology*, 15.

of decisionism. Schmitt did indeed seize on the most significant insights of Hauriou's and Romano's legal institutionalism, but in such a way as to distort and misuse those theories. He put institutionalism at the service of a conception of law that was certainly more robust than the jurisprudence of *Political Theology*, but was still very narrow, obsessed as he was with the homogeneity of the people and with the war on social pluralism.

6

The Politics of Normality

Schmitt's Concrete-Order Thinking

Schmitt's theoretical objective in the early 1930s was quite clear. He wanted to transplant decisionism to a conceptual ground that could grant it new vitality and firm concreteness. Vitality and concreteness were the main properties of Maurice Hauriou's and Santi Romano's institutional thinking. Still, as we shall see, the ideas of life and concreteness that Schmitt poured into his new conception of order were hardly the same as those extolled by the pioneers of legal institutionalism. A quick journey into the theories of these two jurists will allow us to unearth the blatantly idiosyncratic – and at times manipulative – use that Schmitt makes of legal institutionalism in *On the Three Types of Juristic Thought* (1934). This analysis will get us into the heart of Schmitt's concrete-order thinking. Our contention will be that the 1934 text successfully cleared up the shortcomings of the exceptionalist jurisprudence of *Political Theology* and once and for all dispensed with the abstractive notion of exception. However, the 'selective appropriation' of Hauriou's and Romano's institutional theories turned out to be nothing but an attempt to purge decisionism of its exceptionalist bias and to root it in an institutionalist ground.

Our argument in this chapter will be twofold. While Schmitt's institutionalism did succeed in amending his previous jurisprudence, the price he had to pay was too high, since he ended up in a more dangerous kind of decisionism. He came to identify more clearly and more programmatically the origin of the legal order in the (pretty vicious) circle between institutional practices and their selection on the part of a body of officials who oversee the realisation of a societal project. In the end, this proposal looks to us as way more conservative than his exceptionalist jurisprudence. Yet, maybe just because of this despicable nature, Schmitt's institutionalism brings out even more clearly than exceptionalist decisionism one of the most insidious dangers of state law – that is, the tendency to normalise by ways of judicial measures and policy schemes. We shall begin this chapter with a quick summary of the most important traits of Hauriou's and Romano's institutional theories. Based on this account, we shall discuss how Schmitt capitalised on their insights and shall dig out the decisionist residues of concrete-order thinking. The chapter will close by summing up the theoretical advances that, despite the reactionary outcome, make Schmitt's institutionalism more interesting than his exceptionalism to reflect on the nature and the functions of state law.

THE AMBIVALENT RELATION WITH LEGAL INSTITUTIONALISM

Over the course of his long intellectual life,[1] Hauriou pursued a twofold methodological objective. He intended to overcome the objectivism of organicist sociology, from the vantage point of sociology, and the objectivism of state-based public law theories, from the vantage point of jurisprudence.[2] Against sociology, which wanted to penetrate the complex functioning of the social machinery, Hauriou integrated sociological thinking with elements from the field of biology. For the latter does not so much concentrate on objective regularities, but on the irregularities, the phase transitions, the protean forms in which, often unexpectedly, life gets organised. Within biology as well as within the social field, there are no stable laws that can aspire to capture the regularity of the production and reproduction of life. By doing so, Hauriou supplemented his own method of social enquiry with the epistemological model of physical and biological scholarship insofar as they gave up any attempt to grasp the homogeneity and continuity of life to look at the ways in which dynamic, precarious equilibria are obtained. The various forms of life, of any kind, are transitory assemblages, organised in accordance with a formal principle – that is, the principle by which they acquire a form. In the field of social life, those assemblages 'define the institutional fabric of the

[1] As far as Hauriou's theory of the institution is concerned, it originally got underway as early as 1906, the publication year of the sixth edition of the *Précis de droit administratif et de droit public* as well as the important article 'L'Institution et le droit statutaire'. He extensively revised his theory in the two editions of the *Principes de droit public* (1910 and 1916) and eventually gave it a more defined and extensive form in the first edition of the *Précis de droit constitutionnel* (1923) and in *The Theory of the Institution and the Foundation* (1925). See Millard, 'Hauriou et la théorie de l'institution'. For an enlightening interpretation and application of Hauriou's institutional theory, see Loughlin, 'Droit politique' and Loughlin, *Political Jurisprudence*, 109–23.

[2] For a more comprehensive outline of Hauriou's thinking, see, among many other texts, Alonso, Duranthon and Schmit, *La Pensée du doyen Maurice Hauriou à l'épreuve du temps* and Gray, *The Methodology of Maurice Hauriou*. For a more detailed contextualisation, see Blanquer and Milet, *L'Invention de l'état*; Broderick, *The French Institutionalists*, 45–139; Marty and Brimo, *La Pensée du doyen Maurice Hauriou et son influence*.

social space conceived as the stratification of activities and functions'.[3] Here comes the meaning of the term 'organisation': saying that the social is organised amounts to saying that it incarnates 'a formal principle – the institution as an agglutination of the relations that saturate the space of socialisation'.[4]

Therefore, for Hauriou, the social field consists of a series of organisational forms that channel human practices along particular lines and govern individual conduct. With an evident reference to its canon law matrix, the Hauriouvian concept of institution evokes the idea of a 'transubstantiation'[5] whereby a specific conduct metamorphoses into a collective entity. This vitalist system – 'vitalist' in the sense that it identifies an immaterial dynamic principle within life phenomena – turns into a conception of law that breaks with the two most influential traditions of public law, namely the French and the German ones. Much of the French tradition had nurtured the idea of a state produced and animated by an objective, supra-subjective popular will that transcends and generates individual subjects. The German tradition had exalted the ideal of the state as the source of associated life and its condition of possibility. According to these notable examples of state-centred monism, the power of the state (*Herrschaft*) is the true source of its own right to exert power over the populace, while the existence of legal relations between individuals is nothing but the expression of the will of the people incarnated by the state itself. The political power of the state is total and all-encompassing. It can only be lessened by an exercise of self-restraint.

This is a vision that did not fit in with Hauriou's notion of society as a series of forms substantiating spontaneous assemblages. These are forms that derive their origin from singular conducts assembled according to a differential dynamic principle with objective power presiding over them. In this innovative theory, the state does not represent the uniform and constitutive will of a people. Rather, it is a public body that feeds off an acentric multitude of institutionalisation processes. The state collects and directs the vital impulses of the institutions and ensures their integration on a large scale. Consequently, contrary to what the traditional doctrine of the state had long claimed, the law is not the product of the state will, but is a code inherent in the collective forms of interaction performed by social actors. But if normative orders shape up and live according to unpredictable developmental lines, social order is destined to be unstable and to remain sensitive to ongoing tensions. Public law, then, is called on to govern and balance these tensions, though they can never be

3 Chignola, *Diritto vivente*, 172.
4 Chignola, *Diritto vivente*, 172.
5 Salvatore, 'Il diritto della vita', 128.

completely tamed. In this framework, the definition of institution offered by Hauriou reads as follows:

> An institution is an idea of a work or enterprise that is realized and endures juridically in a social context; for the realization of this idea, an organized power equips it with organs; on the other hand, among the members of the social group interested in the realization of the idea, manifestations of communion occur and are directed by the organs of the power and regulated by procedures.[6]

In order that an institution may effectively organise social reality, it must exhibit three constitutive properties: first, an *ordering and project-idea* of social action (*idée directrice*) – that is, a founding idea based on which a social group can carry out its work or enterprise; consequently, the *formation of a structuring power* to design and plan at best the various steps to achieve their aim; finally, a *widespread factual acceptance* of the directing idea within the relevant context – that is, a manifest consensus within the group with respect to the constitutive aim and the means for achieving it. This third element is that which turns a *de facto* situation into a *de jure* condition, since the group can continue to live in peace, and this 'transforms it into an *institution* subsisting by itself and not by force'.[7] Given that institutional forms are subject to constant change, institutional processes are by nature provisional, caught in a constant flux that could erode their strength. To limit contingency, public law deploys public powers of administration and control by which it attests to the 'vitality' or the decline of institutions. The state, then, is a structured political society, a regime of ordered balance that enables the co-existence of multiple processes of institutionalisation that are produced independently of the state's will.

It is impossible in the present chapter to provide a detailed picture of Hauriou's ground-breaking theory as well as its evolutions and shifts as he continually sought to clarify and strengthen his concept of institution. However, one can safely say, without betraying his main lesson, that Hauriou's institutionalism portrays the law as a process of stabilisation of interactional practices requiring a selective (hence, exclusionary) activity meant to reduce the complexity of social life. The law ensures the continuity of community life with an eye to striking a difficult balance: the minimum reduction of expressive richness for the maximum of stability. As is perhaps inevitable for any institutionalist approach, Hauriou's theory fell prey of the

6 Broderick, *The French Institutionalists*, 99.

7 Ibid., 55.

perpetual conflict between the fact of contingency and the need for stability, so much so that he eventually lapsed back into the comfort zone of a state-based idea of institution – one that was 'instrumental in an institutionalist reinstatement of the moral personality of the state more than in a genealogy aimed at deconstructing, or at least relativising, the normative primacy of a sovereign body'.[8]

This is a major sticking point with the other acclaimed initiator of classic institutional thinking, Santi Romano, who bemoaned Hauriou's state-based notion of institution.[9] In his seminal book, *The Legal Order* (1918), Romano recognised that his French colleague had innovated public law like no one else before. However, Romano continued, he 'restricted the concept of institution to one kind of social organization, apt to reach a certain level of development and perfection'.[10] As we shall see, it is precisely this theoretical 'limitation' that makes sense of Schmitt's fascination for Hauriou. However, Romano rejected the objectivist tendency of Hauriou's institutional thinking to obtain a concept of institution that did not reflect the image of the state and did not imply any metaphysical forces. For in Romano's notion there is no reference whatsoever to vital forces or directive ideas. He only drew attention to the organisational nature of interactional contexts – that is, the specific, *technical* task of stabilising interactions – an immanent function, as is the case with Hauriou, but much more machinic. It is almost a technology – one could say in a language that Romano would probably not have used – that requires the deployment of a technical knowledge concerning interactional practices, a knowledge that is not inscribed in those very practices.

A definition of Romano's notion of institution can be obtained by summing up the four characteristics singled out in Section 12 of *The Legal Order*. The institution is an entity endowed with an 'objective and concrete existence' and an 'outward and visible' individuality, 'a manifestation of the social, not purely

8 Salvatore, 'Il diritto della vita', 143.

9 The literature on Romano is too vast to be summarised in a footnote, especially because our quick reconstruction of his seminal theory of law does not have any exegetical intentions. Here we will limit ourselves to the Anglophone literature and will leave aside the critical mass of Italian studies devoted to him. A very informed and detailed introduction is Sandulli, 'Santi Romano and the Perception of the Public Law Complexity'. For a general outline of Romano's theory, see Fontanelli, 'Santi Romano and *L'ordinamento giuridico*'. For a recent reappraisal of Romano's theorising also see Croce and Goldoni, *The Legacy of Pluralism*, 51–98; Loughlin, *Political Jurisprudence*, 109–23; de Wilde, 'The Dark Side of Institutionalism'; Salvatore, 'A Counter-Mine that Explodes Silently'; Vinx, 'Santi Romano against the State?'. Excellent commentaries on the recent translation into English of *The Legal Order* are Cotterrell, 'Still Afraid of Legal Pluralism?' and Fontanelli, 'Review of *The Legal Order*'.

10 Romano, *The Legal Order*, 15–16.

individual, nature of human being', which 'can be considered in itself and for itself precisely because it has an individuality of its own', while 'its identity does not get lost, at least always and necessarily, as its distinct elements vary, as well as its members, patrimony, means, interests, addressees, norms, and so on'.[11] These characteristics lead to an idea of the institution as an interactional context, comprising at least two individuals, which does not depend on the actions of these individuals, and survives their entry or exit. Unlike Hauriou, he envisaged no force or direction at work. The institution is nothing but the accrual of the techniques whereby a practice gets fixed and is less and less exposed to change – or better, change itself gets filtered and administered through these techniques.

For this reason, Romano considered the word 'institution' as nothing more than a juristic term that, in the area of legal studies, was meant to replace the sociological term 'organisation' – as sociology, he firmly believed, should remain distinct from jurisprudence. The institution is an organisational context that acquires independence from the people who transitorily become members. A visible and individual entity, then, not because of concrete, objective characteristics, describable through empirical methods, but because its practices are independent from the agents who transiently engage in them. For example, a group of friends may freely establish the rules designed to govern their interaction, while these rules entirely depend on them. However, one day they may decide to set off a process of specialisation that transforms the group, say, into a private club, where the rules, principles, and procedures can only be changed in compliance with other rules, and thus cannot be freely changed as is the case with a less solidified group. The institution undergoes a transition phase that is also a change of nature through the deployment of specific techniques designed to make it independent of subjective wills. The practice and its standards get separated from the concrete actions that realise them in concrete circumstances, for them to become more and more insensitive to unmindful and careless transformation. The institution:

> takes it upon itself to overcome the weakness and limitedness of their forces, to exceed their feebleness, to perpetuate particular goals beyond their natural life, by creating social entities that are more powerful and durable than individuals. Such entities establish a synthesis, a syncretism in which the individual gets caught. It not only regulates the individuals' activity, but also their position, at times superior and at other times inferior to the others';

[11] Ibid., 17–19.

> things and energies are instrumental in permanent and general ends, and all this with a set of guarantees, powers, subjections, liberties, checks, which systematize and unify an array of scattered elements.[12]

Later we shall see that this conception of institution hardly justifies the 'concretist' misuse Schmitt made of Romano's theory. For now, though, we just want to emphasise that the profound innovation of Romano's proposal lies in his adhesion to 'pan-legalism' – that is, the idea that all normative contexts are *always and already legal*. He insisted that 'institution' is synonymous with 'legal order'. Contrary to Hauriou, he maintained that the institution is not the source of law, as it itself is law. This explains why, in Romano's conceptual framework, the terms 'organisation', 'institution', 'order' and 'law' are perfectly interchangeable. Accordingly, the adjective 'legal' indicates nothing other than the existence of an ongoing organisational process by which an entity fends off the risk of abrupt change. From this ensues the pan-legalist conclusion: all institutions are already and always legal orders. Institution is law, at all levels, whereas the state is but one of many types of law, among many other institutions, smaller and larger. Admittedly, pluralism is inscribed in the genome of Romano's institutionalism.

This makes sense of Romano's rejection of all the definitions of law focusing on the properties that were being discussed in coeval debates. The idea itself that state law could be distinguished from other normative orders because of some inner features of statutory norms and legal procedures, or because of the state's *de facto* monopoly on force, is a mistake due to the poor elaboration of the concept of institution. Norms, sanctions, procedures and the exercise of some type of power are substantive features that an institution might or might not possess, and yet it is not by virtue of them that an institution is an institution. What matters is the organisational process that deploys some techniques (among them, norms, sanctions and procedures) that are meant to oversee internal change and thus restrain unlimited contingency.

Romano's is a purely juristic – that is, neither philosophical nor sociological – attempt to de-objectify the conceptualisation of public law. This is why he was at pains to vindicate the methodological pureness of jurisprudence. In the robust set of footnotes that he published in the second edition of *The Legal Order* (1946) to address the heap of comments and criticisms he had received over a period of thirty years, Romano lamented that his critics had failed to appreciate his firm separation of legal science from

[12] Ibid., 21.

other disciplines. The definition of institution that he aimed to justify in his book was a technical instrument available to the jurist, and as such, it had nothing to do with philosophical and sociological inquiries:

> On my part, I would like to add that it was my aim to include in the legal world a fact of social order that was generally believed to be anterior to the law; to this end, I tried to demonstrate that this mistake is the source of most faults and incongruities of conventional definitions of law, especially as these definitions are all, to different degrees, forced to employ non-legal elements or concepts.[13]

If one juxtaposes Hauriou's and Romano's notions of institution, one can easily conclude that they are certainly not identical, and yet they share two decisive characteristics that are key to pinpointing the limits of Schmitt's institutionalism. First, they both exalt the immanence of the order – an order that is *in re*, and that is 'absorbed' by state law, while it is not for the state to confer normative value on institutions. Second, both Hauriou and Romano put emphasis on the interactional nature of law, in that institutions are nothing other than the conformation that practices take as they change over time. Certainly, one difference between these two scholars is that, within Romano's framework, Hauriou's immaterial vital principle is replaced by the activity of jurists who take it upon themselves to identify the forms that grant stability to social practices.[14] Nonetheless, the practical way in which institutions consolidate and endure should not be confused with their conditions of existence. Another difference – and this was crucial for Schmitt's theoretical purposes – is that Hauriou's institutions must conform to their directive idea, and everything is instrumental in achieving it. On the contrary, for Romano, institutionalisation comes down to a matter of straightforward functionalism, though of a thin type,[15] whereby particular rules, practices, coercive means,

[13] Ibid., 20.

[14] It should also be noted, albeit in passing, and although the theme was not directly addressed by Romano, that a notion of the jurist consistent with his radical pluralism should be able to encompass any individual within a given institution who is called upon to articulate and consolidate the practical knowledge that becomes the 'inner law' of that institution. Only in certain geo-historical circumstances – for example, within complex political structures – can the experts who articulate legal knowledge be members of a recognisable and separate elite. Be that as it may, at least in theory, even in complex structures, legal experts (in the hyper-extensive sense that Romano attributes to this term) are all those individuals who, in a given context, contribute to the stabilisation of that very context.

[15] In 'The Juristic Point of View', Croce highlights the resemblance between Romano's functionalism and the type of functionalism that William Twining calls 'thin functionalism' with reference to Karl N. Llewellyn's theory of law-jobs. See Twining, 'A Post-Westphalian Conception of Law' and Twining, *General Jurisprudence*.

values and principles gradually acquire a more stable form. Nevertheless, however important these differences may be for a thorough comparison of Hauriou's and Romano's conceptions, neither of them ever theorised that the order is *concrete* in a Schmittian sense. Institutions consolidate practices, but they are not meant to crystallise exemplary models and guiding figures that should be made mandatory for the entire political community. Based on this analysis, we can now dive deeper into Schmitt's peculiar institutionalism.

THE SUBSTANTIVE TWIST OF INSTITUTIONALISM

Like Hauriou's and Romano's institutions, Schmitt's concrete order is also an immanent order. But the idea of immanence adumbrated in *On the Three Types of Juristic Thought* is quite different from the one that lies beneath Hauriou's vitalism or Romano's thin functionalism. Doubtless, for Schmitt, too, the law is rooted in a set of practices. However, their rationale is not intrinsic to them. In other words, state law can hardly consider institutions as deserving recognition and protection simply because they are organisational contexts with a normativity of their own. Rather, the institutions to be recognised and protected are only those that conform to the broader historical and socio-cultural context. Like Hauriou and Romano, Schmitt did think that jurisprudence must investigate actual institutionalisation patterns. However, unlike them, he thought that the main jurisprudential task is to identify the criterion whereby some institutions can be selected in while others are selected out. Jurisprudence investigates the interplay of decisions, norms and the concrete order that manifests itself 'in its notions of what is a normal situation, who is a normal person, and what in legal life and legal thought are presumed to be typical concrete examples of the life to be justly judged'.[16] Hauriou and Romano would be hard pressed to theorise an all-embracing, global, totalising order (*Gesamtordnung*) from which a normal situation and a normal individual can be juristically elicited. This is because they dismiss from the very outset the idea that society or the political community are supra-subjective entities. Rather, the community is the precipitate of multiple and acentric processes of institutionalisation. But famously, Schmitt was not a faithful reader and used his sources quite idiosyncratically.

To gauge the extent of Schmitt's (more or less deliberate) misunderstanding, let us pick up the thread of his critique of normativism. In the previous chapter, we showed that his attack on Kelsen's conception of the legal norm

[16] Schmitt, *On the Three Types of Juristic Thought*, 46.

changed significantly between 1922 and 1934. Whereas in *Political Theology*, normativism was charged with purposely dismissing the origin of law (the decision on the state of exception), the critique deployed in *On the Three Types of Juristic Thought* pivoted on the ordinary nature of legal norms. In 1934, Schmitt somehow rehabilitated the normality of ordinary life, in that legal norms are meant to articulate the substantive content of social institutions and thus to fix the decisive traits of a political community's ordinary life. Based on this substantive conception of the normal, the most regrettable error of normativist thinking was found in the identity that it postulated between the order and the norms that comprise it: the order is regarded as nothing other than a complex of norms connected to a basic norm. Schmitt put forward a broader, substantive conception by insisting that the order is much more than a set of norms. The order is something that enlivens norms and that norms struggle to articulate as much as they can. This is why, said Schmitt, the opposite of order is not the simple absence of order, but *disorder* (*Unordnung*). Accordingly, the deviation from just one of the models and guidelines embodied by legal norms is not a mere infringement of the law, but a threat to the overall institutional tapestry of the political community.

This explains Schmitt's rebuke of the normativist tenets that the legal norm is that which associates particular sanctions with particular conducts and that crimes originate from a legislative act that qualifies those conducts as unlawful. In Schmitt's eyes, these tenets reduce the law to a mere impediment to those who wish to carry out prohibited conducts: 'Punishment is an "infringement" on the freedom of the criminal, just as the tax is an infringement on property and military service even on the right to one's own life.'[17] On the contrary, for Schmitt, the violation of a legal norm threatens the whole concrete order: 'Only the concrete peace or a concrete order can be broken; only with this in mind can the concept of crime be salvaged.'[18] In contrast to the image of order as the integration of the plans of action by rational actors, which is much closer to the 'well-regulated traffic on the highways of a modern metropolis',[19] he emphasised the idea of order as a complex of institutional models and guiding figures that we explained in the previous chapter.

It is at this stage that Schmitt believed he could find support in Romano's 'very significant theory',[20] as the latter illustrates the subordination of norms to

17 Ibid., 52.
18 Ibid., 53.
19 Ibid., 53.
20 Ibid., 87.

the legal order.[21] Before introducing what he saw as an excerpt from *The Legal Order* that could confirm his reading, Schmitt offered a rushed summary of Romano's conception: the legal order of a state is not the sum of its norms but a concrete organisational complex, comprising many elements other than norms. Up to this point, Schmitt had been referring to something that Romano never got tired of stressing. However, Schmitt's translation of Romano's text bespeaks a considerable misunderstanding. He refers to a passage of the original Italian edition Romano's book that reads as follows: 'In other words, the legal order, taken as a whole, is an entity that partly moves according to the norms, but most of all moves the norms like pawns on a chessboard – norms that therefore represent the object as well as the means of its activity, more than an element of its structure.'[22]

It should not slip one's attention that Schmitt translated Romano's expression '*comprensivamente inteso*' (taken as a whole) into '*ist ein einheitliches Wesen*' (is a unitary entity). As we argued elsewhere,[23] this fundamentally misreads Romano's conception of institution. According to the Italian jurist, the legal order is not, and could not, be a homogeneous and uniform entity precisely because he emphasised, time and again, the autonomy of the various sub-state orders that make up the state order.[24] For Schmitt, on the contrary, homogeneity is a mode of concreteness. He harboured an essentially ethicist, at times even ethnicist, conception of the order. The legal order is concrete because it puts together and congeals practices in a way that owes much more to Hauriou's directive idea – with the caveat that Schmitt, as we shall see, turned the directive idea into a real, personal Leader. The concrete order pursues the end of perpetuating the political community, while the legal order is the instrument that allows achieving such a supreme objective. The seeming immanence of the concrete order eventuates in an outright transcendence, in that the order is something that lies behind institutions and hovers over them.

[21] In the present context, we cannot dwell on the relationship between Schmitt and Romano. We took up the issue in Croce and Salvatore, *The Legal Theory of Carl Schmitt*, 109–23. See also Croce and Goldoni, *The Legacy of Pluralism*, 126–30; De Wilde, 'The Dark Side of Institutionalism'; Salvatore, 'A Counter-Mine that Explodes Silently'.

[22] Romano, *The Legal Order*, 7.

[23] See Croce and Salvatore, *The Legal Theory of Carl Schmitt*, 116; Croce and Goldoni, *The Legacy of Pluralism*, 128.

[24] See Romano, 'Nota bio-bibliografica', 852, and Police, 'Le autonomie pubbliche come ordinamenti giuridici'.

DECISIONISM REBORN

Based on the analysis thus far, it is easy to spot the decisionist residues of Schmitt's institutionalism. There is no doubt that he regarded Hauriou's directive idea as a living force that confers identity and power on an enterprise and shapes the conduct of the institution members. In this sense, the directive idea might have seemed to him a precursor of the idea of Leadership advanced in *On the Three Types of Juristic Thought*. It is highly likely that while reading Hauriou's books (more than Romano's), Schmitt came to the conclusion that the creative will of a political leader does not express itself in the suspension of normality. Rather, sound political leadership is the one that nourishes normality and ensures its persistence. In that respect, the notion of an *order* is different from that of a *system*. The order implies an idea of law as something that emerges out of people's practices and gets solidified into statutory norms and institutional models. Unlike the system, the order is never entirely artificial; it can be neither created *ex nihilo* nor completely verbalised.[25]

While Hauriou could well be the inspirer of this notion of order, what he could hardly support is that the directing idea corresponds to an actual, personal Leader who is followed by the entire people. Based on this fundamental misunderstanding, Schmitt came up with his peculiar blend of institutionalism and decisionism. Whether this was a way of making his concrete-order thinking compatible with the *Führerprinzip* or a genuine belief, Schmitt dissolved the state into the Leadership:

> The state of the present is no longer a dualistic one separated into state and society, but one built upon the tripartite order of state, movement, people. The state, as a special part of the order within the political unit, no longer has a monopoly on the political, but is only one organ of the *Führer* of the movement. The previous decisionistic or normativistic or positivistic legal thinking combined of both is no longer adequate for a political unit constructed in this way. Now a concrete order and formation thinking is required that will measure up to the numerous new tasks or the governmental, *völkisch*, economic, and ideological conditions and to the new form of community.[26]

25 See Croce and Goldoni, *The Legacy of Pluralism*, 99–135, where the authors adopt the counterpoint between system and order as a lens to approach Schmitt's institutional theory.

26 Schmitt, *On the Three Types of Juristic Thought*, 98.

The order gets embodied into a project of society drawn up by a Leader who knows how to read the institutional dynamics of his people in the light of the community history and traditions. Evidently, there is no room for the unfounded decision of *Political Theology* – the foundation in this new institutional framework is all too solid. Yet, the decisionist element is conspicuous in that the activity of interpreting a societal context is anything but straightforward. As the Leader interprets the history and tradition of an entire society, he[27] shapes it and establishes what does and does not belong in there. Compared to *Political Theology*, the decision in 1934 is to be founded on a pre-existing matter that sets the conditions within which the Leader excises the practices that threaten social homogeneity. Here lies the chasm between *social* and *legal* normativity – and this is as far away from Romano's explicit conclusions as it is from Hauriou's implicit message. As we illustrated in the previous chapter, for Schmitt, society is the formless agglomeration of groups and associations that are pushed by centrifugal tendencies, while the law arises out of the intervention of the Leader on this agglomeration – hence the term 'formation' (*Gestalt*) that figures prominently in the full label of Schmitt's institutional theory: *konkrete Ordnungs- und Gestaltungsdenken*. The Leader's cut shapes an already-existing substance and thereby confers on the latter a stable and enduring conformation. Short of this cut, there is neither stability nor duration. Short of this cut, there is no order.

But what does this cut involve? And how is it performed? While these questions were left unanswered in *Political Theology*, they found quite a resolute response in the early 1930s, especially in *State, Movement, People* (1933), and in some visible, albeit more cursory, traces in *On the Three Types of Juristic Thought*. Unlike *Political Theology*, the decider does not bring about a state of exception, as it would cause havoc in ordinary life and would seriously impinge on its fabric. Instead, the decider operates silently, on a daily basis, through the mediation of a group of reliable and loyal officials. In the previous chapter, we pointed out how such legal tools as general clauses introduced the kind of vagueness that, according to Schmitt, made it possible for legal officials to carry out the project of society drawn up by the Leader. Their general reference to models produced within specific institutional contexts (such as the family, the army and the bureaucracy) granted ample leave to those who are called on to assess, case by case, whether this or that conduct reflected those models and to what extent. Legal officials, as faithful implementers of an image of society, should cut out the products of society

[27] A notorious 'he', ashamedly, in this case.

that did not conform to the models and figures entrenched in legal norms – norms that, thanks to the general clauses, could be differently applied to similar cases if the circumstances require it.

Schmitt intensified his references to everyday normality in that the 'calculability and reliability' of normation rests on 'the presupposedly normal situation'.[28] This is why the solution to the problem of how to regulate social life in its daily aspects certainly could not be found in more detailed legal codes, but in the shrewd use of instruments that are by nature vague by well-trained and devoted state officials. Schmitt's main concern was with legal education and legal training, as the judges should be instructed in how to best apply the new legal instruments. Hence, his reference to the State Secretary of the Reich Ministry of Justice, Roland Freisler, as he stated: '[N]o reform of justice but reform of jurists', and, continued Schmitt, 'it all depends precisely on the *breed* and the *types* of our judges and civil servants'.[29] The law envisaged by Schmitt pivoted on a training for the legal profession that would yield the 'appropriate' type of legal official and would ensure 'the true substance of "personality"'.[30] He certainly offered an oversimplified vision of legal training and law enforcement, entirely dependent on a sort of (hetero-induced) ethno-nationalistic sensitivity to the voice of the Leader. Yet this was contingent on his idea of equality as an *ethnic* equality, one that offered guidance in the application of the rules to concrete cases. The whole judicial and administrative system should have to be revised along these lines, because:

> The idea of the ethnic identity will pervade and dominate all our public law. That is valid for the career civil service, as much as for the legal profession essentially interested in the creation and the shaping of the law, as well as for all the cases in which comrades of the people become active in the management of public affairs, the administration of justice and in jurisprudence. Above all, this will guarantee a fruitful collaboration in the constitution of different new 'councils of leaders.'[31]

The answers to the questions of what the political cut involves and how is it performed are to be found in the answer to the question of *quis iudicabit*. Evidently, in the early 1930s, Schmitt's idea of society, and the law within it, was that of a pyramid with a broader social base and a smaller legal vertex, its various stones being connected to each other by ethical and ethnic homogeneity, designed by the Leader and implemented by his well-trained

28 Schmitt, *State, Movement, People*, 48.
29 Ibid., 50.
30 Ibid.
31 Ibid., 50–1.

delegates. A system of transmission belts that would make it impossible to erode the ethnic identity connecting the lay population to the jurists, the judges and the Leader, 'without which a total leader-State could not stand its ground a single day'.[32]

WAS DECISIONISM A NECESSARY OUTCOME OF CONCRETE-ORDER THINKING?

This is obviously a most despicable conclusion. And yet, it is our claim that it can be uncoupled from Schmitt's reflections that led him to revise his own understanding of social order and its relation to the law. Lest we get misunderstood, the excision of such a regrettable conclusion certainly does not make Schmitt's theory any more useful to rethinking the role of law in liberal democracies. Nonetheless, we think it does illuminate some typical features of the law of post-World War Two constitutional systems, for it casts light on the law's tendency, even within liberal regimes, to embody concrete models of conduct and to make them binding on the whole population. Moreover, it brings out the residues of decisionism that are manifest in liberal legal measures and policy schemes. It should then not be surprising that one of the most famous among the fathers and the mothers of the 1948 Italian Constitution, Costantino Mortati, in 1973 devoted a seminal essay to Schmitt's concrete-order thinking.[33] Without hesitation, Mortati claimed that the acme of Schmitt's thinking is his institutionalism of the 1930s and brought to surface the fruitful tensions it creates within the Schmittian framework. A caveat is needed, though. In his essay, Mortati's interpretation is so liberal that it turned Schmitt into a lucid and coherent Mortatian. However, since we believe that meticulous exegesis is not the only way to gain access to how an author can be relevant to understating the present, it is undoubtedly worth taking stock of his interpretation.

[32] Ibid., 52.

[33] Mortati, *Brevi note sul rapporto fra costituzione e politica nel pensiero di Carl Schmitt*. Though underestimated in the Anglophone debate, Mortati's theory offered a ground-breaking conception of law, and particularly of the constitution. In this footnote we will limit ourselves to mentioning the texts in English that specifically deal with his thinking. See Colón-Ríos, *Constituent Power and the Law*, 186–225; Corduwene, 'Gerhard Leibholz, Costantino Mortati and the Ideological Roots of Postwar Party Democracy in Germany and Italy'; della Cananea, 'Mortati and the Science of Public Law'; Goldoni and Wilkinson, 'The Material Constitution'; La Torre, 'The German Impact on Fascist Public Law Doctrine'; Rubinelli, 'Costantino Mortati and the Idea of Material Constitution'; Rubinelli, *Constituent Power*, 141–75.

He paid no heed to Schmitt's exceptionalism, and straightforwardly saw Schmitt's work (of 'singular charm and scientific excellence'[34]) through the prism of the institution. Certainly, Mortati modelled Schmitt's institution after his own conception of it. Despite this, it helps exhibit the strengths of concrete-order thinking as an innovative jurisprudential paradigm that in the early 1930s introduced a corrective to Schmitt's earlier work and eliminated the hyperbolic conclusions of *Political Theology*. Mortati writes that Schmitt's novel theory was indebted to 'the study of the works of Hauriou and Romano' whereby he came to elaborate on a type of institutionalism that overcame some of the theoretical flaws of his two inspirers.[35] Indeed Schmitt recognised the existence of a hierarchy between the three constitutive elements of law – namely, the decision, the norm and the concrete order. Although the three of them are equally essential for there being a legal order, Mortati thought Schmitt was right in believing that the concrete order precedes and transcends both the decision and the norm. In his hyper-concretist reading, Mortati made a strong case that Schmitt's conjuring of Leadership and ethnic identity was anything but the natural outcome of his concrete-order thinking.

For Mortati, the concrete order is the 'facticity' or 'effectiveness' that substantiates a system of norms. He thus returned to the root cause of Schmitt's anti-normativism and teased out the theory of norms that in *On the Three Types of Juristic Thought* remained largely unexpressed. By criticising Kelsen's rigid separation between validity and effectiveness, Schmitt recovered the latter as an 'internal character' of the former. For a system of norms exists only in a dimension in which particular 'underlying' ends and values yield particular patterns of conduct and particular relations of supremacy and subjection. Just as the norms are the mere reflection of the concrete order, so is the decision. Not only can the latter be considered divorced from an underlying order only in exceptionally rare constituent moments; but even in those uncommon circumstances, the decision must prove to be the expression of a tacit, pre-existing material order:

> But this original decision, once realised, can only operate as an element of a social structure and as the source of its development, ordered not only in an organisational sense, due to the necessary permanence over time of the same supreme authoritative will, but also by a minimum of coherence in the content of the acts through which power is expressed.[36]

[34] Mortati, 'Brevi note', 131.
[35] Ibid., 131.
[36] Ibid., 132.

Much in line with the position advocated in the present book, Mortati thought that the notion of concrete order was a remedy to the abstractness of an unjustified, unfounded, self-referential decision of *Political Theology*. The decision, too, even when it expresses itself in the form of a constituent power, must be able to bring to the surface an order of some kind, one that is prior to the decision and is preliminary to it – especially if it is intended to replace a previous order.

In a way that resonates with his own influential theory of law, Mortati grasped a core claim of Schmitt's understanding of jurisprudence and its objectives as a science. Inasmuch as everything that concerns the law originates from a concrete order, jurisprudence ought to be first and foremost the study of it. This puts an end to those disciplinary distinctions (such as sociology vs legal science, political vs legal theory) that seriously limit the scope of the study of organisational processes. On this account, even the opening line of the third chapter of *Political Theology*, concerning the sociology of legal concepts, was limited and limiting, because it centred on too general a relation between a form of life and its conceptual tapestry. In Mortati's eyes, the concrete order that Schmitt introduced in 1934 was much more tangible – the 'material constitution', in Mortati's parlance, that jurisprudence is required to unearth and study in order to turn it into a fully fledged normative structure.

One friction between Schmitt's and Mortati's theories concerns the identity between the concrete order and the legal order, which is a decisive element in the latter's theoretical framework but does not at all reflect the clear Schmittian separation between society and the law. For Mortati, the structure of society, based on a *de facto* organisation that is already operational, is the backbone of the state legal order:

> In order to understand the link [between politics and law] that I am advocating, it is necessary to configure the society underlying the legal order as characterised by its own internal structure in which, alongside a system of economic relations, various factors of aggregation converge of a natural, religious, cultural nature. These factors determine differences in the positions of subjects towards each other, in the sense that they give rise to relations of supremacy and subjection, a hierarchical distribution of power resulting from the prevalence of certain classes and certain forces vis-à-vis each other: classes and forces that gather around interests and values which are perceived as essential by their members, which are imposed, and imposed effectively, as the unifying element that turns a social group into a political unity.[37]

37 Ibid., 134–5.

This, after all, lays bare one of the most relevant limits of concrete-order thinking. Schmitt recognised the value of sub-state associations and organisations, but he never made out the immediate connection they have with the organisation of the state. Therefore, he neglected the most remarkable and most typical lesson of classic institutionalism. But let us stick to Mortati's line of interpretation. Although, contrary to what Mortati writes, for Schmitt society and the state are not 'two manifestations of the same essence', for Schmitt, too, the concrete order builds on a lively organisational activity, which no sovereign decision can bring into life *ex nihilo* and no system of norms can fully encapsulate. *The order is a substance*: it brings together certain goals so as to homogenise and to protect them. In this new framework, the decider becomes the shrewd interpreter of social reality who identifies the ends and the values around which social forces can aggregate and those that instead exert a disruptive potential.

Mortati suitably presents the homogeneity of the political community as the element of continuity in Schmitt's legal and political thought – an element that after his institutional turn Schmitt believed could be achieved through the meticulous administration of law's selective power.[38] And it is precisely in this regard that Mortati's reading strengthens Schmitt's proposal. The identification of the practices that are relevant to the continuity of social life does not require a project of society or a whole body of well-trained and obedient implementers. Rather, it is the imprint of concreteness, inscribed from the outset in the constitution, which infiltrates all interstices of the social world. Here lies the counterpoint between inclusive openness and exclusionary selection that is in no way anti-democratic or conservative by nature. Liberal-democratic law of the twentieth century is an instrument for delineating a shared project where social pluralism is contained within margins that allow its reproduction and at the same time prevent its implosion. It is a mechanism that orients the life of a community from inception, since no genesis or foundation (no matter how revolutionary and abrupt) can do without a pre-existing social grammar – one that could lie unexpressed, or be a minority practice that is destined to develop, but, in any case, has to prove capable of contributing substance to the formal constitution.

38 On the other hand, we doubt that Schmitt really conceived homogeneity as the prerequisite for 'an equal chance for political forces that, although divided among themselves, agree on the fundamental structure of the regime in force' (ibid., 137). While the competition between parties within a framework of political homogeneity might have been a concern of Schmitt's in the 1920s, his allegiance to Nazism swept away any genuine interest in democratic agonism.

The decisionist conclusion of Schmitt's institutionalism in the 1930s is therefore an unfortunate, and theoretically unnecessary, compromise with the Nazi regime. Without that appendix, his theory would have certainly not qualified as a liberal theory, because it remained a highly conservative understanding of how the law does the selection of social practices to attain political homogeneity. Yet, it would have come closer to Mortati's realist institutionalism, which is important for its theoretical and meta-theoretical orientation. On a theoretical level, he thought the legal order as oriented towards a collective end inscribed in the constitution, as a normative juice that feeds the constitution and draws it to an end when it dries out. On the meta-theoretical level, jurisprudence is the science that investigates the legal order in the light of this very collective end, so as to understand both its origin and the way in which it animates and perpetuates the constitution.[39]

It is a vision that differs, and not by a small margin, from the teachings of Hauriou and Romano, and that makes one aspect of the former's theory (i.e. the directing idea) an element that drowns out all the others. Although amended in a Mortatian sense, Schmitt's institutionalism portrays the concrete order as a collective guiding force, whereas legal norms and procedures do nothing but translate and implement this force. If one dared to give it a critical twist, one could say that the concrete-order theory unveils an enduring tendency of post-World War Two substantive constitutions, which can be described as a pool of values and principles that are the at core of a political community – and thus also serve as a sieve that, inevitably, has to filter out potential alternatives or to make sure that these alternatives subscribe to constitutional values and principles. But this is not the appropriate context to give a critical twist to Schmitt's theory, nor do we believe that his theoretical proposal is the ideal candidate to advance a critique of the potentially illiberal tendencies of democratic regimes. So, we leave it here.

[39] It is worth clarifying that here we are not subscribing to Mortati's conception of the material constitution. Instead, our argument is that Mortati's understanding of Schmitt's concrete order could solve some of the problems that beset the latter. For a critique of the material constitution in a Schmittian-Mortatian sense, see Croce, 'What Matter(s)?'.

7

Doing Away with Politics

Schmitt's Juristic Institutionalism

Although it goes often unnoticed, Schmitt's output did not end with his voluntary exile in his native Plettenberg after the end of the war, the tribulations of his two periods of imprisonment and his firm refusal of any de-Nazification procedure; nor can his thought be reduced to his diary entries, sometimes just resentful, other times quite telling. Despite the difference in nature and theoretical relevance, in 1950 four works hailed the controversial return into the limelight of the scholar who had been labelled the 'Führer's supreme jurist'[1] – just a few months after the entry into force of the Basic Law (Grundgesetz) of the newly founded Federal Republic of Germany. If not a new beginning, these works marked a new, somewhat unprecedented approach in Schmitt's persistent obsession with the nature of law and the concrete possibilities of implementing a stable legal order. These works were published in a time span of less than nine months: *The Plight of European Jurisprudence* (March), *Ex Captivitate Salus* (August), *Donoso Cortés Interpreted in a Pan-European Perspective* (October), *The 'Nomos' of the Earth in the International Law of the 'Jus Publicum Europaeum'* (November).

A parallel reading of these works, which at first glance look divergent even in the genre (a pamphlet, a memoir, a synthesis and a treatise), seems to attest

[1] This term – which soon turned into an enduring (and at least partially misleading) label – was originally coined by Schmitt's former student Waldemar Gurian, who in 1934 published a brief article titled 'Carl Schmitt, der Kronjurist des III. Reiches' in *Deutsche Briefe*, a widely read resistance journal for Catholic *émigrés* (26 October 1934). As we have noted, the literature on Schmitt and the Nazi regime is abundant. In the present context, we would like to suggest Blasius, *Carl Schmitt. Preußischer Staatsrat in Hitlers Reich*; Cumin, *Carl Schmitt*, Ch. 5; Koenen, *Der Fall Carl Schmitt*; Mehring, *Carl Schmitt: Aufstieg und Fall*, Part III; Rüthers, *Carl Schmitt im Dritten Reich*; Tielke, *Der stille Bürgerkrieg*.

to a substantial continuity with the paradigm shift that we detected in the early 1930s. It can be rightly defined as 'continuity' if only because there is no trace of exceptionalism. But there is more than meets the eye. From the post-war years onwards, even the residues of decisionism came to vanish. After the major amendment that we analysed in the previous chapters, whereby the decision turned into a selective filter, rather than a creative act, decisionism was expunged once and for all (the diary note of 13 October 1947 opens with a laconic and revealing notation: 'Association with Hauriou (instead of Bodin and Hobbes)'[2]). So, while the concrete-order thinking was still marked by a difficult cohabitation of decisionism and institutionalism, the post-war works did away with it completely so as to provide the grounds for what could be defined as a *juristic* institutionalism (which culminated in the greatly underrated *The Plight of European Jurisprudence*[3]).

In the post-war works, the authentic, truly effective and reliable driving force of *Rechtsverwirklichung* (the realisation of the law) is no longer identified with the polemical logic of the political, let alone with a sovereign figure. Rather, it is the constant, widespread and polycentric work of contextual mediation carried out by the jurists (and now, contrary to the writings of the 1910s, by legal professors and scholars ahead of judges). By dint of their sensitivity to history, rather than their legal training, jurists are called upon to actualise the two fundamental tasks of law – that is, the need for stability and the governing of social change. The stability of the order and the unity of the political community can only be ensured by the pondered and flexible fulfilment of the needs of the legal system on the part of the jurists. The residue of decisionism that could still be found in Schmitt after World War Two gradually gave way to a more fundamental juristic activity – that is, the incessant struggle to define and redefine the interactional practices that are already in place, though they are in need of an ordered structure that only the meticulous work of the jurists can provide them with and turn into a superior and self-conscious unity.

2 Schmitt, *Glossarium*, 25.

3 For an overview of this important and still generally overlooked text, see Bogdandy, 'Die heutige Lage der europäischen Rechtswissenschaft im Spiegel von Schmitts Schrift'; Carrino, 'Carl Schmitt and European Juridical Science'; Di Marco, 'A proposito del saggio di Carl Schmitt *Die Lage der europäischen Rechtswissenschaft (1943–1944)*'; Garofalo, 'Carl Schmitt e la *Wissenschaft des römischen Rechts*'; Mehring, 'Carl Schmitts Schrift *Die Lage der europäischen Rechtswissenschaft*'; Piccone and Ulmen, 'Schmitt's "Testament" and the Future of Europe'; Salvatore, 'A maggior gloria della *scientia iuris*'. More generally on the changing uses of Roman law in Schmitt's Weimar, Nazi and post-war thought, see Suuronen, 'Mobilizing the Western Tradition for Present Politics'.

NOMOS, OR THE LONG GOODBYE TO DECISION

Schmitt was not allowed to return to an academic job after 1945 and took to voluntary exile in his native Plettenberg. Such a long period was marked by the appearance of a seemingly new notion, the *nomos*. 'Seemingly new', because the first reference to this notion can be found in a rather minor passage of *Constitutional Theory*, in which he alluded to 'the general character of the legal norm',[4] which is to be contrasted with the narrower concept of norm as the outcome of a statutory procedure formally regulated by the legal order. Schmitt returned to the *nomos* in *On the Three Types of Juristic Thought*, as he tried to conceptualise the order in its concrete development within a structure endowed with a form. Here the *nomos* was nothing other than the law conceived as the inseparable union of norm, decision and – 'above all', Schmitt specifies quite significantly – the concrete order.[5] With a pithy style that is difficult to find in subsequent treatments of this concept, *On the Three Types of Juristic Thought* defines the *nomos* as the concrete order of a concrete community.[6] In such a core text of Schmittian institutionalism, the *nomos* is treated as synonymous with institutional order. On this account, statutory law is to be viewed as the tip of an iceberg emerging out of the vast ocean of spontaneous interactions. The concept of *nomos*, therefore, importantly antedates the *magnum opus* that more completely outlines its nature and boundaries – that is, *The 'Nomos' of the Earth*. And this should not go unnoticed. Despite a few differences with Schmitt's characterisation in *The 'Nomos' of the Earth*, from the 1930s onwards the *nomos* can be regarded as a normative feature that is intrinsic and co-essential to the original appropriation of a physical space. As such, it predetermines the ordered structure of that space and orients all subsequent explicit regulations. This view places considerable stress on concreteness. For the way in which a given community appropriates, through an original act, a given context (which is first and foremost a physical, spatial, concrete context) already contains within itself an ordering potential, one that is actualised – that is, made effective and put in force – through subsequent and explicit law-making. As Schmitt stated in the passage that comes closest to a definition, the *nomos* is 'the full immediacy of a legal power not mediated by laws'.[7]

4 Schmitt, *Constitutional Theory*, 184.

5 Schmitt, *On the Three Types of Juristic Thought*, 50.

6 On Schmitt's engagement with the Greek *nomos* in *On the Three Types of Juristic Thought*, see van den Berge, 'Law, King of All'.

7 Schmitt, *The 'Nomos' of the Earth*, 73.

Let us make a short digression on such a key concept, since it is as fascinating as it is elusive. Most probably, Schmitt's philosophy of the *nomos* could have been much more robust if he had given up evocative images of theological-political figures and reactionary conceptions of world history. He could have focused on a more detailed *jurisprudential* account of how the essential elements of an ordered context combine and coalesce to set the social and epistemic conditions for successful interactions taking place within, and made possible by, stable institutions. There is no shred of doubt that Schmitt ultimately failed, or did not event try, to explain why and how the concept of *nomos* should be regarded as the link between his institutional thinking and a theory of shared social meanings able to support, from an epistemic standpoint, the concept of concrete order. Because of this flaw, the concept of *nomos* was doomed to remain an untidy patchwork quilt out of different artworks, the last remnants of the glorious and bygone age of modern sovereignty. While the original relationship between concrete spaces and effective ordering is more complicated and interesting than Schmitt suggested by simplistically referring to the etymological combination of *Ordnung* (juristic ordering) and *Ortnung* (spatial orientation), the fact remains that his discussion of it is at best superficial. Therefore, the potentially groundbreaking concept of *nomos* remained grossly underdeveloped. Oversimplification and vagueness undermine such a promising insight, which is torn between considerable potential and serious lack of detail. The intertwining of spatial laws and legal spaces as discussed in *The 'Nomos' of the Earth*, fascinating and interesting as it may appear, can be at best regarded as a working project, but it is short of a complete theory, let alone a fully fledged paradigm. While the apodictic sentence 'All law is law only in a particular location'[8] – a late reformulation of the original 'All law is "situational law"'[9] – deserves attention, it should be interrogated much more thoroughly than Schmitt was willing (or able) to do.[10]

8 Ibid., 98.

9 Schmitt, *Political Theology*, 13.

10 Serious doubts on the validity of Schmitt's concept of *nomos*, from both a historical and a theoretical standpoint, have been raised by Cercel, 'Exploring Carl Schmitt'; Chandler, 'The Revival of Carl Schmitt in International Relations'; Colombo, 'The "Realist Institutionalism" of Carl Schmitt'; Dean, 'A Political Mythology of World Order'; Elden, 'Reading Schmitt Geopolitically'; Hooker, *Carl Schmitt's International Thought*; Jacques, 'From *Nomos* to *Hegung*'; Loughlin, '*Nomos*'; Meyer, Schetter and Prinz, 'Spatial Contestation?'; Minca and Rowan, 'The Question of Space in Carl Schmitt'; Koskenniemi, 'International Law as Political Theology'; Müller, 'Carl Schmitt's Method'; Palaver 'Carl Schmitt on *Nomos* and Space'; Simons, 'Carl Schmitt's Spatial Rhetoric'; Teschke, 'Fatal Attraction'; Vinx, 'Carl Schmitt and the Analogy between Constitutional and International Law'.

In the light of the above, and to go back to the original issue, the crucial question here is whether the legal power evoked by Schmitt, which is not mediated by laws, springs from an original act of decision. To put it otherwise, the question is whether the *Landnahme* – the appropriation of land that *The 'Nomos' of the Earth* locates at the heart of the entire process of development of the *nomos* – should be interpreted as the reviviscence of the early 1920s decisionist approach. In our opinion, this is only half-true. There is no denying that emphasis on the cut, the break, the establishment of boundaries that delimit an inside and an outside, are manifest in Schmitt's argument. And yet, on the one hand, the decisionism of the *Landnahme* relativises the constitutive link with any identity-yielding opposition to an enemy. On the other hand, this type of decision lacks three fundamental features of the decisionism of the early 1920s. First, it is no longer a sovereign who decides, in that emphasis is placed as much on the article as it is on the noun – and indeed the personalistic element of the decision withers away to such an extent that one is left wondering how the collective subject who decides on the occupation of land was originally constituted (the idea of a founding hero does not stand any serious chance). Second, the decision is conditional on the factual nature of space, which is at variance with the claimed pre-existing nothingness of Schmitt's erstwhile decisionism. Third, the decision loses its demiurgic *fiat*, which was unable to go beyond the singularity of the moment pointed out by Schmitt in his occasional self-critique – an attitude which was rare in him. The law-making act of Schmitt's former decisionism is now replaced by (or reshaped as) the gradual development of a legal system that originates from, but does not coincide with, the deciding act. Therefore, if it is true that the notion of decision pops up in *The 'Nomos' of the Earth*, it is also true that it is noticeably different and institutionally refashioned, pre-existing legal instances temper its demiurgic omnipotence.

However, no matter what one may think of the affinities between *Entscheidung* and *Landnahme*, what concerns us here is that, despite its decisionistic nature, the *Landnahme* does not account for the birth and development of that *jus publicum europaeum* in which the potential of the order underlying the *nomos* becomes concrete. Indeed, one is hard pressed to understand how a set of individual appropriative decisions – which are obviously individual, as they belong to communities that are not (and should not be) identifiable with each other – can give rise to a *jus publicum* that makes, and holds together, an entire continent as a legal community and a political entity of its own. If the *Landnahme* is to be interpreted as a form of decisionism, then it is beset by the same limits that twenty years before had led

Schmitt to ditch it and to endorse an institutional approach. In either case, it is pretty unclear how individual, distinct sovereign decisions – at the domestic level in *Political Theology*, at the supra-state level in *The 'Nomos' of the Earth* – can give rise to something more homogeneous than a simple contextual (that is, limited in space and time) formulation. According to Schmitt's former decisionism, the constitution of a political unity presupposed, though by negation, a pre-existing communitarian substratum with respect to the sovereign decision. According to Schmitt's new (alleged) decisionism, the constitution of the juridical unity, here at a continental level, presupposes that a group of individuals share an interactional space that not only pre-exists any appropriation of land, but must also circumscribe the space for action and guide the methods of intervention – if one is to explain the convergence (indeed a spontaneous one) on a common juridical heritage.[11]

If we look closer, the concept of appropriation in Schmitt's texts underwent an oscillation – if one does not want to see it as an evolution – that is far from negligible. A few years later, in the essay titled 'Nehmen/Teilen/Weiden', the concept of *Landnahme* is displaced in a largely different framework than the rhapsodic reconstruction of the first chapter of *The 'Nomos' of the Earth*.[12]

[11] This is why, while many scholars have convincingly argued that Schmitt's fascinating counter-narrative provided in *The 'Nomos' of the Earth* and other minor works of the same period is both empirically and conceptually flawed, we think that his approach suffers from a more fatal flaw, at once ideological and logical, which makes his concept of *nomos* highly defective. It is the complete lack of a sociological investigation of those practices, experiences, links, processes and even conceptual devices that make an order – especially if defined as *concrete* – possible and functioning. Despite Schmitt's rhetorical claims, in the end, spatial dimension and social relations still remain separate from one another. Short of a comprehensive account of what 'concrete legal ordering' actually means, Schmitt's account of *nomos* is doomed to be grounded on acts of disruptive foundational violence – a perspective that is as historically untenable as politically unacceptable. To put it metaphorically, by reducing the emergence of social order to an original act of appropriation, Schmitt may be able to account for the opposition between pieces on the chessboard, but he can hardly advance a proper understanding of the chessboard itself. Why such an original land appropriation? Why do certain individuals team together to act politically if not on the basis of a more original commonality, which is left unexplained? Why the primacy of an original divide (the conquest as separation between two territories, a familiar and a threatening one) over a detailed account of the process of group formation? Schmitt writes: 'There are neither spaceless political ideas nor, reciprocally, spaces without ideas or principles of space without ideas' (Schmitt, 'The *Großraum* Order of International Law with a Ban on Intervention for Spatially Foreign Powers', 87). However, contrary to what he puts in dialectical terms, Schmitt only explores one way of such a two-way path – that is, the direction from an already shaped social unity to a coherent conception of space – but he never provides us with an explanation of how and whence an original conception of space may emerge in the absence of shared social meanings.

[12] In this sense, one should not forget that that part of Schmitt's book was meant to be an introduction to the reconstruction of European expansionism, as the full title of the work clarifies.

First, he no longer speaks of *Landnahme* but of *Nahme*, implying that the land is not the only thing one appropriates (even less so, if one reduces the strategies for appropriation to invasion or conquest). Secondly, appropriation is only one of the three features of the legal order, which is to be supplemented with the other features of *division* and *production*. Thirdly, depending on the contexts and spheres involved, the appropriation does not necessarily precede the other two features. The appropriation of land is therefore only one of the modes of appropriation, and moreover – as Schmitt explicitly states[13] – the oldest and primeval. It is the first in a historical succession that ties the moment of taking possession not to the use of violence (which is only one of the modes, the most rudimentary), but to a monopolistic management of resources of various kinds (land, soil, means of production, labour power, social product, monetary regulation), which are necessary for the reproduction of an order. This more general framework is replicated in Schmitt's last essay expressly devoted to the concept of *nomos*, '*Nomos* – *Nahme* – Name', published in 1959.[14]

Whether or not decisionism is a colour of the *Landnahme*, the *nomos* can be understood, at least in the author's intentions and despite its flaws, as an attempt to rearticulate the concrete-order thinking in a more realistic, three-dimensional configuration by adding the idea of space.[15] The two-dimensionality of Schmitt's institutionalism of the 1930s resulted from the combination of the spontaneity of institutional practices and the selective

[13] 'The world history is a history of progress – or perhaps just change – in the means and methods of appropriation: from the appropriation of the land in nomadic and agrarian-feudal times, to the appropriation of the sea in 16th and 17th centuries, to the industrial-technical age and its distinction between developed and undeveloped areas, and finally to the appropriation of the air and space in present times. . . . The present essay deals with a constitutional aspect of the issue of nomos, which becomes more and more relevant since the most important function of the state comes to be the distribution or redistribution of the social product. This is the case with industrialised countries, in which the administrative state provides public services on a mass scale. . . . Before distributing or redistributing the social product, such a state must take possession of it, whether it does so through taxes or contributions, through the distribution of jobs, through currency devaluation or in some other direct or indirect ways. In any case, the positions where one can distribute and redistribute are real political power positions that are also taken and distributed' (Schmitt, 'Nehmen/Teilen/Weiden', 503). On the nasty habit of replacing argumentative reasoning with etymological resonance, see Stergiopoulou, 'Taking *Nomos*'.

[14] Schmitt, *The 'Nomos' of the Earth*, 336–50.

[15] This is a point well captured by a recent interpretation of Schmitt's thought as a whole: 'Order is *nomos* made visible, and *nomos* is the development of communities of men in space thanks to the natural relationships between them, to labor and tradition, and to man's natural way of being, as well as that of a particular people' (Herrero, *The Political Discourse of Carl Schmitt*, 63).

activity of the decisional filter – although it should be noted that the filtering activity robs the *nomos* of the spontaneity of practices. In the face of it, the anchorage to space ensures greater concreteness, in the sense that the description of the *nomos* looks more realistic, whereas the order that characterises a given context enjoys more stability. The space is determined and shaped by institutional contexts, while institutional contexts are determined and shaped by the space that they organise. The order is thus redefined in that it is materially affixed to an extension, a territory, a combination of physical elements and logistics that reinforces its stability and at the same time limits, as it were, its volatility.

Although burdened by the decisionist tinge that Schmitt includes here for the last time (and in any case, only in the first of the various writings devoted to the subject), the concept of *nomos* provides an answer, however rudimentary, to a question that the concrete-order thinking left unresolved: why are some institutional aggregates created and not others? What explains that the spontaneity and plurality of interactional practices operate in such a way as to allow the formation of institutional arrangements that are cohesive enough and are distinct from those of other realities? This question is twofold. On the one hand, it asks why and how certain forms of organisation integrate with each other to the extent that they give rise to a political community. On the other hand, it asks why the same happens in other contexts without leading to further integration between different communities. The concept of *nomos* unfolds as the answer, or a possible answer, to both problems. The dialectic between the historical nature of the original act of appropriation and the specific character of the different territorial contexts explains (at least in part – that is, as far as plurality is concerned) why some institutional instances give rise to a coherent organisational reality and differentiate themselves from others that exist and are not integrated in that they are part of another history and another place. In short, concrete orders are multiple and plural because the places and histories of the earth are multiple and plural.

In Chapter 1 of this book, we drew attention to a matter of fact – that is, the non-decisionist character of Schmitt's early works. Let us close the book with another matter of fact: the decision as the founding act of an order makes its last appearance in the first pages of *The 'Nomos' of the Earth* (significantly written in the mid-1940s). In later writings, the term *Entscheidung* recurs more and more rarely and most often with the generic meaning of 'resolution'.[16] The publication in 1950 of the collection of articles devoted to Donoso Cortés

[16] As an illustrative example, since what is at issue is the opposition between two irreducible identity blocks, see Schmitt's untranslated essay 'Die Einheit der Welt' (The Unity of the World), originally published in 1952.

should not mislead us in this respect. For it rather demonstrates that Schmitt was steadily moving away from the decisionist approach of the early 1920s. Again, it is significant that the title of the book is, not by chance, the only one of the four essays not written in the 1920s, but in 1944, the same year in which Schmitt wrote the first complete version of *The Plight of European Jurisprudence*. Donoso is conjured not as the counter-revolutionary father of decisionism (as he was still presented – quite implausibly – in Chapter 4 of *Political Theology*), but as the first who unveiled a crisis in European civilisation that had been worsening over the course of a century. According to Schmitt, the only remedy, though little more than wishful thinking, is the mediatory activity of the jurists who finally gain awareness of the role they ought to play once the nihilistic advance of technique becomes more and more threatening and the decisionist state order has proven ineffective.

A JURIST APPEALING (AGAIN) TO JURISTS

As we have seen, this was not the first time that Schmitt emphasised the role of the jurists. He had done so in the 1910s and in the 1930s, although the context was different. In his desperate search for order and stability within a parlous world, the works and circumstances in which Schmitt conjured judges, jurists and legal specialists outnumber those in which he entrusted his hopes to political authorities – whether they were embodied by a sovereign, the people or the Führer. In addition to those Schmittian pages that evoke irrevocable decisions, supreme resolutions and original acts that create order, there are passages and statements, certainly less emphasised and yet no less crucial, in which the order is taken to be contingent on the implementation of certain legal practices, both in the interpretation and in the application of the law. Nothing demonstrates better the importance Schmitt assigned to the role of the jurists than the telling passage where he stated: 'A people that do not have a class of jurists has no Constitution'[17] – a statement that looks even more relevant if one considers that the text in which it features was designed to legitimise the Führer's absolute power. Even in the heart of the most unabashed arbitrariness and in the only genuine *plenitudo potestatis* of twentieth-century Europe, no order is given without the jurists.

But the essay in which Schmitt's eulogy of the juristic science is the most crystal-clear is *The Plight of European Jurisprudence*. To fully appreciate the originality of this writing, it is imperative to briefly recall the theoretical

[17] Schmitt, 'Aufgabe und Notwendigkeit des deutschen Rechtsstandes', 183.

acquisitions of the two previous circumstances in which Schmitt placed emphasis on juristic wisdom: *Statute and Judgment* (1912) and *On the Three Types of Juristic Thought* (1934). In 1912, reference was to the *esprit de corps* shared by the entire class of jurists and to the professional conscience, as it were, of the modern cultivated jurist or legal specialist. They were deemed to be fully conscious of how complex the legal order is as well as of the need to reinterpret it radically when it fails to keep pace with social change and the fundamental task of protecting the order as a whole. In 1934, however, with a radical twist, Schmitt spoke of a 'new concept of the jurist', called upon to rise above and overcome 'the earlier positivistic tearing apart of law and economy, law and society, law and politics'.[18] This is a brand-new figure, a faithful executor of the spirit of the people that could find in the Führer the sole and unquestionable interpreter. This latter type of jurist should make use of the various references to ordinary practice that are contained in the text of the norms as a judicial means to the end of subverting the existing legal order from within so as to adjust its socio-political orientation to the Nazi ideology – this explains the key role of the general clauses, as discussed in Chapter 5 of this book.

The figure of the jurist praised in Schmitt's post-war writing – in the text that he tellingly defined as his 'testament' – shows clear continuity with the jurist who carries out a 'normalising' activity in his prior writings. However, there are two notable differences that make it impossible to juxtapose *The Plight of European Jurisprudence* with the 1912 and 1934 texts (and even more so with the jurist in the brown shirt). First, jurists are no longer confined to the domestic sphere of state-based legal systems; for they now refer, by training and vocation, to a Continental tradition founded on their common belonging to a *depositum iuris* that exceeds national boundaries: 'The "reception of Roman law" is the great recurring event in the history of jurisprudence.'[19] Importantly, for the first time in Schmitt's overall output, jurisprudential activity is completely unfettered by the state legislative authority (and therefore, more or less directly, by the political decision-maker). Second, and this is a striking difference, the compositional activity of the jurists is taken to be the guarantor of the unity of a political space no longer confined within territorial borders. The territory is now a political space that overlaps perfectly, without any friction, with a porous and elastic legal context, exclusively bounded by jurisprudence. Schmitt's words are unambiguous: '*Jurisprudence is itself the true source of law.*'[20]

[18] Schmitt, *On the Three Types of Juristic Thought*, 97.
[19] Schmitt, *The Plight of European Jurisprudence*, 39.
[20] Ibid., 57.

In *The Plight of European Jurisprudence*, therefore, one can appreciate a landmark conclusion of the Schmittian reflection, one that is difficult to underestimate. Schmitt affirmed nothing less than the independence of jurisprudence from any external orderings and thereby postulated its self-sufficiency. Concretely, this comes under the guise of a relation of mutual belonging between legal science and the political community, which comes to encompass the whole of Europe and thus reduces the risk of conflict by virtue of a common political and institutional history. It also ensures a mediation between incompatible international practices so as to neutralise potentially destructive centrifugal forces and to preserve the unity of the system by minimising internal divisions. One's being alien to a tradition, therefore, is no longer a matter of one's identity vis-à-vis an original, monolithic community. Rather, alienness stems from the impossibility of translating juristic contextual practices into a shared communitarian language, since their inherent particularism precludes the pre-eminence of the common traditional matrix that holds together the remaining components of the community. If that is the case, it is evident that a decisionist interpretation of these jurist practices would be completely off-topic. For a decision should separate either something that is already and always separate or something that is composed of the same legal texture as the unity from which it is to be separated. In the former case it would be utterly useless, in the latter completely ineffective. It is the *suturing* activity of juristic knowledge that best fits this picture, in that it sutures international wounds that can still be healed by means of a shrewd and responsible mediation. If some of the components of the legal order resist any integration, they can then be cut out without compromising the rest of the tissues.

Such an activity of selection is exactly the kind of activity that a sovereign decision cannot carry out, and this makes decisionism completely unserviceable. In other words, within the same component refractory to the order (or rather: ordered in keeping with a different normative code), a sovereign decision would fail to discriminate that which can be rescued from that which cannot be reintegrated. Moreover, a sovereign decision cannot evaluate the actual possibility of permanence within the order of the component that is being cut out for it to be remodelled, at least in part, in the light of the needs and organisational characteristics of the refractory component. But it is obviously the more general approach to the problem of the legal order that needs to be reset here. Those who put things in order – that is, those who contribute to making a legal order an effective system for the governing of social interactions – ought in the first place to be able to conceive the parts that they affect as a fabric consisting of a multiplicity of threads. These are to be untangled and recombined, without giving in to the radicality of a final cut.

The flash of lightning of the sovereign decision is replaced by the fishing lamp of jurisprudence – that is, a penetrating, meticulous and inherently acephalous legal practice that buttresses the evolution of social practices. Jurisprudence gives them legal form according to a dual criterion: internal coherence and the sustainability of the institutional complex (a sustainability that now also applies, and this is a sheer novelty, to conflict-resolution procedures). While jurisprudence is thus held responsible for maintaining the order, this Herculean activity is entirely left down to the body of jurists. It is no coincidence that in the plot of *The Plight of European Jurisprudence* political decision-makers are reduced to background actors, who cannot be chosen 'according to our own tastes'[21] – added Schmitt, not without a hint of bitterness (possibly with hindsight), speaking on behalf of the whole body of jurists. Political decision-makers come and go, jurists are here to stay and to create something that will be there long after they will be gone; this is the reason why jurisprudence itself is a fine example of an institution (that is, a social enterprise that outlives its founders). It is the politicians, Schmitt seems to suggest, who should be chosen by the jurists, and not the other way round. Although we have already stressed it, it is worth repeating that the depersonalisation and the decentralisation of the order do not imply its depoliticisation. It is still a decision that settles jurisprudential controversies, as previously did social conflicts. And yet, the difference with the sovereign decision is striking in terms of procedures, modes of intervention and ordering criteria.

The Plight of European Jurisprudence represented a real turning point in Schmitt's output. Though it was exposed to a few fluctuations, these are mostly inessential, as we shall see. Indeed, it is in this essay that a theory of the order (or, if you wish, an orderly direction) is thoroughly outlined, with no reference whatsoever to the decision as the act of a political authority. In this novel view, legal science no longer depends on a political will that determines its structure and the modes of its existence. Rather, it takes upon itself the task of making decisions, while at the same time it limits the absoluteness and pervasiveness of these very decisions. These find its concrete implementation in the management of those conflicts that occur within the different social micro-contexts comprising the broader social realm. It is thus no coincidence that in the essay we are discussing the term 'decision' never occurs (except once, with the meaning of 'legal adjudication').

[21] Ibid., 66.

It goes without saying that decisions and politics do not disappear at all. However, they are explicitly taken away from the authority that holds the monopoly on force (whether this is the sovereign demiurge, an executive legitimated by plebiscite or a charismatic leader) and placed under the rubric of legal science. Decisions and politics are rethought according to an interpretative and operative code that is now entirely juristic. Basically, legal science is no longer called upon to co-operate with the political, whether consensually or not. Jurisprudence takes over politics and attends to the activity of selecting the international practices that translate and actualise the decision. If one now rereads the thundering conclusion of the first chapter of *Political Theology* ('authority proves that to produce law it need not be based on law'[22]), one can better appreciate the chasm between the decisionist perspective that it iconically denotes and Schmitt's juristic institutionalism. In 1950 he went so far as to task jurisprudence with no less than seeing to the destiny of the whole Europe, which at the time was engulfed with the debris of war.

In truly institutionalist fashion, *The Plight of European Jurisprudence* portrays law not so much as decision and norms, but first and foremost as a practice, as a process of mediation between regularity and regulation that includes and rearticulates both the decision and the norms. In this sense, it is very significant that Schmitt's jurisprudential plea in 1950 indirectly refers back to the methodological *ralliement* advanced in 1912 in *Statute and Judgment* – as if he were to draw a link with the theorisation that the decisionism of the early 1920s had briskly interrupted. Despite the differences that will be discussed below, the recognition of legal science as a source of law finds in *Statute and Judgment* a clear precedent in that it theorised the functional self-sufficiency and methodological autonomy of jurisprudence: 'Legal practice, in other words, justifies itself through itself.'[23] Yet, while in 1912 the legal practice is conceived as a dialogue among jurists, who ought to make their decisions mutually consistent with reference to what is considered as normal in their own domain, in the post-World War Two the chief jurisprudential task is to support and orient the social evolution of a community by countering the aimless and alienating forces of technique. To put it another way, in 1912 legal practice is the replication, in juristic terms, of a political unity already present, whereas in 1950 (and beyond) legal practice takes it upon itself to guard the political substance of a society that, enthralled by the song of technique, runs the serious risk of losing its own identity.

[22] Schmitt, *Political Theology*, 13.

[23] Schmitt, *Statute and Judgment*, 115.

The 1950 essay thus shares with *Statute and Judgment* the centrality of law-applying activities as they confer order, while order here is to be understood primarily as the stabilisation and widest possible inclusion of the various models of interaction present in a given context. As such, it is opposed to the political sphere as the holder of disruptive power and hence as a source of constant uncertainty. But the task – the vocation of the scholar, one might say – is much broader and much more delicate. It is no longer the merely judicial task of applying normative indications in a coherent and uniform way, one that could thus be assigned to the judges. Rather, it is the much more demanding task of translating into jurisprudential terms and legal forms the social practices that are widely adopted within the social realm and yet are ignored or deformed by statutory law as it is subservient to the imperatives of technology. Jurisprudential law should grant an organic structure to a form of life that is inscribed into unexpressed customs and that is threatened by the systemic logic of technocracy. The protagonists of such a juristic activity are no longer the judges alone (if only because the picture is broader and goes beyond their legal competence to include the *jus condendum*), but the jurists more generally. On this account, the jurist is anyone who contributes, with her professional as well as intellectual skills and expertise, to providing social reality with concrete, juristically supervised normative structure. Once institutionally organised, a community is perfectly equipped to settle its internal conflicts and contradictions and at the same time to preserve its cultural identity and political specificity. Sovereign deciders, in their different institutional forms, are consigned to the past once and for all.

THE LAST BATTLE: LAW IN CONTEXT VS BORDERLESS TECHNIQUE

One thing should be made explicit. No political philosopher's (let alone jurist's) theoretical productions and scholarly activities are more ambiguous, multiple, multifaceted, elusive, allusive, often contradictory, than Carl Schmitt's. Where disorder reigns, everything, or almost everything, can be said or done. Therefore, we certainly give up hope of an all-encompassing reconstruction that accounts for all Schmitt's writings and sayings – which he himself sometimes amended and even had to remind himself of, as happens in his diaries. When it comes to hermeneutical enterprises, one is allowed a great deal of interpretive freedom by which one favours some texts to the detriment of others, minimises some writings and emphasises others, establishes connections and parallels, as we did in this book. If one then establishes connections between works that are very different from each other (and are spread over a period of seventy years) with the various Schmitt self-interpretations, a hermeneutic that is more arbitrary than subjective becomes a serious threat – a threat that can never be fully neutralised. Based on what, then, can we vindicate the interpretative line that holds together Schmitt's initial writings, his concrete-order thinking and his later juristic institutionalism? Does this institutional interpretative key withstand scrutiny? Or is it as far-fetched as (we claimed) the exceptionalist reading? Finally, why should *The Plight of European Jurisprudence* be considered anything more than a jurist's plea – somehow out of time – to the body of jurists?

The grounds for all this, in short, are the following. As Schmitt obsessively reiterated in almost all his post-war writings, when the state-form proves more and more unable to create, stabilise and perpetuate social order, juristic institutionalism is all that is left for bringing order to this political scenario. Statehood is withering away, and along with it the shaping force of sovereign decision-making. In the face of it, it is necessary to 'promote' the entire class of jurists. It is therefore a context-specific need, a necessary and almost desperate step, yet the only step that is available to Schmitt, if one thinks of his scepticism in *The 'Nomos' of the Earth* as to the possibility of a new concrete order – an order that in various subsequent writings, and right from the title, he announced, prefigured, invoked, went so far as to divine and yet never managed to delineate or determine. As we mentioned, this is a daunting challenge. Indeed, for Schmitt the end of statehood coincides with the triumph of technology, and technology imposes itself first and foremost as a highly effective regulatory system for governing social flows and exchanges by relying on a self-correcting system of automatisms. The clash that looms large is between the technology of law and the law of technology, between a legal science that knows how to assert its special character (and based on it, the political nature of individual contexts) and a technology that parasitically appropriates the mediatory function of the law. It is worth delving deeper into this issue.

The peculiar nature of technology and its relevance for the political are originally debated by Schmitt in the essay *The Age of Neutralizations and Depoliticizations* (1963), later published as an appendix to *The Concept of the Political.* In the pursuit of a neutral sphere that suddenly disappears, technique marks a point of no return (and of no continuation) in that it appears at first sight as totally neutral, for it is used and shared by everybody in the same way and for the same instrumental reasons. It therefore paves the way for an epochal (and for Schmitt always distrustful) general consensus. Nonetheless, Schmitt warned, such a neutrality is but apparent. Technology is by nature a means that can be instrumental in any end, and for this reason it is neither interested in, nor capable of, setting goals. Therefore, technology is unable to determine an effective convergence of the goals and beliefs of those who make use of it. On the other hand, the ends that technical means make possible, without being able to determine or influence, are divergent. Schmitt commented: 'So far the hope that a politically dominant elite would develop out of the community of technical inventors has not been fulfilled. ... Neither a political question nor a political answer can be derived from purely technical principles and perspectives.'[24]

However, while technology cannot by nature perform the primarily political task of setting goals, the problem is that it can compromise their concrete implementation of them.[25] This is what Schmitt pointed out, originally in *The Guardian of the Constitution* and then again in the second edition of *The Concept of the Political*, while considering a particular meaning of the notion of political neutrality, according to which the state is in fact reduced to 'a technical means, which must function in a concretely predictable way and must offer everyone the same possibilities of use'.[26] The state (here a figure of political unity in general) thus becomes a simple administrative apparatus, whose purpose is to provide certain services to anyone who complies with the procedures that regulate their provision. Within the scope of this functionalism, the only remaining difference between one state and another is the number, the quality and the efficiency of the services they provide. This does away with the need for a territorial partition of spaces, which come to be considered as mere logistical extensions. It is from this perspective that in 1950 Schmitt conjured the spirit of Donoso Cortés, the first prophet of technical misfortune and its tragic irresistibility (and the fact that the situation was very serious is confirmed by the fact that Schmitt went so far as to say that even anarchy is preferable to the nihilism of a centralised order: it may sound as a paradox, but it is an unprecedented one in Schmitt's writings[27]).

It is finally the last text of the quadrilogy, *Ex Captivitate Salus*, that marked Schmitt's return to the public scene and completed the portrayal of the challenge that jurists must confront. At the heart of this very special booklet – generally neglected by critics and merely regarded as a resentful memoir, despite its theoretical relevance – Schmitt traced a sort of genealogy of jurisprudence.[28] It was a vehicle for the political and institutional history of modern Europe, which also replaced politics at some crucial junctures –

[24] Schmitt, *The Concept of the Political*, 92.

[25] On the connection between technology and liberalism, both understood by Schmitt as anti-political forces, see McCormick, *Carl Schmitt's Critique of Liberalism*.

[26] Schmitt, *Der Hüter der Verfassung*, 112.

[27] Schmitt, *Donoso Cortés*, 9–10. Also significant is the explicit disavowal, on the same pages, of the essay 'The Philosophy of the State of the Counterrevolution: De Maistre, Bonald, Donoso Cortés', originally added, as the last chapter, to *Political Theology*.

[28] Schmitt, *Ex Captivitate Salus*, Ch. 5

especially during the transition from the universalism of the Church's spiritual power to the particularism of the state system. The ubiquity of technology, Schmitt argued, confronted jurists with a radical alternative: irrelevance vs subjugation to the 'new objectivity of pure technicity'.[29] Together with statehood, it is the function itself of jurisprudence that risks disappearing even more disgracefully than the state. For while the latter collapses because of internal erosion, jurists will be remembered for the shadow cast on them by their unforgivable betrayal. They have been reduced to silence – '*Silete jurisconsulti!*'[30] – by the impersonal but unequivocal command of technology. Yet, they can always disobey, Schmitt seems to imply – though he never did so when it was his turn.

What counts here is not the chance of success, which Schmitt already considered slim, but the fact that the residual hopes of victory are now definitively placed in the hands of the jurists – and certainly not in the hands of any political entity or authority, although Schmitt never tired of evoking it in spite of his increasing scepticism. It is a confrontation between the *longue durée* of the law, which only the jurists can turn into an enclosed and bounded totality, and the serial, almost mechanised production of executive measures; between the permeation of an order that grows with the organism it nurtures and the homogenising infiltration of regulatory automatisms. The efficiency of this latter form of mechanical law ensures a more and more fluid network of exchanges and connections and thus requires a growing indistinction between territories and contexts (along with the unfulfillable promise of a conflict-free society). There is no decision here that can carry out the ordering task. Rather, Schmitt's plea is for the institutional nature of the order against automatisms of technique, the new and more algid Leviathan. Technique, Schmitt claimed, ensured with greater efficiency and less waste of resources the same ordering functions that once it was up to jurisprudence to provide. In the new scenario, the jurists themselves end up acting, even unconsciously,[31] as technicians of the law – that is, as mere advisers who offer legally executable solutions for the functional needs of the technical apparatus. The jurists, on their part, can neither check the system nor assess the risks it entails. And what role could Schmitt play in his post-World War Two writings, and particularly

[29] Ibid., 60.

[30] Ibid.

[31] It is with brisk tones that Schmitt refers to the fact that, '[w]ithout being aware of it, toward the end of the 19th century European international law had lost the consciousness of the spatial structure of its former order. Instead, it had adopted an increasingly more superficial notion of a universalizing process that it naively saw as a victory of European international law. It mistook the removal of Europe from the center of the earth in international law for Europe's rise to the center' (Schmitt, *The 'Nomos' of the Earth*, 233).

from the mid-1950s on, other than that of a jurist who struggled hard to awake his colleagues from a deep sleep, while jurisprudence – he thought – proved unable to understand the present?

The risk of jurisprudence falling short of its vocation goes hand in hand with the risk of the disappearance of that 'pluralism of spiritual life'[32] that Schmitt considered as the political precondition for every meaningful existence.[33] On this account, legal science is first and foremost called upon to become aware of itself precisely as legal *science* – that is, as a repository of the knowledge that is necessary to furnish the legal order with a coherent set of norms which characterise a specific historical-cultural context ('historical-spiritual', Schmitt would have said) against any attempt to reduce law to the machinic functioning of unrelated regulatory segments. In conclusion, with the political enemy gradually turning into the chameleonic figure of an other-than-self devoid of radically oppositional substance, in his late works Schmitt went to great lengths to remind jurists, who were facing the radical challenge posed by technique, of the solemn and decisive responsibility to which they are called by the entire community they belong to and that was at risk. It is a responsibility that is at once a vocation and a duty – that of ensuring an exact correspondence between, and an intimate connection with, the regulatory needs of a given legal order and the distinctive traits, in terms of political identity and personal self-recognition, of the community life that it is meant to govern, strengthen and perpetuate.

32 Schmitt, *The Concept of the Political*, 95.

33 For the relevance of this assumption for the whole of Schmitt's thinking, see Marder, *Groundless Existence*.

Conclusion

Demythologising Carl Schmitt

During his long and controversial life as a man and as a scholar, Schmitt presented himself in very different guises and with varying degrees of credibility. This attitude goes far beyond his countless, protean self-portraits (sometimes detailed, other times just sketched, and yet always revealing) which he created, mostly for self-serving reasons, throughout an existence and a career that were all but smooth – including those that were meant to debunk rather fanciful interpretations. On several occasions Schmitt engaged steadily in sustained confrontations with a number of authors, more often than not to the point of identifying himself with, and even of wearing the mask of, the counterpart. This is the case with at least six figures, each one being halfway between an *alter ego* and a *Doppelgänger*: three political philosophers, two fictional characters and a jurist. In order of historical appearance (real or fictional): Epimetheus (in the Christian version), Niccolò Machiavelli, Thomas Hobbes, Juan Donoso Cortés, Friedrich Carl von Savigny and Benito Cereno. Still, sooner or later, everyone loses their magic, and Schmitt was no exception. This is why in his last long interview – he had just turned 95 and his health was failing – Schmitt took all his masks off and proudly claimed: 'I feel one hundred percent a jurist and nothing else. And I do not want to be anything else. I am a jurist and I remain a jurist and I die as a jurist . . . .'[1] This is his last will as well as his last self-interpretation.

It is our claim that it is also the most consistent and convincing one. To live up to Schmitt's legacy, scholars have offered no fewer portraits of an author who has been confusingly interpreted (more than once with his complicity) as a historian, a theologian, a philosopher, a political scientist (if not also a politician *tout court*, flirting with various shades of authoritarian regimes)

[1] Schmitt, 'Un giurista davanti a se stesso', 34.

and even a prophet, but seldom as a jurist (and only a jurist) – although he insisted many a time, and over many years, with particular emphasis that he was nothing other than a legal scholar. Based on what we have argued in this book, we genuinely believe that this statement should not only be re-evaluated, but even considered as the key to reading and understanding his entire work. However unexpected, disorienting and occasional his oscillations and changes of mind may be, these should not be only interpreted in purely legal terms. More radically, they should be observed from an entirely juristic standpoint for readers to be able to decipher them properly. By 'legal terms' and 'juristic standpoint' we refer to an institution-centred perspective meant to draw attention away from all Schmitt's references to numinous events, theological figures and tortuous etymologies – which we think are far from essential – and focus on how and why Schmitt's institutional conception proves more effective when it comes to his genuine obsession: the stability of the order.

On more than one occasion, scholars have looked overconfident, and to a large extent have been, about the wisdom of some of Schmitt's best-known and allegedly illuminating insights. One need only think of the demiurgic act that creates social order out of nothingness, the trans-historical and all-embracing basic definition of the political, the imaginative diagnosis of the end of the state history (and eventually of Western civilisation as such), the ultimate battle between opposite (and quite changing) forces in an ever-forthcoming conflict, with a present trapped in the tension between a past that does not pass and a prophesised (usually threatening) future that never materialises. Enchanted or repelled by the siren song of mythological creatures – exceptions more lasting than the rules they break, institutional settings described as about to collapse for decades if not centuries, crises almost coeval to the orders that have fallen into crisis – a significant number of interpretations, some critical some eulogistic, lose sight of the operational relevance of the Schmittian approach to law and politics. This could explain why, following distinct but converging paths, scholars generally demand too much and too little of Schmitt's theorising. Too much because his exceptionalist decisionism placed too much emphasis on extraordinary circumstances, to the extent that the theory of a near-permanent state of exception is claimed to be able, somewhat mysteriously, to generate normality. Too little because, owing to the self-evident weakness of exceptionalism as both a (faux) political theory and methodological framework, comparatively little attention has been paid to other insights, perhaps less inspiring but certainly far more inspired.

Once Schmitt is demythologised and considered from a 'purely' legal standpoint, his theory turns out to be first and foremost an attempt to uncover the grammar of social order with a view to providing practical solutions to preserve or restore it. In this light, normality – which should be conceived descriptively as the normal functioning of a self-reproducing order – comes to be more important than any exceptional case and ontologically prior to it. By isolating the socially relevant, fundamental elements of an interactional context (elements that are considered to be essentially juristic in the institutional perspective we are discussing), Schmitt's major concern was to explain how an order emerges, how it can be maintained and how it should be preserved. Beyond (or rather beneath) Schmitt as a reluctant or willing prophet, there exists another Schmitt – namely, the legal scientist who collects the raw material from the juristic field and disassembles it in order to offer an explanatory account of social order. Schmitt's intentions regarding a given social order and his partisan and active participation in defending or debunking a certain state of affairs are far less relevant than Schmitt's radical deconstruction of social order – a deconstruction that is to be conceived in a literal sense. This includes all the exegetic interpretations of his works meant to demonstrate that in this or that work he is conspiring against this or that political regime.

By concentrating on the operational and legal relevance of Schmitt's insights (that is, on the different institutional solutions he proposed from a juristic standpoint in order to establish and strengthen an up-and-running legal order), we have tended to centre our analysis on certain texts at the expense of others, which perhaps are the most debated in the literature. We have emphasised the specifically jurisprudential concerns that lie at the heart of *Political Theology*, against those readings that conceive of it as part of Schmitt's larger theological, metaphysical or political project. At the same time, we have relocated attention to his early works, those that made him earn an enduring reputation as a prominent jurist well before the publication of *Dictatorship* and *Political Theology*. Along with *The Value of the State and the Significance of the Individual* (which we culpably did not consider enough in the present work), Schmitt's approach during the 1910s, we claimed, was incompatible with his exceptionalist decisionism of the 1920s – though, as we insisted, it does not graph onto his later institutionalism in any easy manner.

For the same reasons, moving on to the other extreme of Schmitt's output, we have stressed the cogency and the salience of his late works as a refined development of his concrete-order thinking. Well beyond *The 'Nomos' of the Earth*, several largely neglected works – above all *The Plight of European Jurisprudence*, but the analysis needs to be extended to other previous and coeval texts – are worth musing on. While these texts are valuable on their own, they also played a crucial role in the transition from the institutional decisionism of the 1930s to the juristic institutionalism of the following forty years. This transition, which looks to us more as an evolution than a turn, is also to be interpreted as an attempt to switch from a 'two-dimensional' to a 'three-dimensional' (hence more realistic) approach to the legal foundation of social order. In this latter context, the exception ceases once and for all to be more interesting than the norm, whereas its key role comes to be replaced by the political potential of a normality that in its turn is always in need of stability. If one broadens one's perspective and shifts one's gaze to both ends of Schmitt's production (that is, before 1922 and after 1950), the received view can be compellingly challenged and, in a way, reversed. Schmitt's exceptionalist decisionism of the early 1920s, and not the institutional approach of the early 1930s, is a phase transition which is replete with red herrings and dead ends. Schmitt then tried to evolve towards a more concrete and workable theory of social order and espoused an institutional view that he never abandoned until the end of his literary career.

Doubtless, one should not look at it to gain inspiration for the construction of a fair and pluralistic society, as one will find the opposite – that is, a despicable, misleading conception of pluralism as the arch-enemy of political stability. However, one will certainly find instructive musings on how the law contributes to a politics of normality that inheres in the law's intrinsic task of providing stability. Unfortunately, Schmitt did not take full stock of the claim of one of his inspirers, Santi Romano, as the latter downplayed the conservative nature of law. 'Like all buildings', Romano observed, the law 'has foundations, walls, roofs that ensure its stability, and in a way close it off. But it has doors, windows, pipes, fans that keep it open to the external world.'[2] The legal order cannot be subservient to a sheer politics of normality lest it dry out and grind to a halt. The idea of law being an institution was meant to reflect the fact that it is 'an entity which, although it remains identical to itself, as long as it is alive all its elements get continually renewed whether abruptly or gradually'.[3] All in all, Schmitt espoused institutionalism half-heartedly, as he seized on the idea of stability and jettisoned the correlated idea of constant renewal. And yet, we claim, his half of legal institutionalism still has to teach an important lesson – one that we cannot but extrapolate from Schmitt's framework as a warning to those who fail to see how the law, even within liberal states, inevitably includes someone to the detriment of someone else.

[2] Romano, *Frammenti di un dizionario giuridico*, 86.
[3] Ibid., 86.

References

Adair-Toteff, Christopher, *Carl Schmitt on Law and Liberalism* (Cham: Palgrave Macmillan, 2020).

Agamben, Giorgio, *State of Exception* (University of Chicago Press, 2005).

Alonso, Christophe, Duranthon, Arnaud, and Schmitz, Julia (eds.), *La Pensée du doyen Maurice Hauriou à l'épreuve du temps: quel(s) héritage(s)?* (Aix-en-Provence: Presses Universitaires d'Aix-Marseille, 2015).

Arato, Andrew, 'Multi-track Constitutionalism beyond Carl Schmitt', 18 *Constellations* 324–51 (2011).

Arvidsson, Matilda, Brännström, Leila, and Minkkinen, Panu (eds.), *The Contemporary Relevance of Carl Schmitt: Law, Politics, Theology* (Abingdon: Routledge, 2017).

Balakrishnan, Gopal, *The Enemy: An Intellectual Portrait of Carl Schmitt* (London: Verso, 2000).

Barnes, Barry, 'Social Life as Bootstrapped Induction', 17 *Sociology* 524–45 (1983).

Bates, David, 'Political Theology and the Nazi State: Carl Schmitt's Concept of the Institution', 3 *Modern Intellectual History* 415–42 (2006).

Baume, Sandrine, 'On Political Theology: A Controversy between Hans Kelsen and Carl Schmitt', 35 *History of European Ideas* 369–81 (2009).

Bellamy, Richard, and Baehr, Peter, 'Carl Schmitt and the Contradictions of Liberal Democracy', 23 *European Journal of Political Research* 163–85 (1993).

Bendersky, Joseph W., *Carl Schmitt: Theorist for the Reich* (Princeton University Press, 1983).

Berge, Lukas van den, 'Law, King of All: Schmitt, Agamben, Pindar', 12 *Law and Humanities* 198–222 (2019).

Berthold, Lutz, *Carl Schmitt und der Staatsnotstandsplan am Ende der Weimarer Republik* (Berlin: Duncker & Humblot, 1999).

Blanquer, Jean-Michel, and Milet, Marc, *L'Invention de l'état. Léon Duguit, Maurice Hauriou et la naissance du droit public moderne* (Paris: Odile Jacob, 2015).

Blasius, Dirk, *Carl Schmitt. Preußischer Staatsrat in Hitlers Reich* (Göttingen: Vandenhoeck & Ruprecht, 2001).

Bloor, David, *Wittgenstein, Rules and Institutions* (London: Routledge, 1997).

Böckenförde, Ernst-Wolfgang, 'The Concept of the Political: A Key to Understanding Carl Schmitt's Constitutional Theory', 10 *Canadian Journal of Law & Jurisprudence* 5–19 (1997).

Bogdandy, Armin von, 'Die heutige Lage der europäischen Rechtswissenschaft im Spiegel von Schmitts Schrift. Grundfragen in einer irreführenden, aber erkenntnisträchtigen Perspektive', *Jahrbuch des Öffentlichen Rechts der Gegenwart* 409–38 (2020).

Brännström, Leila, 'Carl Schmitt's Definition of Sovereignty as Authorized Leadership', in Matilda Arvidsson, Leila Brännström and Panu Minkkinen (eds.), *The Contemporary Relevance of Carl Schmitt*, 19–33 (Abingdon: Routledge, 2017).

Broderick, Albert (ed.), *The French Institutionalists: Maurice Hauriou, Georges Renard, Joseph T. Delos* (Cambridge, MA: Harvard University Press, 1970).

Calabrese, Alessio, 'Colpa e decisione negli scritti giuspenalistici di Carl Schmitt (1910–1912)', 7 *Logos* 45–64 (2012).

Carrino, Agostino, 'Carl Schmitt and European Juridical Science', in Chantal Mouffe (ed.), *The Challenge of Carl Schmitt* 180–94 (London: Verso, 1999).

Cercel, Cosmin Sebastian, 'Exploring Carl Schmitt: Space, Power and the Law in Contemporary Debates', 3 *Romanian Journal of Constitutional Law* 117–35 (2012).

Chandler, David, 'The Revival of Carl Schmitt in International Relations: The Last Refuge of Critical Theorists?' 37 *Millennium: Journal of International Studies* 27–48 (2008).

Chignola, Sandro, *Diritto vivente. Ravaisson, Tarde, Hauriou* (Macerata: Quodlibet, 2020).

Colliot-Thélène, Catherine (1999), 'Carl Schmitt versus Max Weber: Juridical Rationality and Economic Rationality', in Chantal Mouffe (ed.), *The Challenge of Carl Schmitt*, 138–54 (London: Verso, 1999).

Colombo, Alessandro, 'The "Realist Institutionalism" of Carl Schmitt', in Louiza Odysseos and Fabio Petito (eds.), *The International Political Thought of Carl Schmitt: Terror, Liberal War and the Crisis of Global Order* 21–35 (New York: Routledge, 2007).

Colón-Ríos, Joel, *Constituent Power and the Law* (Oxford University Press, 2020).

Corduwener, Pepijn, 'Gerhard Leibholz, Costantino Mortati and the Ideological Roots of Postwar Party Democracy in Germany and Italy', 26 *Journal of Political Ideologies* 101–19 (2020).

Cotterrell, Roger, 'Still Afraid of Legal Pluralism? Encountering Santi Romano', 45 *Law & Social Inquiry* 539–58 (2020).

Croce, Mariano, 'Governing Through Normality: Law and the Force of Sameness', 28 *International Journal of Politics, Culture, and Society* 303–23 (2015).

'Afterword: The Juristic Point of View: An Interpretive Account of The Legal Order', in Santi Romano, *The Legal Order* 111–28 (Abingdon: Routledge, 2017).

'What Matter(s)?', in Marco Goldoni and Michael A. Wilkinson (eds.), *The Cambridge Handbook on the Material Constitution* (Cambridge University Press, forthcoming).

Croce, Mariano, and Goldoni, Marco, *The Legacy of Pluralism: The Continental Jurisprudence of Santi Romano, Carl Schmitt, and Costantino Mortati* (Stanford University Press, 2020).

Croce, Mariano, and Salvatore, Andrea, *The Legal Theory of Carl Schmitt* (Abingdon: Routledge, 2013).

'After Exception: Carl Schmitt's Legal Institutionalism and the Repudiation of Exceptionalism', 29 *Ratio Juris* 410–26 (2016).

'Normality as Social Semantics. Schmitt, Bourdieu and the Politics of the Normal', 20 *European Journal of Social Theory* 275–91 (2016).

'Little Room for Exceptions: On Misunderstanding Carl Schmitt', 47 *History of European Ideas* 1169–83 (2021).

Cumin, David, *Carl Schmitt. Biographie politique et intellectuelle* (Paris: Cerf, 2005).

Dahlheimer, Manfred, *Carl Schmitt und der deutsche Katholizismus, 1888–1936* (Paderborn: Schöningh, 1998).

Dean, Mitchell, 'A Political Mythology of World Order: Carl Schmitt's *Nomos*', 23 *Theory, Culture & Society* 1–22 (2006).

della Cananea, Giacinto, 'Mortati and The Science of Public Law: A Comment on La Torre', in Christian Joerges and Navraj Singh Ghaleigh (eds.), *Darker Legacies of Law in Europe: The Shadow of National Socialism and Fascism over Europe and Its Legal Traditions*, 321–35 (Oxford and Portland: Hart Publishing, 2003).

de Wilde, Marc, 'The State of Emergency in the Weimar Republic Legal Disputes over Article 48 of the Weimar Constitution', 78 *Tijdschrift voor Rechtsgeschiedenis/Revue d'Histoire du Droit/The Legal History Review* 135–58 (2010).

'The Dark Side of Institutionalism: Carl Schmitt Reading Santi Romano', 11 *Ethics & Global Politics* 12–24 (2018).

Diamanteis, Marinos and Schütz, Anton, 'Political Theology beyond Schmitt', in Marinos Diamanteis and Anton Schütz (eds.), *Political Theology: Demystifying the Universal* 78–114 (Edinburgh University Press, 2017).

Di Marco, Giuseppe Antonio, 'A proposito del saggio di Carl Schmitt *Die Lage der europäischen Rechtswissenschaft (1943–1944)*', 6 *Diritto e cultura* 41–70 (1996).

Duarte d'Almeida, *Luís, Gardner, John, and Green, Leslie, Kelsen Revisited: New Essays on the Pure Theory of Law* (Oxford: Hart Publishing, 2013).

Dyzenhaus, David, *Legality and Legitimacy: Carl Schmitt, Hans Kelsen and Hermann Heller in Weimar* (Oxford University Press, 1997).

The Constitution of Law: Legality in a Time of Emergency (Cambridge University Press, 2006).

'Kelsen, Heller and Schmitt: Paradigms of Sovereignty Thought', 16 *Theoretical Inquiries in Law* 337–66 (2015).

Eisenberg, Avigail, 'Pluralism and Method at the Turn of the Century', in Marc Bevir (ed.), *Modern Pluralism: Anglo-American Debates since 1880*, 60–80 (Cambridge University Press, 2012).

Elden, Stuart, 'Reading Schmitt Geopolitically: *Nomos*, Territory and *Großraum*', 161 *Radical Philosophy* 18–26 (2010).

Fatovic, Clement, *Outside the Law: Emergency and Executive Power* (Baltimore, MD: John Hopkins University Press, 2009).

Fioravanti, Maurizio, 'Kelsen, Schmitt e la tradizione giuridica dell'Ottocento', in Gustavo Gozzi and Pierangelo Schiera (eds.), *Crisi istituzionale e teoria dello Stato in Germania dopo la Prima guerra mondiale*, 51–104 (Bologna: il Mulino, 1987).

Fontanelli, Filippo, 'Santi Romano and *L'ordinamento giuridico*: The Relevance of a Forgotten Masterpiece for Contemporary International, Transnational and Global Legal Relations', 2 *Transnational Legal Theory* 67–117 (2011).

'Review of Santi Romano, *The Legal Order*', 31 *European Journal of International Law* 1537–44 (2021).

Galli, Carlo, 'Carl Schmitt's Antiliberalism: Its Theoretical and Historical Sources and Its Philosophical and Political Meaning', 21 *Cardozo Law Review* 1597–617 (2000).

Genealogia della politica: Carl Schmitt e la crisi del pensiero politico moderno, 2nd ed. (Bologna: il Mulino, 2010).

'La gloria e i nemici della Chiesa cattolica', in Carl Schmitt, *Cattolicesimo romano e forma politica*, 83–96 (Bologna: il Mulino, 2010).

Garofalo, Luigi, 'Carl Schmitt e la *Wissenschaft des römischen Rechts*. Saggio su un cantore della scienza giuridica europea', 11 *Anuario da Facultade de Dereito da Universidade da Coruña* 299–323 (2007).

Gibbs, Nathan, 'Modern Constitutional Legitimacy and Political Theology: Schmitt, Peterson and Blumenberg', 30 *Law and Critique* 67–89 (2019).

Goldoni, Marco, and Wilkinson, Michael A., 'The Material Constitution', 81 *Modern Law Review* 569–97 (2018).

Gray, Christopher Berry, *The Methodology of Maurice Hauriou: Legal, Sociological, Philosophical* (Amsterdam and New York: Rodopi, 2019).

Gross, Oren, 'The Normless and Exceptionless Exception: Carl Schmitt's Theory of Emergency Powers and the Norm–Exception Dichotomy', 21 *Cardozo Law Review* 1825–68 (2000).

Guastini, Riccardo, 'Kelsen on Validity (Once More)', 29 *Ratio Juris* 402–9 (2016).

Hampsher-Monk, Iain, and Zimmerman, Keith, 'Liberal Constitutionalism and Schmitt's Critique', 28 *History of Political Thought* 678–95 (2007).

Hell, Julia, '*Katechon*: Carl Schmitt's Imperial Theology and the Ruins of the Future', 84 *Germanic Review* 283–326 (2009).

Heller, Hermann, 'Bemerkungen zur Staats- und rechtstheoretischen Problematik der Gegenwart', 55 *Archiv des öffentlichen Rechts* 321–54 (1929).

'Political Democracy and Social Homogeneity', in Arthur J. Jacobson and Bernhard Schlink (eds.), *Weimar: A Jurisprudence of Crisis*, 256–65 (Berkeley: University of California Press, 2000).

Herrero, Montserrat, *The Political Discourse of Carl Schmitt: A Mystic of Order* (Lanham, MD: Rowman & Littlefield).

Hoelzl, Michael, 'Ethics of Decisionism: Carl Schmitt's Theological Blind Spot', 20 *Journal for Cultural Research* 235–46 (2016).

Holmes, Stephen, *The Anatomy of Antiliberalism* (Cambridge, MA: Harvard University Press, 1996).

Honig, Bonnie, *Emergency Politics: Paradox, Law, Democracy* (Princeton University Press, 2009).

Hooker, William, *Carl Schmitt's International Thought: Order and Orientation* (Cambridge University Press, 2009).

Jacques, Johanna, 'From *Nomos* to *Hegung*: Sovereignty and the Laws of War in Schmitt's International Order', 78 *The Modern Law Review* 411–30 (2015).

Kahn, Paul W., *Political Theology. Four New Chapters on the Concept of Sovereignty* (New York: Columbia University Press, 2011).

Kelsen, Hans, *Über Grenzen zwischen juristischer und soziologischer Methode* (Tübingen: Mohr, 1911).

Introduction to the Problems of Legal Theory: A Translation of the First Edition of the Reine Rechtslehre or Pure Theory of Law (Oxford University Press, 1997).

Kennedy, Ellen, '*Hostis* not *Inimicus*: Toward a Theory of the Public in the Work of Carl Schmitt', 10 *Canadian Journal of Law & Jurisprudence* 35–47 (1997).
Constitutional Failure: Carl Schmitt in Weimar (Durham, NC: Duke University Press, 2004).
'Emergency and Exception', 39 *Political Theory* 535–50 (2011).
Koenen, Andreas, *Der Fall Carl Schmitt. Sein Aufstieg zum 'Kronjuristen des Dritten Reiches'* (Darmstadt: Wissenschaftliche Buchgesellschaft, 1995).
Koskenniemi, Martti, 'International Law as Political Theology: How to Read *Nomos der Erde?*' 11 *Constellations* 492–511 (2004).
Kraft-Fuchs, Margaret, 'Prinzipielle Bemerkungen zu Carl Schmitts Verfassungslehre', 9 *Zeitschrift für öffentliches Recht* 511–41 (1930).
Krebs, Thomas, *Restitution at the Crossroads: A Comparative Study* (London: Cavendish Publishing, 2001).
Kuhn, Helmut, 'Carl Schmitt, *Der Begriff des Politischen*', 38 *Kant-Studien* 190–6 (1933).
Laborde, Cecile, *Pluralist Thought and the State in Britain and France, 1900–25* (Houndmills, UK: Palgrave Macmillan, 2000).
Langford, Peter, and Bryan, Ian, 'Hans Kelsen's Concept of Normative Imputation', 26 *Ratio Juris* 85–110 (2013).
La Torre, Massimo, 'The German Impact on Fascist Public Law Doctrine – Costantino Mortati's Material Constitution', in Christian Joerges and Navraj Singh Ghaleigh (eds.), *Darker Legacies of Law in Europe: The Shadow of National Socialism and Fascism over Europe and Its Legal Traditions*, 305–20 (Oxford and Portland: Hart Publishing, 2003).
Lazar, Nomi Claire, *States of Emergency in Liberal Democracies* (Cambridge University Press, 2009).
Lievens, Matthias, 'Theology without God: Carl Schmitt's Profane Concept of the Political', 72 *Bijdragen. International Journal for Philosophy and Theology* 408–31 (2011).
Loughlin, Martin, 'The Concept of Constituent Power', 13 *European Journal of Political Theory* 218–37 (2014).
'Nomos', in David Dyzenhaus and Thomas Poole (eds.), *Law, Liberty and State: Oakeshott, Hayek and Schmitt on the Rule of Law*, 69–95 (Cambridge University Press, 2015).
'*Politonomy*', in Jens Meierhenrich and Oliver Simons (eds.), *The Oxford Handbook of Carl Schmitt*, 570–91 (New York: Oxford University Press, 2016).
'Droit politique', 17 *Jus Politicum* 295–335 (2017).
Political Jurisprudence (Oxford University Press, 2017).
Löwith, Karl, 'The Occasional Decisionism of Carl Schmitt', in Karl Löwith, *Martin Heidegger and European Nihilism*, 137–69 (New York: Columbia University Press, 1995).
McCormick, John P., 'Political Theory and Political Theology: The Second Wave of Carl Schmitt in English', 26 *Political Theory* 830–54 (1998).
Carl Schmitt's Critique of Liberalism (Cambridge University Press, 2009).
'From Roman Catholicism to Mechanized Oppression: On Political-Theological Disjunctures in Schmitt's Weimar Thought', 13 *Critical Review of International Social and Political Philosophy* 391–8 (2010).

'Teaching in Vain: Thomas Hobbes, Carl Schmitt, and the Theory of the Sovereign State', in Jens Meierhenrich and Oliver Simons (eds.), *The Oxford Handbook of Carl Schmitt*, 269–90 (New York: Oxford University Press, 2016).

Marck, Siegfried, '"Existenzphilosophische" und idealistische Grundlegung der Politik', 9 *Die Gesellschaft* 441–50 (1932).

Marder, Michael, *Groundless Existence: The Political Ontology of Carl Schmitt* (New York: Continuum, 2010).

Marty, Gabriel, and Brimo, Albert (eds.), *La Pensée du doyen Maurice Hauriou et son influence* (Paris: A. Pédone, 1969).

Maus, Ingeborg, 'The 1933 "Break" in Carl Schmitt's Theory', 10 *Canadian Journal of Law and Jurisprudence* 125–40 (1997).

Mehring, Reinhard, *Carl Schmitt: A Biography* (Cambridge: Polity Press, 2014).

'Carl Schmitts Schrift *Die Lage der europäischen Rechtswissenschaft*', 77 *Zeitschrift für ausländisches öffentliches Recht und Völkerrecht* 853–75 (2017).

Meier, Heinrich, *Carl Schmitt and Leo Strauss: The Hidden Dialogue* (University of Chicago Press, 1995).

The Lesson of Carl Schmitt: Four Chapters on the Distinction between Political Theology and Political Philosophy, expanded edition (University of Chicago Press, 2011).

Meierhenrich, Jens, 'Fearing the Disorder of Things', in Jens Meierhenrich and Oliver Simons (eds.), *The Oxford Handbook of Carl Schmitt*, 171–216 (New York: Oxford University Press, 2016).

Meierhenrich, Jens, and Simons, Oliver (eds.), *The Oxford Handbook of Carl Schmitt* (New York: Oxford University Press, 2016).

Meyer, Robert, Schetter, Conrad, and Prinz, Janosch, 'Spatial Contestation? The Theological Foundations of Carl Schmitt's Spatial Thought', 43 *Geoforum* 687–96 (2012).

Millard, Éric, 'Hauriou et la théorie de l'institution', 30–1 *Droit et Société* 381–412 (1995).

Minca, Claudio and Rowan, Rory, 'The Question of Space in Carl Schmitt', 39 *Progress in Human Geography* 268–89 (2015).

Minca, Claudio, and Rowan, Rory, *On Schmitt and Space* (Abingdon: Routledge, 2016).

Mortati, Costantino, 'Brevi note sul rapporto fra costituzione e politica nel pensiero di Carl Schmitt', in *La teoria del potere costituente*, 131–52 (Macerata: Quodlibet, 2020).

Motschenbacher, Alfons, *Katechon oder Großinquisitor? Eine Studie zu Inhalt und Struktur der Politischen Theologie Carl Schmitts* (Marburg: Tectum, 2000).

Müller, Jan, 'Carl Schmitt's Method: Between Ideology, Demonology and Myth', 4 *Journal of Political Ideologies* 61–85 (1999).

Neocleous, Mark, 'Friend or Enemy? Reading Schmitt Politically', 79 *Radical Philosophy* 13–23 (1996).

Nicholls, David, *The Pluralist State: The Political Ideas of J. N. Figgis and His Contemporaries* (London: Macmillan, 1975).

Nicoletti, Michele, *Trascendenza e potere. La teologia politica di Carl Schmitt* (Brescia: Morcelliana, 1990).

Nino, Carlos Santiago, 'Some Confusions around Kelsen's Concept of Validity', 64 *ARSP: Archiv für Rechts- und Sozialphilosophie / Archives for Philosophy of Law and Social Philosophy* 357–77 (1978).

Ohana, David, 'Carl Schmitt's Legal Fascism, Politics, Religion & Ideology', 20 *Politics, Religion & Ideology* 273–300 (2019).

Ojakangas, Mika, *Philosophy of Concrete Life: Carl Schmitt and the Political Thought of Late Modernity* (Jyväskylä: Minerva, 2006).

Palaver, Wolfgang, 'Carl Schmitt on *Nomos* and Space', 106 *Telos* 105–27 (1996).

Paulson, Stanley L., 'Hans Kelsen and Carl Schmitt: Growing Discord, Culminating in the "Guardian"', in Jens Meierhenrich and Oliver Simons (eds.), *The Oxford Handbook of Carl Schmitt*, 510–46 (Oxford University Press, 2016).

Paulson, Stanley L., and Litschewski Paulson, Bonnie, *Normativity and Norms: Critical Perspectives on Kelsenian Themes* (Oxford University Press, 1999).

Pavlakos, George, 'Kelsenian Imputation and the Explanation of Legal Norms', 37 *Revus – Journal for Constitutional Theory and Philosophy of Law* 47–56 (2019).

Piccone, Paul and Ulmen, Gary L., 'Schmitt's "Testament" and the Future of Europe', 83 *Telos* 3–34 (1990).

Police, Aristide, 'Le autonomie pubbliche come ordinamenti giuridici', in Roberto Cavallo Perin et al. (eds.), *Attualità e necessità del pensiero di Santi Romano*, 101–18 (Naples: Editoriale Scientifica, 2019).

Portinaro, Pier Paolo, 'Che cos'è il decisionismo?' 59 *Rivista internazionale di filosofia del diritto* 247–67 (1982).

La crisi dello ius publicum europaeum. Saggio su Carl Schmitt (Milan: Edizioni di Comunità, 1982).

Posner, Eric and Vermeule, Adrian, 'Demystifying Schmitt', in Jens Meierhenrich and Oliver Simons (eds.), *The Oxford Handbook of Carl Schmitt*, 612–26 (New York: Oxford University Press, 2016).

Rae, Gavin, 'The Real Enmity of Carl Schmitt's Concept of the Political', 12 *Journal of International Political Theory* 258–75 (2015).

'The Theology of Carl Schmitt's Political Theology', 17 *Political Theology* 555–72 (2016).

Raz, Joseph, *The Authority of Law*, 2nd ed. (Oxford: Clarendon Press, 2009).

Richter, Emanuel, 'Carl Schmitt: The Defective Guidance for the Critique of Political Liberalism', 21 *Cardozo Law Review* 1619–44 (2000).

Roberts, Aaron B., 'Carl Schmitt: Political Theologian?' 77 *The Review of Politics* 449–74 (2015).

Romano, Alberto, 'Nota bio-bibliografica', in Santi Romano, *L'"ultimo' Santi Romano* 843–85 (Milan: Giuffrè, 2013).

Romano, Santi, *The Legal Order* (Abingdon: Routledge, 2017).

Rubinelli, Lucia, 'Costantino Mortati and the Idea of Material Constitution', 40 *History of Political Thought* 515–46 (2019).

Constituent Power: A History (Cambridge University Press, 2020).

Runciman, David, *Pluralism and the Personality of the State* (Cambridge University Press, 1997).

Rüthers, Bernd, *Carl Schmitt im Dritten Reich: Wissenschaft als Zeitgeist-Verstarkung?*, 2nd ed. (Munich: C. H. Beck, 1990).

Salvatore, Andrea, 'A Counter-Mine that Explodes Silently: Romano and Schmitt on the Unity of the Legal Order', 11 *Ethics & Global Politics* 50–9 (2018).

'Il diritto della vita. Sull'inquietudine di Hauriou', in Maurice Hauriou, *La teoria dell'istituzione e della fondazione*, 125–50 (Macerata: Quodlibet, 2019).

'A maggior gloria della scientia iuris. L'istituzionalismo giurisprudenziale di Carl Schmitt', in Carl Schmitt, *La situazione della scienza giuridica europea*, 79–124 (Macerata: Quodlibet, 2020).

Scheppele, Kim L., 'Law in a Time of Emergency: States of Exception and the Temptations of 9/11', 6 *University of Pennsylvania Journal of Constitutional Law* 1001–83 (2004).

'Legal and Extralegal Emergencies', in Gregory A. Caldeira, R. Daniel Kelemen and Keith E. Whittington (eds.), *The Oxford Handbook of Law and Politics*, 165–86 (Oxford University Press, 2008).

Scheuerman, William E., 'Review: Carl Schmitt and the Nazis', 23 *German Politics & Society* 71–9 (1991).

Between the Norm and the Exception: The Frankfurt School and the Rule of Law (Cambridge, MA: The MIT Press, 1994).

'Carl Schmitt's Critique of Liberal Constitutionalism', 58 *The Review of Politics* 299–322 (1996).

'States of Emergency', in Jens Meierhenrich and Oliver Simons (eds.), *The Oxford Handbook of Carl Schmitt*, 547–69 (New York: Oxford University Press, 2016).

Carl Schmitt: The End of Law, 2nd ed. (Lanham, MD: Rowman & Littlefield, 2019).

Schmitt, Carl, *Der Hüter der Verfassung* (Tübingen: Mohr, 1931).

'Aufgabe und Notwendigkeit des deutschen Rechtsstandes', 6 *Deutsches Recht* 181–5 (1936).

Donoso Cortés in gesamteuropäischer Interpretation. Vier Aufsätze (Cologne: Greven, 1950).

'Die Einheit der Welt', 6 *Merkur* 1–11 (1952).

'Freiheitsrechte und institutionelle Garantien der Reichsverfassung (1931)', in Carl Schmitt (ed.), *Verfassungsrechtliche Aufsätze aus den Jahren 1924–1954. Materialien zu einer Verfassungslehre*, 140–73 (Berlin: Duncker & Humblot, 1958).

'Grundrechte und Grundpflichten (1932)' in Carl Schmitt (ed.), *Verfassungsrechtliche Aufsätze aus den Jahren 1924–1954. Materialien zu einer Verfassungslehre*, 181–231 (Berlin: Duncker & Humblot, 1958).

'Nehmen/Teilen/Weiden. Ein Versuch, die Grundfragen jeder Sozial- und Wirtschaftsordnung vom Nomos her richtig zu stellen', in Carl Schmitt (ed.), *Verfassungsrechtliche Aufsätze aus den Jahren 1924–1954. Materialien zu einer Verfassungslehre*, 489–504 (Berlin: Duncker & Humblot, 1958).

'*Nomos – Nahme –* Name', in Siegfried Behn (ed.), *Der beständige Aufbruch. Festschrift für Erich Przywara*, 92–105 (Nuremburg: Glock & Lutz, 1959).

Über Schuld und Schuldarten. Eine Terminologische Untersuchung, 2nd ed. (Frankfurt am Main: Keip, 1977).

'Un giurista davanti a se stesso. Intervista a Carl Schmitt', 3 *Quaderni costituzionali* 5–34 (1983).

'The Plight of European Jurisprudence', 83 *Telos* 35–70 (1990).

Glossarium. Aufzeichnungen aus den Jahren 1947 bis 1958 (Berlin: Duncker & Humblot, 1991).

Roman Catholicism and Political Form (Westport, CT: Greenwood, 1996).

'The Visibility of the Church: A Scholastic Consideration', in Carl Schmitt (ed.), *Roman Catholicism and Political Form*, 45–59 (Westport, CT: Greenwood Press, 1996).

'State Ethics and the Pluralist State', in A. J. Jacobson and B. Schlink (eds.), *Weimar: A Jurisprudence of Crisis*, 300–12 (Berkeley: University of California Press, 2000).
State, Movement, People: The Triadic Structure of the Political Unity (Corvallis, OR: Plutarch, 2001).
'A Pan-European Interpretation of Donoso Cortes', 125 *Telos* 100–15 (2002).
The 'Nomos' of the Earth in the International Law of the 'Jus Publicum Europaeum' (New York: Telos Press, 2003).
Legality and Legitimacy (Durham, NC: Duke University Press, 2004).
On the Three Types of Juristic Thought (Westport, CT: Praeger, 2004).
Political Theology: Four Chapters on the Concept of Sovereignty (University of Chicago Press, 2005).
The Concept of the Political, expanded edition (University of Chicago Press, 2007).
Constitutional Theory (Durham, NC: Duke University Press, 2008).
Political Theology II: The Myth of the Closure of any Political Theology (Malden, MA: Polity Press, 2008).
'The Großraum Order of International Law with a Ban on Intervention for Spatially Foreign Powers: A Contribution to the Concept of Reich in International Law (1939–1941)', in *Writings on War* 75–124 (Cambridge: Polity Press, 2011).
Dictatorship: From the Origin of the Modern Concept of Sovereignty to Proletarian Class Struggle (Cambridge: Polity Press, 2014).
'The Guardian of the Constitution', in Lars Vinx (ed. and trans.), *The Guardian of the Constitution: Hans Kelsen and Carl Schmitt on the Limits of Constitutional Law*, 79–173 (Cambridge University Press, 2015).
Ex Captivitate Salus: Experiences, 1945–47 (Cambridge: Polity Press, 2017).
Der Begriff des Politischen. Synoptische Darstellung der Texte, ed. Marco Walter (Berlin: Duncker & Humblot, 2018).
'Statute and Judgment', in Lars Vinx and Samuel Zeitlin (eds.), *Carl Schmitt's Early Legal-Theoretical Writings: Statute and Judgment and The Value of the State and the Significance of the Individual*, 39–155 (Cambridge University Press, 2021).
'The Value of the State and the Significance of the Individual', in Lars Vinx and Samuel Zeitlin (eds.), *Carl Schmitt's Early Legal-Theoretical Writings: Statute and Judgment and The Value of the State and the Significance of the Individual*, 159–242 (Cambridge University Press, 2021).
Schupmann, Benjamin, *Carl Schmitt's Constitutional and State Theory: A Critical Analysis* (Oxford University Press, 2017).
Seitzer, Jeffrey, *Comparative History and Legal Theory: Carl Schmitt in the First German Democracy* (Westport: Greenwood Press, 2001).
Simons, Oliver 'Carl Schmitt's Spatial Rhetoric', in Jens Meierhenrich and Oliver Simons (eds.), *The Oxford Handbook of Carl Schmitt*, 776–802 (New York: Oxford University Press, 2016).
Stears, Marc, 'Guild Socialism', in Marc Bevir (ed.), *Modern Pluralism: Anglo-American Debates since 1880*, 40–59 (Cambridge University Press, 2012).
Stergiopoulou, Katerina, 'Taking Nomos: Carl Schmitt's Philology Unbound', 149 *October* 95–122 (2014).

Storme, Tristan, 'Maintenir l'histoire en mouvement. Carl Schmitt, penseur de l'historicité moderne', 117 *Vingtième Siècle. Revue d'histoire* 119–32 (2013).
Strauss, Leo, 'Notes on Carl Schmitt: The Concept of the Political', in Carl Schmitt, *The Concept of the Political*, expanded edition, 97–122 (University of Chicago Press, 2007).
Surdi, Michele, 'Critica della categoria del politico: 1932–1937', 170–1 *aut-aut* 197–228 (1979).
Suuronen, Ville, 'Carl Schmitt as a Theorist of the 1933 Nazi Revolution: 'The Difficult Task of Rethinking and Recultivating Traditional Concepts', 20 *Contemporary Political Theory* 341–63 (2021).
'Mobilizing the Western Tradition for Present Politics: Carl Schmitt's Polemical Uses of Roman Law, 1923–1945', 47 *History of European Ideas* 748–72 (2021).
Teschke, Bruno, 'Fatal Attraction: A Critique of Carl Schmitt's International Political and Legal Theory', 3 *International Theory* 179–227 (2011).
Tielke, Martin, *Der stille Bürgerkrieg. Ernst Jünger und Carl Schmitt im Dritten Reich* (Berlin: Landtverlag, 2007).
Tushnet, Mark, 'Emergencies and the Idea of Constitutionalism', in Mark Tushnet (ed.), *The Constitution in Wartime: Beyond Alarmism and Complacency* 39–54 (Durham, NC: Duke University Press, 2005).
Twining, William, 'A Post-Westphalian Conception of Law', 37 *Law and Society Review* 199–258 (2003).
General Jurisprudence. Understanding Law from a Global Perspective (Cambridge University Press, 2009).
Vermeule, Adrian, 'Our Schmittian Administrative Law', 122 *Harvard Law Review* 1095–149 (2009).
Vinx, Lars, *Hans Kelsen's Pure Theory of Law* (Oxford University Press, 2007).
'Carl Schmitt and the Analogy between Constitutional and International Law: Are Constitutional and International Law Inherently Political?' 2 *Global Constitutionalism* 91–124 (2013).
'The Incoherence of Strong Popular Sovereignty', 11 *International Journal of Constitutional Law* 101–24 (2013).
'Introduction', in Lars Vinx (ed. and trans.), *The Guardian of the Constitution: Hans Kelsen and Carl Schmitt on the Limits of Constitutional Law*, 1–21 (Cambridge University Press, 2015).
'Carl Schmitt and the Problem of Constitutional Guardianship', in Matilda Arvidsson, Leila Brännström and Panu Minkkinen (eds.), *The Contemporary Relevance of Carl Schmitt*, 34–49 (Abingdon: Routledge, 2017).
'Santi Romano against the State?' 11 *Ethics & Global Politics* 25–36 (2018).
Vinx, Lars and Zeitlin, Samuel Garrett, 'Carl Schmitt and the Problem of the Realization of Law', in Lars Vinx and Samuel Garrett Zeitlin (eds.), *Carl Schmitt's Early Legal-Theoretical Writings: Statute and Judgment and The Value of the State and the Significance of the Individual* 1–36 (Cambridge University Press, 2021).
Wolin, Richard, 'Carl Schmitt: The Conservative Revolutionary Habitus and the Aesthetics of Horror', 20 *Political Theory* 424–47 (1992).

Index

For EU product safety concerns, contact us at Calle de José Abascal, 56–1°,
28003 Madrid, Spain or eugpsr@cambridge.org.

www.ingramcontent.com/pod-product-compliance
Lightning Source LLC
LaVergne TN
LVHW011815200926
848484LV00005B/1208
* 9 7 8 1 3 1 6 5 1 1 3 8 1 *